D1432773

Lester Young

Twayne's Music Series

Developed and edited in cooperation
with Chris Frigon and Camille Roman

Lester Young

Lewis Porter

Twayne Publishers

Lester Young

Lewis Porter

Copyright © 1985
By G. K. Hall & Company
All Rights Reserved
Published by Twayne Publishers
A Division of G. K. Hall & Company
70 Lincoln Street
Boston, Massachusetts 02111

First Printing

Book production by Marne B. Sultz
Book design by Barbara Anderson

This book was typeset in
Century Oldstyle
by Compset, Inc.

Photograph of Lester Young in 1942
courtesy of Don Schlitten

Printed on permanent/durable
acid-free paper and bound in
the United States of America

Library of Congress Cataloging in Publication Data

Porter, Lewis.
Lester Young.

(Twayne's music series)
Bibliography: p. 114
Discography: p. 181
Includes index.
1. Young, Lester, 1909–1959. 2. Jazz musicians—
United States—Biography. I. Title. II. Series.
ML419.Y7P7   1985   788'.66'0924[B]   85-5416
ISBN 0-8057-9459-X
ISBN 0–8057–9471–9 (pbk)

Contents

About the Author

Lewis Porter is assistant professor of music at Tufts University, where he directs all bands, including the Jazz Ensemble, and teaches courses and graduate seminars in jazz history and jazz research. He has two more books forthcoming—a history of jazz, coauthored with Michael Ullman, to be published by Prentice-Hall, and a study of the music of John Coltrane. He has been jazz editor and a regular contributor to the *Black Perspective in Music.* Recent publications include a history of women in jazz for *Music Educators Journal,* a study of jazz drumming for *Percussive Notes,* biographies of jazz musicians including Young for *The New Grove's Dictionary of Music in the United States,* and a liner-note essay for *Louis Armstrong and Sidney Bechet in New York, 1923–1925* (Smithsonian R026).

Mr. Porter has performed on saxophone (and piano) in New York City and San Francisco and now performs regularly in the Boston area with Alan Dawson and others. He leads his own small groups, free-lances, and presents solo recitals, workshops, and clinics. He holds the Bachelor of Arts degree in psychology from the University of Rochester, where he studied at the Eastman School of Music; the Master of Education degree from Northeastern University; the Master of Arts degree in music from Tufts University; and the Ph.D. in musicology from Brandeis University.

Preface

All jazz fans know that Lester Young, the black American tenor saxophonist known as "Pres" (or "Prez"), was one of the greatest artists in jazz. This book will give the reader a fuller sense of exactly what was so great about him. It is hoped that it will inspire the reader to listen to more of his recordings and thus will foster better appreciation. If my book serves to heighten the general interest in the music of Lester Young, I will feel very gratified. Young's music has been poorly served by other authors, and too few people recognize its depth, beauty, and brilliance. The English critic Benny Green put it well: "Lester is every bit as great as fashion today decrees but it is not commonly known why" (from the collection *Just Jazz,* 1959).

The musicians and critics who heard "Pres" at his peak knew best. Thousands of jazz performers have attested to Young's influence in words and, of course, in their music. As another brilliant saxophonist, Dexter Gordon, described it to writer Russ Russell in the article "Bebop" (reprinted in *The Art of Jazz*), 'Hawk [Coleman Hawkins] was the master of the horn, a musician who did everything possible with it, the right way. But when Pres appeared, we all started listening to him alone. Pres had an entirely new sound, one that we seemed to be waiting for." Charlie Parker, universally recognized as one of the geniuses of jazz, said, as quoted in *Hear Me Talkin' to Ya,* "I was crazy about Lester. He played so clean and beautiful." Alto saxophonist Lee Konitz heard Parker warming up by playing one of Young's famous solos by heart—and very fast. Young was among the five names voted the most important in the history of jazz by ten leading critics in March 1955, and 100 leading jazz musicians voted him "Greatest Tenor Saxophonist Ever" (reported in *The Encyclopedia of Jazz*). Konitz summed up the feelings of many musicians about Young when he said, in *Hear Me Talkin' to Ya,* "How many people he's influenced, how many lives! Because he is definitely the basis of everything that's happened."

Since Young's death in 1959, however, the younger generations of musicians and listeners display none of the adulation that their predecessors had toward Young. If they have heard his music at all, they typically describe it in such mildly positive terms as "mellow and real swinging." The decline of Young's reputation contrasts greatly with that of his successor, Charlie Parker. The mention of Parker's name still elicits awestruck responses to this day.

Part of the problem with Young is his inconsistency. Every solo he recorded from 1936, his debut year, through 1941 is a gem, but younger listeners, musicians or not, may have little empathy with the dated fidelity of those recordings, or with the Swing Era style employed by Young's colleagues. On later recordings, Young played in a somewhat different style that remains controversial to this day. And during his last years, in the 1950s, Young was sometimes in poor health, resulting in a few deficient recordings, which, unfortunately, were widely available. No wonder that the younger audience remains unimpressed!

The evaluation of Young's work after 1941, and particularly after 1945, remains one of the major problems of jazz criticism. Many writers have maintained that there is little of interest in this large body of work, that only the earliest works are of value, and that the later style is a corruption of the early one. A growing minority believes, with this author, that the later works have their own value, independent of the early works. Obviously, those few recordings that display Young under physical duress are not the best ones with which to assess his later achievements. There is no question that he was not as consistent in later years as before, but he was still capable of marvelous things. One of the major concerns of this book will be the delineation and detailed analysis of the components of Young's style at different times. In the last chapter I review the critical opinions at length and weigh them against the results of my analysis. I leave the final evaluation of Young's work to each reader, feeling content that the reader will now have the information needed to make that evaluation.

Perhaps as a result of the lack of unanimity regarding Young's legacy, only three short books were written about him, none over 100 pages, only one in English, all mainly biographical and based on unreliable sources (Burkhardt and Gerth; Franchini; and Dave Gelly, published too late for my Bibliography). Some fine articles exist—among them Lawrence Gushee's wide-ranging treatment of *Shoe Shine Boy* (1981), Louis Gottlieb's analysis of the early music entitled "Why So Sad, Pres?" (1959), Don Heckman's comparison of Young with Coleman Hawkins (from *Down Beat,* 1963), and thorough and provocative articles on Young's life story by Nat Hentoff (1957) and John McDonough (1980). But most of the jazz history books devote a page or so to Young, as compared with whole chapters on Louis Armstrong, Duke Ellington, and Charlie Parker.

This book is a step toward rectifying the situation of Lester Young in jazz scholarship. I concentrate on the music because I respect Lester's feeling that "[my life] was all music; that's all there was" (from *Down Beat,* 1949). But I have also included a substantial biographical chapter and a comprehensive listing of Young's recorded titles, both of which contain material never before published. The biography presents portions of Young's last known interview, in Paris about one month before his death. This interview has appeared many times in print, but only in edited form or incorrectly transcribed. I also draw upon other Young interviews, interviews with his family and colleagues, and new research, with thanks to my fellow researchers. Through the generosity of other discographers, the record listing mentions unissued and alternate takes and broadcasts only recently discovered and clarifies some confusion with regard to dates. The Selected Bibliography and the Catalog incorporate information received through November 1984.

The meat of the text, chapters 2 through 6, consists of analysis of Young's music. Basically the reader will grow to understand Young's style and its development through a close examination of its facets—melody, rhythm, and so forth. Perhaps most important, an overall picture emerges from this analysis. Young modified certain aspects of his style considerably during his career, especially his tone quality and the ways that he tied his ideas together. In fact, his style changed enough that we may discern three distinct style periods—an early period, from the first recordings of 1936 through 1942; a middle period, from 1943 through about 1950; and a late period, covering 1950 through 1959. Obviously Young gradually modified his style during each period, not all at once. But the changes are most drastic between 1942 and 1943 and around 1950.

Of equal importance to our awareness of Young's style periods is the realization that certain musical concerns never changed. His constant preoccupations were with structural unification, openness of tone, relaxed swing, and singing melodies, and these made Lester who he was despite the different methods he used to achieve these goals during each period. These are the four omnipresent areas in which his genius shone brightest. In preparing my analysis, I examined all of Young's recorded solos, including all bootleg issues and some unissued private tapes. I then selected a sample of thirty-four solos to examine more closely and subjected them to an array of analytical procedures, including computer analysis. A list of the thirty-four solos follows this preface; I refer to solos from this list quite often.

In order to help the reader follow the analytical portions, conclusions are presented two ways—chronologically for each style element (e.g., development of tone or rhythm through the years) and horizontally for each style period (e.g., a summary of tone, rhythm, and so forth, as they appear during one particular period). Furthermore, chapter 5 consists of analyses of three complete solos, one from each period. By the end of the book the reader will be able not only to hear aspects of Young's style as they changed over the years, but also to pick any particular year and summarize what qualities characterized Young's music at that time.

Since Lester Young was a jazz musician, it is important for us to have a common understanding about what jazz is. Jazz is a form of art music developed by black Americans around 1900 that draws upon a variety of sources from Africa, Europe, and America. Jazz has borrowed from black folk music, and all kinds of popular music have borrowed from jazz, but these types of music remain distinct and should not be confused with one another.

From its beginnings, jazz has branched out into so many styles that it is difficult, and unnecessary, to find one description that fits them all. But a few generalizations can be made that apply to the vast majority of jazz performances since about 1930, including all of Young's performances:

1. Musicians create within the conventions of their chosen style, usually accompanied by the repeated framework of a popular song or original composition.

2. Instrumentalists emulate black American vocal styles.

3. Each performer tries to develop his or her own sound or tone color. (Lester certainly did!)

4. The rhythms are characterized by constant syncopation and create swing, a sensation of pull and momentum.

With regard to the last point, the reader will note that the transcribed examples in this book show a preponderance of eighth notes. On the recordings, these are "swung" so that they actually approximate triplets, ♩♪ ♫ . But it is a convention of jazz notation to write eighth notes as such. Triplets are used only when they are heard as distinct from "swung" eighth notes. I have attempted to indicate details of performances on my transcriptions by using a number of symbols, each of which is explained at its first occurrence. The symbols and their meanings are collected at the end of this preface.

Unless concert key is specified, all musical examples and text references are in the tenor saxophone key, that is, one whole step above concert key. Notes played on the tenor saxophone sound a major ninth lower than written.

The study of Young's music has continued relevance for anyone interested in jazz. His early style marked the beginning of modern jazz and directly inspired Charlie Parker in the creation of bebop. John Coltrane, a great genius of the tenor saxophone who is the model for most of today's performers on the instrument, said that Young was, along with Johnny Hodges, his first major influence (*Jazz Review,* 1959). He was referring to Young's middle-period work of the 1940s. Another major saxophonist, Sonny Rollins, when asked to choose his favorite jazz records, included *Lester's Savoy Jump,* from Young's middle period (*Boston Real Paper,* 1976). Young's influence was so extensive that his formulas became commonplace among players of all instruments. Big band arrangements to this day employ melodies and riffs directly out of the Young tradition. It would be no exaggeration to say that the language of modern jazz developed out of the music of Lester Young.

Lewis Porter

Tufts University

List of Transcribed Solos

The following is a list of the thirty-four transcribed solos that were the focus of the analysis and are the sources of the musical examples in this book:

1. *Lady Be Good* (11/9/36)
2. *Shoe Shine Boy* (11/9/36, Take 1)
3. *Shoe Shine Boy* (11/9/36, Take 2)
4. *Boogie Woogie* (11/9/36)
5. *Honeysuckle Rose* (1/21/37)
6. *One O'Clock Jump* (7/7/37)
7. *Honeysuckle Rose* (1/16/38, concert)
8. *Jumpin' at the Woodside* (8/22/38)
9. *Jive at Five* (2/2–4/39)
10. *Clap Hands, Here Comes Charlie* (8/4/39)
11. *Lester Leaps In* (9/5/39, Take 1)
12. *Lester Leaps In* (9/5/39, Take 2)
13. *Dickie's Dream* (9/5/39, Take 1)
14. *Dickie's Dream* (9/5/39, Take 2)
15. *Dickie's Dream* (9/5/39, Take 3)
16. *Tickle Toe* (3/19/40)
17. *Easy Does It* (3/20/40)
18. *Indiana* (7/15/42, 1st solo)
19. *I Can't Get Started* (7/15/42, 1st solo)
20. *I Got Rhythm* (12/21/43, 2nd solo, 3 choruses)
21. *Hello, Babe* (12/21/43, Master)
22. *Hello, Babe* (12/21/43, Alternate)
23. *After Theatre Jump* (3/22/44)
24. *These Foolish Things* (12/45)
25. *I Want to Be Happy* (3 or 4/46, 1st solo, 1st chorus)

26. *I Want to Be Happy* (3 or 4/46, 2d solo, 2d chorus)

27. *Jumpin' with Symphony Sid* (2/18/47, 1st solo)

28. *Jumpin' with Symphony Sid* (2/18/47, 2d solo)

29. *Destination Moon* (2/22/50)

30. *Just You, Just Me* (8/4/52, 2d solo)

31. *Neenah* (1/10/53, 1st four choruses)

32. *The Modern Set (Chris 'N Diz,* probably 1955, concert, 3d chorus)

33. *Pres Returns* (1/13/56, 2d solo)

34. *Lester Leaps In* (10/56, private recording, 1st three choruses)

Since I refer to these solos often, I omit the date except in the case of *Lester Leaps In* (10/56), which must be distinguished from the 1939 version. For example, I cite *Honeysuckle Rose* (concert) and *Shoe Shine Boy* (Take 2) in various places. I give the full date when referring to recordings not listed above. All recordings appear in the Catalog of Recorded Works. I always count measure numbers from the beginning of Young's solo chorus, not the beginning of the recording.

Note on the Music Examples

The following diacritical markings are employed to indicate details of performance:

$\hat{\mathsf{P}}$ Accent and hold less than full value

(P) Barely audible, "ghosted" note

$\mathsf{P}^{\sim}$ Pronounced vibrato—symbol placed approximately where vibrato occurs

$\mathsf{\dot{I}}$ Indefinite sound due to slip of fingers or tongue

$\nearrow\mathsf{P}$ Slide into pitch from below by adjusting embouchure, sometimes combined with a fingered grace note

$\mathsf{P}^{\frown}$ Note ends in a downward glissando (falloff)

$\mathsf{P}^{\smile}$ Note ends in an upward glissando (doit)

$\mathsf{J}\!\!\sim\!\!\!\frown\mathsf{P}$ Notes connected by glissando, too fast for individual notes to be transcribed

$\mathsf{\dot{P}}$ Flat by less than one half step

$\mathsf{\uparrow P}$ Sharp by less than one half step

$\mathsf{P}^{\rightarrow}$ Delayed by less than one sixteenth note

$\mathsf{P}^{\leftarrow}$ Anticipated by less than one sixteenth note

$\mathsf{\overset{!}{P}}$ "Honk"

$\mathsf{\overset{x}{P}}$ Timbre changed by alternate fingering

Acknowledgments

I began my research on Lester Young in 1978, and I owe many thanks to Dr. T. J. Anderson of Tufts University who supported this project from its inception, and to Professors Jane Bernstein and Jeff Titon, also of Tufts, who made many helpful suggestions. The format of the analysis was largely inspired by Dr. Titon's book *Early Down Home Blues: A Musical and Cultural Analysis* (University of Illinois Press, 1977). Dr. George Stalker designed computer programs that enabled me to perform portions of the analysis.

I acknowledge my great debt to Dan Morgenstern, director of the Rutgers Institute of Jazz Studies, for making the resources of the Institute available to me, for tracing requested recordings and articles, and for his support. During the ealy stages of my writing, jazz saxophonist Lee Konitz spent several hours sharing with me his thoughts and feelings about Young's music. Seth Rubin proofread my musical transcriptions.

Lester's brother Lee was a great help with the biographical chapter, as were the generous researchers John McDonough, John Chilton, and Dr. Douglas Henry Daniels, and musicians Norman Simmons, Jerry Potter, and Buzzy Drootin. Lester Young, Jr., also read this chapter, and Loren Schoenberg and Phil Schaap shared with me information about Young's life as well as his recorded works.

Collector-discographer Bill Miner, who graciously reviewed the Catalog of Recorded Works and made numerous comments on its content and presentation, receives my heartfelt gratitude. Valuable assistance for the Catalog also came from Tony Shoppee and Chris Sheridan (author of a Basie discography forthcoming from Greenwood Press)—both of whom worked closely on portions of it—and Jan Evensmo, Norman Saks, Ralph Berton, Don Manning, Harry Schröder, Helmut Schwarzer, Bill Savory, Bill Potts, Rainer Lotz, Malcolm Walker, Jack Woker, Harry Swisher, Ira Berger, Lloyd Rauch, and Doug Dreishpoon. Record producers John Hammond, Jerry Valburn, Norman Granz, Bob Porter, Art Zimmerman, Don Schlitten, and J. R. Rowland took time out from their busy schedules to respond to my queries. Fred Turco of Oak Lawn Jazz worked beyond the call of duty to locate obscure LPs and publications for me.

Finally I would like to thank four people behind the scenes who were essential to this book—my editor, John LaBine; my typist, Susan Wood; my music copyist, Armand Qualliotine, and my wife, Gail.

Some of the material in chapters 3 and 4 appeared in different form in an article, "Lester Leaps In: The Early Style of Lester Young," *Black Perspective in Music,* Spring 1981.

An award from the Faculty Research Fund of Tufts University partially supported the preparation of the manuscript. Last minute help came from Thierry Trombert, Robert Perlongo, Torbjørn Lidtveit, Karl Knudsen, and Bob Redcross. I hope anyone I have inadvertently omitted will forgive me.

Chronology

1909 Lester Willis Young born in Woodville, Mississippi, August 27. Shortly after, the family moves to New Orleans.

1919– Young moves to Memphis, then to Minneapolis. Plays drums, later
1927 alto saxophone in family band.

1928 Tours with Art Bronson's Bostonians, adopts tenor saxophone.

1929 Returns to family band; probably plays with Eli Rice's Cotton Pickers toward the end of the year.

1930 Plays with Walter Page's Blue Devils, returns to Bronson's Bostonians from June until November, then moves to Minneapolis.

1931 Plays at Nest Club in Minneapolis under Eddie Barefield, Frank Hines, and Leroy White. Works in Eugene Schuck's Cotton Club Orchestra in summer, then returns to the Nest Club; also plays with Paul Cephas at South Side Club.

1932 Signs with "Thirteen Original Blue Devils" early in the year; plays with them in spring at Ritz Ballroom in Oklahoma City, then tours extensively.

1933 Blue Devils disband in the fall. Young moves to Kansas City and plays with Bennie Moten–George E. Lee band, Clarence Love, and King Oliver. In December, plays with the visiting Fletcher Henderson Orchestra for one night, taking the place of Coleman Hawkins, and plays against Hawkins at a marathon "jam session."

1934 Joins Count Basie early in the year. Transfers to Fletcher Henderson Orchestra in Detroit, March 31; leaves in July and plays with Andy Kirk en route to Kansas City, then with Boyd Atkins and Rook Ganz in Minnesota.

1935 Returns to Kansas City and freelances.

1936 Plays with Count Basie at the Reno Club in Kansas City. In September, visits sick father in Los Angeles. Makes first recordings in Chicago including *Lady Be Good* and *Shoe Shine Boy*. John Hammond arranges contract for Basie with Music Corporation of America, which begins with an engagement in Chicago, November 7 to December 3; Buffalo, December 7; New York City debut, December 24.

1937 First recordings with full Basie band for Decca, New York City, January 21; first recordings with vocalist Billie Holiday January 25—she dubs him "President" or "Pres." Performs with Basie in and around New York City, also in Pittsburgh in February. At the Savoy (New York) in April and June, Ritz-Carlton of Boston in July, Meadowbrook (New Jersey) in November.

1938 Plays at Benny Goodman Carnegie Hall concert, January 16. Performs with Basie at Famous Door, New York City, July through October, then on tour, Nashville, St.Louis, and elsewhere; at "Spirituals to Swing" concert, Carnegie Hall, December 23.

1939 January, Geneva Armory, New York. Herschel Evans dies on February 16. Performs with Basie at Southland Café, Boston, between February and March; Hotel Sherman, Chicago, in June, with many broadcasts; Famous Door, New York City, in July and August. Records *Lester Leaps In,* September 5. Probably to California in October. Performs with Charlie Christian at second "Spirituals to Swing" concert, Carnegie Hall, December 24.

1940 Basie band in New York City, January; in Boston, February 13 into March (mostly at Southland Café); in New York City, April to June; in Chicago on July 15; in California, August to October. Records informally with Benny Goodman and Charlie Christian, October 28 in New York. Leaves Basie band in December.

1941 Leads band at Kelly's Stables in New York, February 27 through March 17. Moves to Los Angeles in May to join band of brother Lee; debuts at Billy Berg's Club Capri.

1942 Lee and Lester Young at Capri from February 24; to Trouville Club in spring, then residence at Café Society Downtown, New York City, September 1 to December 29.

1943 Lee goes to Los Angeles after death of father February 6; stepmother dies soon after and band is dissolved. Lester plays at Minton's Playhouse and Village Vanguard in New York. Joins Al Sears band in spring for USO tour and other performances. Plays with Count Basie in October, then rejoins Basie in December at Lincoln Hotel.

1944 Performs with Basie on one-nighters in Northeast in January, February; New York in March, and at Hotel Lincoln, New York City, April and May; in Chicago June 12 to 22; Ohio, Kansas City, in July. Opens in Los Angeles August 1, then San Francisco, Oakland, back to Los Angeles on September 7. Appears in film *Jammin' the Blues* in August. Inducted into the army on September 30 and stationed at Fort McClellan, Alabama, on December 1. Wins first place in *Down Beat* poll at end of year.

1945 Court-martialed for possession of drugs, February 16. Sent to detention barracks, Fort Gordon, Georgia; discharged from army in December. Returns to recording in Los Angeles. Wins *Esquire* Silver award.

1946 Signs personal management contract with Norman Granz, appears at Granz-produced JATP concerts in Los Angeles, January and April, Chicago, May 14, and at Carnegie Hall, New York City, on four Mondays beginning May 27. Back to Chicago, June 22. Records in Los Angeles in August; performs with own group in Chicago during October, New York City in November.

1947 Records *Jumpin' with Symphony Sid* February 18. On tour—one or two weeks each in St. Louis, Detroit, Washington, D.C., New York City (May 11 through 17 at the Savoy), Boston, and so on. Records in New York City at end of year. Wins *Esquire* Silver Award.

1948 January to February 16, Seattle; February 17 to March 1, San Francisco; March to November, tour of East Coast. Cleveland, November 11 through 17. Performs at Royal Roost, New York City, November 25 to December 8.

1949 On tour in January. Performs in Chicago February 14 to March 13, then New York's Royal Roost March 17 to April 13. JATP concert, Carnegie Hall, September 17. At Birdland opening, December 15.

1950 At Birdland, January and February; Chicago in April, then back to New York. Appears at Norman Granz concert, Carnegie Hall, September 16.

1951 Performs at Birdland, New York City, throughout the year. Also at Carnegie Hall, February 21; Chicago, August 10 to 23; two JATP concerts (Newark, and midnight at Carnegie Hall) on October 19. Philadelphia, December 3 to 8.

1952 First tour of Europe for Young and for JATP leaves March 26, returns April 21. Young then appears at Birdland through June; Washington, D.C., June 30 through July 5; Philadelphia, July 7 through 12.

Back to Birdland from July 24, including guest appearances with the Basie band. JATP American tour begins September 13 in Carnegie Hall, working west to Los Angeles and Honolulu.

1953 Performs at Birdland in January, with own groups and as guest of Count Basie band; JATP in Europe from early February, including concerts in London and Paris in March; back at Birdland in July; JATP concert, September.

1954 Performs in San Francisco, March 9 to 29; at first festival in Newport, July 18. Makes guest appearances with Basie at Carnegie Hall, September 25, and at Birdland in December.

1955 Plays with Birdland All-Stars in February, and at Charlie Parker Memorial Concert, April 2, Carnegie Hall. Performs with Billie Holiday at Carnegie Hall, May 6; at Birdland most of May; in Chicago from July 22. JATP concert tour including Chicago, October 2. Hospitalized in winter.

1956 Reunites with Teddy Wilson at recording sessions, January 12 and 13; Chicago, April 20 to May 4; tours Europe with Birdland All-Stars in November. Plays in December in Washington, D.C., then at Café Bohemia, New York City.

1957 Hospitalized again. Birdland tour begins February 15 at Carnegie Hall, through March. Appears with Count Basie band at Newport Jazz Festival, July 7; Granz concerts include Hollywood Bowl, August 22, and JATP tour opening September 14, Carnegie Hall, ending in Los Angeles in October. Appears on television program "The Sound of Jazz" with Basie and Billie Holiday, December 8.

1958 Hospitalized again; moves to Alvin Hotel in Manhattan in spring. Appears at Newport Jazz Festival, July 5, and has birthday tribute at Birdland on August 27, then begins to perform more frequently, including two weeks at the Five Spot, New York City, in November, and a return scheduled there in December.

1959 Begins engagement at the Blue Note, Paris, on January 23; makes last commercial recordings March 4. Returns to New York City March 14 and dies at three A.M., March 15. Posthumously elected to *Down Beat* Hall of Fame.

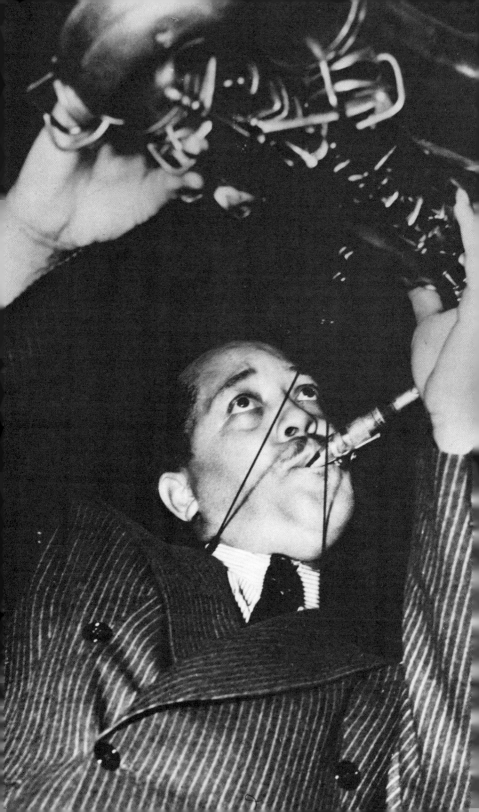

1

"It Was All Music"

Lester Young lived in a unique world of his own design. It was a highly private world and he allowed only a few others inside it, almost all of them members of his culture, black America. Ironically, most of the writing about Young has been by whites, who sometimes speak of him as taciturn, uncommunicative, even psychologically disturbed. Those who were close to him speak instead of his tremendous wisdom, expressed with ample wit.

Eighteen-year-old pianist Bobby Scott (today well known also as a singer and composer) was one of the few whites Young took under his wing, as they toured together with Jazz at the Philharmonic in the fall of 1955. He found that it didn't work to push one's friendship onto Young:

"You don't find God, you lose yourself until God finds you." That is the quality of understanding Lester required, if in your search for him you eventually noticed that he had found you. . . . As he spoke less than almost anyone I have ever known, I came to read his silences, hoping to see what it was that he wasn't saying. He once said to me, "The best saxophone section I ever heard is the Mills Brothers." That made me laugh, and made me think. The Mills Brothers, a vocal quartet, had a blend one rarely heard in the sax section of a band. . . . He had an ability to see through many fictions ("Walter Cronkite and the seven o'clock white folks news," he called it). Once I asked Prez why he didn't play certain licks, which everyone I knew did, knocking out a few of them on the piano for him. His face took on a great incredulity, and he fired back, "That's the way Bird [Charlie Parker] played!" He paused, and then he said, "He plays those licks, I play my licks, you play your licks." I nearly fell off the piano bench from the weight of his truth.

Guitarist Barney Kessel, another sensitive white colleague, observed that "he had great insight into the forces of life and the elements of daily living, and his commentaries were not only rich in wisdom, but also outrageously humorous. Musicians loved to gather around Lester and listen to him talk about anything and everything. There was always a lesson in what he said, and always that superb wit. His words are still passed from musician to musician."[1]

Young's wit marked some musicians for life, because he had a talent for devising nicknames that stuck. Harry Edison became "Sweets" Edison, Billie Holiday became "Lady Day," and Charles Thompson became, and still is, "Sir Charles," all because of Young. He devised cryptic expressions for every situation. He had "big eyes" for things he liked, and "no eyes" for those he didn't. When it was time to perform, he would go "to get all his little claps" from the audience. If he wanted one of his musicians to play longer he would invite him to "have another helping."

Young's speech was also sprinkled generously with four-letter words. I quote extensively from Young in this chapter, and I trust the reader will understand the importance of presenting his words uncensored and unedited. But all agree that Young's speech was not offensive. The Reverend John Gensel, quoted by Rudi Blesh in *Eight Lives in Jazz/Combo: U.S.A.,* avowed that, at least in the 1950s, "Young was the most profane man I'd ever heard—and I've heard a few. Lester's flow of obscenity was magnificent. Nor was it really obscene, because it was not aggressive and was said as his personal poetry. No one, surely, but Prez could say 'mother-fucker' like music, bending the tones until it was a blues."

John Lewis, a major black jazz pianist and composer who worked with Young in the 1950s, pointed out that Young's seemingly eccentric speech and other habits had a cultural context, and were not the result of haphazard whims:

I don't think he consciously invented his special language. It was part of a way of talking I heard in Albuquerque from my older cousins, and there were variations of it in Oklahoma City and Kansas City and Chicago in the late twenties and early thirties. These people also dressed well, as Lester did—the porkpie hats and all. So his speech and dress were natural things he picked up. They weren't a disguise, a way of hiding. They were a way to be hip—to express an awareness of everything swinging that was going on.[2]

Lewis and others from certain parts of black America could see Young's behaviors as creative extensions of the norm for his subculture. Those from outside Young's subculture would naturally interpret his behaviors as expressions of a peculiar personality.

Young's story tempts writers to invoke the all too familiar romantic stereotype about the sensitive soul who has difficulty communicating with the real world and suffers at the hands of other people; this soul manages to create out of his suffering a rich and moving artistic legacy. Admittedly, this stereotype is somewhat appropriate, for Young clearly became more and more unhappy as his life went on, and was seriously alcoholic toward the end. Even those who knew him well agree that he was highly introverted, and rarely discussed personal matters. Nor, indeed, did he display much interest in anything besides music, except for marijuana (never hard drugs) and certain diversions such as crap shooting. It seems fair to describe him as an escapist when it came to personal difficulties.

But Bobby Scott helps us to see this life in another aspect:

The uninitiated might think that what one saw in Prez was the defeat of the human spirit, or the surrender to alcoholism. . . . I came to think his was the exquisite loneliness that comes of a splendid type of isolation. His heart was an Islandman's heart, the heart of one unhappy on a mainland. It put him outside the temporal stream of life. . . . The quiet that surrounded and covered Lester was of a contemplative nature and origin. The one observation I could make about him was that the peace that emanated from him was a glowing proof of a *balanced* personality.

This balanced personality began with a childhood in the South that seems to have been perfectly happy. His father's father was a blacksmith, his father's mother an Evangelist. That side of the family was based in Thibodaux, Louisiana, near New Orleans.[3] Lester's father, Willis Handy "Billy" Young (born ca. 1872, died February 6, 1943), was his musical inspiration. He knew how to play and teach many instruments, including violin, cornet and trumpet, saxophones, and drums, as well as voice. (He reportedly studied at Tuskegee Institute.) The cornet appears to have been his main performing instrument. Lee Young, Lester's younger brother, recalls hearing that their father was a high-school principal in Thibodaux, but this is unconfirmed. Willis Young mostly earned his living as a free lance musician, especially with traveling carnivals. His wife was named Lizetta (or Lyzetta).

The Young family stayed in the vicinity of New Orleans for some years, and Lester Willis Young was born in nearby Woodville, Mississippi, on August 27, 1909. Apparently some of the older family members lived there, as Lester explained: "My mother was scared, you know, so she wanted to go back home to the family, in case something happened—that type. So after I was straight, and she made it, and everything was cool, then she take me to New Orleans and we lived in Algiers."[4] The Algiers section is just across the Mississippi River from New Orleans proper, and Lester was raised there for his first ten years. His first sibling was a sister, Irma, followed in 1917 by his brother, Lee.

New Orleans was full of all kinds of music—symphonies, operas, black folk music—and it was the main center of a new kind of music, jazz. The now legendary jazz greats "King" Oliver, Louis Armstrong, Sidney Bechet, and many others were born there and were active there during Lester's childhood. Lester couldn't help being drawn to music in this environment. Bands would advertise their upcoming dance engagements by playing on the back of a truck while driving through the city, and Lester would follow the trucks and pass out handbills for the musicians. "I'd be running ['round] giving out the handbills," he said, "and I just loved that music, I'd be just running till my tongue was hanging out like this."

Mr. Young, Sr., was away much of the time performing with traveling shows. In fact, Lester once said, "I didn't even know my father until ten years old—I didn't know I had one." He described himself as "a good kid. I would never steal. I got to the third or fourth grade at school [Ed: fourth is correct] but I've been earning my own living since I was five—shining shoes, selling papers."

Lester's schooling ended and his father returned when Mr. and Mrs. Young divorced in 1919. (Lizetta stayed in New Orleans, remarrying to become Lizetta Grey, and moved to Los Angeles around 1944.) This meant big changes for Lester and his two siblings. Mr. Young married a woman named Sara and took the family to Memphis, then settled in Minneapolis by 1920, living in a mostly Swedish neighborhood. Lee described Sara as "a great lady" who "had quite an effect on all our lives" and "was the guiding light for my dad." She was also a musician—saxophonist (baritone and others) and banjoist—and she and Mr. Young decided to form a family band, the Billy Young Jazz Band. The three Young children were taught a variety of musical instruments and went on the road as soon as they were old enough. (Willis appears to have had some new children with Sara.) Two cousins from New Orleans, children of the father's brother, joined the family band for tours, both playing saxophones—Isaiah "Sport" Young and Austin "Boots" Young. "Boots" also played trombone, and eventually became known as a bassist, recording in the 1940s. He and "Sport" were older, and it seems that even their wives played saxophones in the band.[5] The family show included comedy and song as well as the saxophone band and toured with magicians and other acts.

Lester studied violin, trumpet, and drums with his father. The drums were his favorite, and had been ever since New Orleans, but he didn't stay with them long:

Like I was telling you about them trucks that was playing when I [sent] out the hand-bills—he was the onliest person I liked up there was the drums, you dig? (Laughs) Everytime I'd be in a nice little place and meet me a nice little bitch—dig?—her mother says, (mimicking) "All right, Mary, come on, let's go." Goddamn, I'm trying to pack these mother lumpers fast, and shit like this, cause I want this little bitch, you dig? . . . She called her once, and twice, and I'm trying to get this shit straight, so I just said, "Fuck it! I'm through with drums! Mother fuck [them] drums, all the other boys got those clarinet cases, trombone cases, trumpet cases, and here I am wiggling around with all this shit. . . . *Fuck* these motherfuckers!"

And I really played them, Lady Kansas. [Ed.: Drummer Kansas Fields was present.] I could play my ass off, I'm playing for a year. You know, with that strap around you up here? Shit (imitates), "hivey-divey, oobie-doobie, ivey—*hi*tty, *ro*oty, *po*oty!"

Lee Young remembers that Lester's individuality expressed itself even in the way he held his drumsticks. Lester didn't bother to hold the sticks between the "correct" fingers specified by drumming traditions.

Young took up the alto saxophone at about age thirteen, and, he claimed, "just picked the motherfucker up and just started playing it." When he played it in the family band, he frequently found himself in conflict with his father, a stern taskmaster who wouldn't tolerate Lester's casual attitude to technique and reading practice. Mr. Young would apply the razor strap to his children when they misbehaved, but Lester didn't respond to that kind of discipline. Lee remembers that Lester ran away from home on several occasions during his teenage years—once, when he was about seventeen, for as long as two months.

The elder Young would write musical exercises on a blackboard and test his children on their reading, but Lester would try to get by just by using his ears:

When I was coming up playing in the band I wasn't reading music, I was bullshitting, but I was in the band. And my sister, see, she was playin' and I'd get close to her and pick up on the part—you know? Playin' marches and all that shit like that. And finally my father said one day, he said, "Kansas, play your part." [Ed.: He uses "Kansas" as an example.] I knew goddam well I'd lose my ass, he knew I wasn't reading. "Play your part, Kansas." (hums Kansas's part) "tatatalup—dudaladaladulup. . . ." He say, "Now play your part—go!" Say, "Now, Lester, play *your* part."

I couldn't read a motherfuckin' note, not a goddamn note. He said, "Get up"—you know, he don't curse like I do—"get up and get your fuckin' ass and [work] you some scales. Get out.". . . Left them in a hurry. Now you know my heart was broke, you dig. I went and cried and gave up my little teardrops and [said], I said, "Well, I'll come back and catch these motherfuckers if that's the way they want it." Like that, you know? So I went away and learned how to read music—*still* by myself—and then I came back in the band. Played this music and shit, and all the time I was coppin' on the records also with the music so I could fuck these motherfuckers *completely* up.

So I went [in the band] and they took the goddamn marches out and I read the music and shit and everything was great. But what was in *my* heart, why all the motherfuckers laughed when they kicked me out when I couldn't read, [then come] up and say, "Won't you show me how this goes—you play like that?" Sure, I'll show you shit—rusty mother-fucker! So that's the way that went down.

Young's competitive spirit is evident from this story. He also displayed it one night that he sneaked into a dance where his cousin Boots was playing, jumped on stage, and proceeded to demonstrate his superiority on the saxophone. Only Mrs. Young's intervention stopped Boots from whipping Lester.

Lester had not escaped the pain of racism while growing up. Lee recounted an incident in which one of the cousins had to flee a lynch mob (presumably while they still lived in Louisiana), and Lester was sent to help. Late in his life, Lester admitted to a psychiatrist that he had always believed that blacks could not attain salvation as a result of a church he and his father had attended where only whites could come up to the mourners' bench.

Young's stormy relationship with his father became aggravated by a racial issue when the father booked the family band for an extended tour that would take them through Texas and the South before a planned stay in New Mexico. Lester argued against going—"I told him how it would be down there"—but to no avail. Finally, he left, and went out on his own in Salina, Kansas, and while at the Wiggly Café there he met bandleader Art Bronson.

From January 1928 Young toured with Art Bronson's "Bostonians," covering the Dakotas, Nebraska, Colorado, and other states. He played baritone saxophone with Bronson and apparently alto, too, and then adopted the tenor. His reason for switching was refreshingly pragmatic:

We were a nice little group, about eight or ten pieces. The bossman's name was Art Bronson, he played piano . . . I was playing alto and they had a old evil-assed motherfucker [Ed.: he played tenor]. He had a nice beautiful background, you know, mother and father [made] whole lot of bread and all that shit like that. So, everytime we'd get a job—this was in Salina, Kansas—so everytime we'd go to see this motherfucker we'd all be ready, we're waiting for ninety years to get us a gig, you know? And he'd go (mimicking), "Ohhh, wait for me while I put my shirt on, get my tie on." . . . Oh yeah, everybody's waiting disgusted.

So I told the bossman . . . I said, "Listen, let's don't go through this shit." I said, "You buy me a tenor saxophone and I'll play this motherfucker and we'll be straight then." And he worked at a music store—so all he had to do was go and get me a tenor saxophone—and we split. *Fuck* that motherfucker! So that's how I started playing it. Soon as I heard this bitch I knew it was for me. That alto was a little too high, you know.

Young left Bronson in January 1929 to return to the family band for a spell. Lee remembers his brother's alto style as "running a lot of scales . . . he used to run all over the horn a lot," but found his tenor style was "more mellow—he did change considerably." The family had moved to New Mexico, where they seem to have enlarged the group with some new recruits, including Ben Webster. Webster was playing piano, but Willis Young inspired him to specialize in saxophone (on which he later achieved fame). By this time, brother Lee was on drums and Irma played alto saxophone. Some veteran musicians, including Cootie Wiliams and Paul Quinichette, recollected Irma's playing with enthusiasm and even suggested that Lester may have drawn some inspiration from her.

The pianist John Lewis recalls the band staying in Albuquerque for a while, although he would only have been about eight years old at the time: "They . . . had come in with a tent show and been stranded. There was a very good local jazz band, called St. Cecilia's, that Lester played in. He also competed with an excellent Spanish tenor player and housepainter named Cherry. I barely remember Lester's playing. He had a fine, thin tone." In Albuquerque, Young met a woman named Beatrice, who became his first wife.

Next, the Youngs relocated to Phoenix for a long residency, playing regularly in a park and at dances. They would eventually work their way to Los Angeles, where Lee and Irma grew up. But Lester stayed behind, losing touch with them for many years. Late in 1929 he probably played briefly with Eli Rice's Cotton Pickers and, in 1930, joined Walter Page's Blue Devils. Ralph Ellison recalled having seen Young during this period:

A tall, intense young musician . . . arrived in Oklahoma City. . . . With his heavy white sweater, blue stocking cap and up-and-out-thrust silver saxophone, [he] left absolutely no reed player and few young players of any instrument unstirred by the wild, excitingly original flights of his imagination. . . . Lester Young . . . with his battered horn upset the entire Negro section of the town. . . . I first heard Lester Young jamming in a shine chair, his head thrown back, his horn even then outthrust, his feet working the footrests, as he played with and against Lem Johnson, Ben Webster . . . and members of the old Blue Devils Orchestra.[6]

He rejoined Bronson from June to November 1930, then went to Minnesota, working at the Nest Club in Minneapolis under various leaders, including Frank Hines, Eddie Barefield,and Leroy "Snake" White. "Band at the

Nest Club wasn't anyone's, really," said Young; "they gave it to different people every week." He played in Eugene Schuck's Cotton Club Orchestra in the summer of 1931, then returned to the Nest Club. During this period he also played with pianist Paul Cephas at the South Side Club.

Eddie Barefield remembers the twenty-two-year-old Young as "pretty straight. He hadn't developed that strange way of talking. . . . He was quiet, very talented . . . didn't curse, or drink even." Lee Young supports the last comment, saying that "no one in our family ever drank or smoked." Young was about six feet tall, with a light complexion and greenish eyes. He was sometimes called "Red," either because of his complexion or his auburn hair, darkened by the "conking" that blacks employed to straighten their hair in those days. He weighed about 180 pounds. Benny Carter, one of the greatest jazz alto saxophonists (also trumpeter and composer), heard Young playing alto in Minneapolis around 1931, and supported Lee Young's assertion that Lester was more flashy on alto than on tenor:

When I was on the road with McKinney's Cotton Pickers . . . we hit Minneapolis and somebody told us about a wonderful alto player in a local club. I went to hear Prez and was enraptured. It was the greatest thing I'd ever heard. He had a definition and a mastery that I don't think he ever felt necessary to display on the tenor.[7]

According to veteran saxophonist Budd Johnson, McKinney's Cotton Pickers even offered Young a job if he would play alto all the time, but he declined because of his preference for the tenor instrument.[8] These stories indicate that Young was developing a reputation. Jo Jones, who was working in Nebraska at the time, claims that entertainer Clarrie Cammell played him a silver record of Lester's music, and that it was good enough to inspire him to seek out the saxophonist. (There is also an unconfirmed report that Young went to Natchez, Mississippi, sometime in 1931 or 1932 and played with one Bud Scott—not the famous guitarist.)

Early in 1932, while working at the Nest Club with Frank Hines, Young was signed as a member of "The Thirteen Original Blue Devils," the descendant of Walter Page's group, now led by a respected alto saxophonist known as Buster Smith. Leroy White had told Smith, in town for a performance, about Young. The band played a residency at the Ritz Ballroom in Oklahoma City in the spring. The Ritz was a white ballroom and the black players went to Slaughter's Hall to "jam" after hours; the after-hours "jam session," where musicians would get together just to play for themselves, was an important part of Young's life throughout the 1930s. During this engagement he met

Charlie Christian, then fifteen or sixteen years old, who was later to gain recognition as a brilliant jazz guitarist. "We used to go out in the alley and jam," Young said.

After the Ritz residency the Blue Devils toured extensively, but black jazz bands led a hard life in those Depression years, accepting any engagment they could get, and playing at empty clubs in obscure towns for low pay. In the fall of 1933, the band undertook a disastrous tour into Kentucky and West Virginia. They did so poorly that they did not have enough money to return home and had to keep searching for other bookings. Finally they received an offer of a steady job at a white night club in Beckley, West Virginia. Buster Smith lamented that they accepted the offer with the promise of a certain salary, only to discover that they were working for a share of the door receipts, which were variable and could be as low as thirty dollars a night. They had been riding taxicabs to work, on credit, and the cab company had their instruments impounded by the police when they failed to pay their bills. Their instruments were returned each night for them to work off their debt, and then returned to the police. Finally they were thrown out of their hotel.[9] Lester recalled:

They took us right to the railroad track and told us to get out of town. There we were sitting around with these hobos, and they showed us how to grab the train. We got to Cincinnati, no loot, no horns, all raggedy and dirty, and we were trying to make it to St. Louis or Kansas City. I found a man who had an alto and he loaned it out for gigs, so I managed to play a couple of dates. Finally we all had a meeting . . . and we decided it was "every tub," every man for himself.

Well, I got to Kansas City, got hold of a tenor, borrowed some clothes from Herschel Evans—he was playing with Bennie Moten. Moten was stranded too, and all the men put him down: Count Basie had been playing with him but they'd been squabbling, so Count cut out and took over most of the band while Bennie Moten and George Lee formed another group and I went with them.

In addition to the Bennie Moten–George E. Lee band, Young played in Clarence Love's band, probably played with Gene Coy, and, along with trombonist Otto "Pete" Jones, toured in King Oliver's band. Jones had played in the Young family band and had briefly been married to Irma, so he and Lester were old friends. Now Jones was a sort of business manager for Oliver, and got Lester the job. Oliver, a celebrated trumpeter, was now past his prime at the age of forty-eight. He had dental problems and only played a few numbers each set, but according to Young, "he was playing well. . . . His tone was full when he played. . . . He could play some nice blues. He was a very nice fellow, a gay old fellow. He was crazy about all the boys, and it wasn't a drag playing for him at all."[10]

Beatrice, Young's first wife, seems to have come to Kansas City with him, but the marriage soon failed and little else is known because Young never talked about it.

Kansas City Years (1933–1936)

By the early 1930s Kansas City had established itself as one of the most important centers for jazz. Mayor Tom Pendergast encouraged the consumption of liquor and drugs, even during Prohibition, because he arranged to reap a healthy profit for those businesses. He had close connections with Kansas City gangsters who made sure that the proper amounts of money went to the Pendergast machine. (Pendergast's regime ended in 1938 when he was sent to prison for massive tax evasion and for his involvement in several gangland killings.) In this freewheeling atmosphere there was plenty of demand for live music at all hours of the night. After most of the larger bands finished around one o'clock in the morning, jazz musicians congregated at jam sessions. The emphasis at these sessions was on the creativity of the individual soloist, and many of the greatest soloists of the time were associated with Kansas City, although not necessarily born there. In addition to Young, they included bandleader-pianist William Basie (known as "Count" from around 1935), tenor saxophonists Herschel Evans (Young's friend) and Ben Webster, pianist-composer Mary Lou Williams, and, later, alto saxophonist Charlie Parker.

Most tenor saxophonists played within the traditions established by Coleman Hawkins (1904–1969). Hawkins used a rich, throaty tone and wide, fast vibrato. His style was heavily ornamented and rhythmically and harmonically complex. In many ways, it was the antithesis of the style Young was developing around this time and for which he was to become famous.

Early in December 1933 Hawkins came to Kansas City as part of the Fletcher Henderson band, one of the leading bands in the country at that time. This was Young's first opportunity to hear him in person:

I'd always heard so much about Hawk [Hawkins]—he was from St. Joseph, Missouri—and while I was working at the Paseo Club [El Paseo Ballroom—perhaps with the Moten-Lee band] in K.C., Fletcher Henderson was in town. I ran over to dig him between sets; I hadn't any loot so I stayed outside listening. Then one night Fletcher said his tenor man hadn't showed up, and wanted to know if there was someone around that could blow.

The story continues from the unedited interview with Postif:

I ran a million miles to hear Coleman Hawkins play and he wasn't there. So Fletcher Henderson ran out [the door], saying, "Don't you have no tenor players here in Kansas City? Can any of you motherfuckers play?" You know, that type of shit like that? Herschel [Evans] was out there—you dig—but he couldn't *read.* Herschel played *good,* but *he* couldn't read. So them motherfuckers just said, "Red"—they called me "Red" then—say, "Red, go [on in there] and blow this goddamn saxophone." And I'm coming to see Coleman Hawkins, they told me how great he was, I ain't seeing the fuck how great he *is.* You know? That type of shit.

So they shoved me on in there and I get up and grabbed his saxophone and played the motherfucker and read the music and read his clarinet parts and *everything.* Now I got to run back to my job where there's thirteen people in it. Run ten blocks back to get to them.

Sometime later during that engagement, Hawkins showed up at an after-hours jam session at the Cherry Blossom.[11] As the word spread, Young and other tenor saxophonists such as Ben Webster and Herschel Evans appeared. Reportedly they took turns playing with Hawkins all night long, giving him a much greater challenge than he had anticipated. Mary Lou Williams recalled that "Lester's style was light and . . . it took him maybe five choruses to warm up. But then he would really blow; then you couldn't handle him."[12] Clearly, Young's mastery was already evident by this time.

Basie had formed his own band, and Young joined up early in 1934, leaving Kansas City with them for a tour. He was very happy, saying, "I'd sit up all night and wait to go to work." But while playing with them in Little Rock, Arkansas, he received an offer of a permanent job with Fletcher Henderson's band. Hawkins had left in mid-March to go to England, and Henderson remembered the "strange young tenor man" from the Kansas City engagement the previous December. It is usually reported that Young received a telegram. George Dixon, fellow saxophonist, says he had received an airmail special delivery letter from Young expressing interest in any good offer outside Kansas City. Dixon remembers showing the letter to Henderson, then going right to the phone and getting Young on the line. A telegram may have followed.[13] This account is interesting, because Young never declared that he had actively sought to leave Basie. In any case, he was finally swayed by the greater prestige of the Henderson band, and the financial rewards—about seventy-five dollars per week as compared to fourteen with Basie, who was just starting out as an independent leader.

Young joined up with the Henderson group at the Graystone Hotel in Detroit on March 31, 1934. This was the first performance in a tour that took the band through numerous cities in Ohio, Iowa, Missouri, Kentucky, West Virginia, and elsewhere. They touched base in New York City at the end of April, only to go right out again on more one-nighters, in the East Coast area. At the end of May, the band settled in to the Apollo Theater in New York City.

Young was already collecting good notices from the press. John Hammond wrote in *Melody Maker* on June 2, "Hawkins' successor is a sensation I am told. I haven't heard this redheaded star. . . . No less than ten swell 'Harlemites' have told me that he swings more than Hawkins, and has actually 'cut' the Master on occasions." The *Chicago Defender* of June 16 reported that Young was "rated by many to be the equal of the old master [Hawkins]." But Henderson's musicians complained constantly about Young's style. John Hammond, Henderson's record producer, described the situation:

The whole sax section rebelled. They said that he sounded like another alto, that the section didn't have any body: they hated him! And Fletcher was too weak to stand up to them. I was absolutely entranced. Pres would get up and I had never heard anything like it in my life. And I'd say to Fletcher, "He's the best saxophone player I ever heard," and Fletcher would reply, "I know, John, but nobody likes him."[14]

Young, who stayed at the Henderson's New York home, told his side of the story:

I got bruised because I didn't play like Hawkins. They rang the bell on me. So I really did a lot of teardrops there, you know?

And this bitch would take me down, Fletcher Henderson's wife, take me down in the basement and play one of them old windup [record players] and shit, and actually said, (mimicking) "Lester, can't you play like this?" Coleman Hawkins playing. (Feigning boredom) "Umm, ivey-divey." "But I mean, don't you hear this? Can't you get with this?" You dig? I split! Every morning that bitch would wake me up at nine o'clock to try to teach *me* to play like Coleman Hawkins. And she played trumpet herself—circus trumpet! (Laughs) Fuck these motherfuckers! I'm *gone*!

The motherfuckers was whispering on me everytime I played. I can't make that. I won't say nothing while you're playing, nothing like that; you hear a group of motherfuckers whispering—Jesus! So [I] split. So I went to Fletcher and asked him, I said, "Would you give me a nice recommendation? I'm going back to Kansas City." This type of shit, you know. He said, "Oh, yeah!" right quick. (Laughs) I said, "Thank you."

An engagement at the famous Cotton Club fell through in mid-June, and the band was forced to go out on tour again, much to their disappointment. When they returned to New York early in July, they had no work for a little while, and Young probably left around this time, or while on tour. Young next joined the Andy Kirk band en route back to Kansas City. Kirk told this author in 1983 that Young played "some gigs" with the band during that short stay and "used to jam all night on the bus." By November Young was playing with the bands of Boyd Atkins and Rook Ganz in Minneapolis (and possibly Milwaukee), staying into 1935. Drummer Jo Jones and trumpeter Joe Keyes also appear to have been in the Ganz group, and later followed Young back to Basie. Young told a story about hearing Basie's new band, "Count Basie and His Barons of Rhythm" (the band's name seems to have undergone several changes), on a radio broadcast from Kansas City's Reno Club, while he was at the Cotton Club of Minneapolis. Young loved the band but hated the tenor saxophonist, Slim Freeman, and he sent a telegram that Basie later described as "strange and convincing," asking to come back to Basie and work as first tenor, moving Freeman to second. Basie agreed and Young returned to his adopted city. If this story is true, it must have been during 1935. In any case, back in Kansas City, Young worked at the Sunset, the Subway, and other clubs as well as with Basie. Jo Jones remembers a small group with Young at the Yellow Front Saloon. It was probably also during this period in 1935 that Earl Hines, in town with his big band, auditioned Young to replace the late Cecil Irwin (who had died on May 3 in an accident) but declined to hire him.

In 1936 Basie's musicians at the Reno Club made only about two dollars a night working from ten P.M. to five A.M., but they had the benefit of the nightly radio broadcasts, which John Hammond happened to hear on his powerful car radio at one o'clock one morning in Chicago. "I couldn't believe my ears," he recalled. In May 1936 Hammond wrote in *Down Beat* that Basie's group "has the most powerful drive of any band in the country. . . . Lester Young's tenor playing . . . is so good that it seems impossible that it was the same guy who took Hawkins' place in Fletcher's band two years ago and failed to distinguish himself." In July an unsigned article described the band on location at the Reno, "one of the town's most unsavory holes. . . . There they swing some of the country's finest arrangements under the noses of pimps, bags, and shipping clerks who may or may not appreciate them fully. . . . But even in the smoke-filled darkness of the rough'n ready Reno one gets a tremendous boot listening to Basie's riders. . . . Lester Young . . . lackadaisically plays tenor sax 'til 'who laid the chunk.'" The band included four saxes in all, Young, Freeman, Buster Smith, and Jack Washington, as well as three trumpets, one trombone, Basie's piano, guitar, bass (Walter Page) and drums, and two vocalists including Jimmy Rushing. Smith helped lead the band and wrote some of the music. It was a collection of top-notch players who had established themselves together and separately in the best local bands.

Hammond convinced Willard Alexander of Music Corporation of America, a major booking company, to sign a contract with Basie, and arrangements were made for the band to come East. While Hammond tried to negotiate a record contract with American Record Company, a Decca representative persuaded Basie to sign a three-year recording contract that offered no royalties and a minimal flat payment per recording. This contract also stipulated that Basie enlarge the group by several pieces. Buster Smith and trumpeter "Hot Lips" Page, two of the band's major soloists, left Basie for other offers, but among the new members were the outstanding trumpeter Buck Clayton and tenor saxophonist Herschel Evans. Drummer Jo Jones had also rejoined by this time, and his musical contribution became an indispensable element in the future success of Basie and Young.

Young's plans to tour with Basie were interrupted in September by the news that his father had suffered a stroke. Basie lent Lester his car and chauffeur, and Lester drove to Los Angeles (passing through New Mexico, according to John Lewis) and saw his father and the rest of his family for the first time in some years (probably since 1929). In fact, this was the first time, recalls Lee, that "I had seen Lester as an adult . . . Lester looked at me and he said, 'Oh, look at how big he is!' I said, 'He sounds like a girl,' you know, with that high voice he had. . . . He stayed about ten days, I think, and he brought a dog with him, I think—but he left the dog here with me."

Lee was pursuing a successful career as a jazz drummer. Irma had given up the saxophone but continued to perform as a singer and dancer in various shows. (She retired from show business during the 1950s and still resides in California.) Willis Young had continued to run a family band, and the family also played for their Baptist congregation on Sundays. One of the younger grandchildren, Martha, who was born to Irma around the time the family moved to Los Angeles, reminisced about the family's musical life in those days:

I played piano. My older cousins, one played piano, one played trombone, one played trumpet, and the small [kids], like my brother Brownie and the youngest girls, played tambourine, and my grandmother (Sara) played banjo. Papa (grandfather Willis) played cornet. . . . On Fridays we'd have a thing of family music. Papa wrote a lot for the family.

About Lester, "Uncle Bubble (Bubba)—that's the family name for him and that's all I ever called him—he didn't live in Los Angeles. . . .The thing of him coming home was always like, there was gonna be a really hot time! I stayed up later when he was in town so that I could be with him."[15] (Martha today is a fine professional jazz pianist in San Francisco.)

While in Los Angeles, Young took the opportunity to jam with some of the local musicians, and he attracted some notice in the local press. When he left, he brought back with him altoist Caughey Roberts to lead Basie's sax section. (The highest voice is always the leader in a jazz section, irrespective of improvisational ability.)

Count Basie Years (1936–1940)

The *Chicago Defender* newspaper reported in late September 1936 that "Count Bassey" (*sic*) was in Chicago on business. The nature of his business soon became clear. According to trumpeter Buck Clayton, the full and re-vamped Basie band left Kansas City after an engagement on Halloween night, October 31, 1936. The band's first MCA booking was a month at the Grand Terrace in Chicago, from November 7 through December 3, where they received very mixed reviews. It was probably during this engagement that Young's first recordings were made.[16] Hammond had protested the Dec-ca contract unsuccessfully and before it went into effect he wanted the band's sound on record. So he recorded Basie, Young, and four other members of the band, including vocalist Jimmy Rushing, under the pseudonym "Jones-Smith, Inc." (Jo Jones and Carl Smith were the drummer and trumpet player, respectively.) These are among the most celebrated of all jazz recordings.

From Chicago, the band went to the Vendome Hotel in Buffalo to play for a few weeks beginning on December 7, then to New London, Connecticut, and other one-nighters on the way to New York. Their big debut was at the Roseland Ballroom in Manhattan on December 24. By this time, most of the bugs had been worked out, and the band began to build up a following. George Simon, who had originally panned the group for poor intonation, ad-mitted in *Metronome,* February 1937, that "there's some brilliantly con-ceived stuff," and that the band members sounded more relaxed, and the rhythm section "consistently fine." The same month, in *Down Beat,* Ham-mond continued his support of the group, conceding that it was inconsistent, but that it had "the ability to sound magnificent and clean and in tune." More important, he was now convinced that Lester Young was "without doubt the greatest tenor player in the country . . . the most original and inventive sax-ophonist I have ever heard."

As a result of the band's exposure, Young became famous and appeared on several hundred recordings and "live" broadcasts between 1936 and

1940, with Basie as well as with Billie Holiday and others. He began to turn up regularly in the *Down Beat* polls beginning November 1937, usually in fifth or sixth place. Jazz critic Ralph Gleason was among those who were stunned by Young's music one night at the Famous Door on Fifty-second Street, where the Basie band, packed onto a small bandstand, played with its typical vigor: "Out of this acoustical wave Pres, with long and wavy hair and a thin wisp of moustache, rose and whispered, 'How d'you *do* there!' It cut through the brass like a bullet, soft as it was, and hit me right in the pit of my stomach. I almost cried."[17] Those Famous Door days of the second half of 1938 secured the band's reputation. (The reader should consult the Chronology and Catalog for any details of Young's itinerary not mentioned in the text of this chapter.)

Young developed many followers who imitated not only his music but also his mannerisms. As Stanley Dance recalled, "Young wore an incurious, enigmatic expression on a strangely boyish face. . . . He sat farthest from Basie, turning away from the sax section to blow, one shoulder down and horn tilted at an odd angle." One of the most striking mannerisms was this habit of holding the saxophone out to the right at about a forty-five-degree angle when he soloed. He probably developed this habit in his youth—Ralph Ellison remembered seeing the horn "outthrust" around 1930—although reedman Rudy Powell felt that "when he first joined the [Basie] band, he said, 'Herschel [Evans] is playing so much, nobody is paying any attention to me.' So he held his horn a different way." A more pragmatic explanation was offered by Ross Russell: "At the Reno Club with its crowded bandstand . . . Lester acquired his unusual way of holding the saxophone. To avoid poking fellow musicians in the back, Lester would twist in his chair, turn the horn at an angle of forty-five degrees and project it through an opening in the front line, so that he could play without interference and be heard by the dancers." According to Earle Warren, the angle did not help Young to be heard. Upon first encountering the Basie band early in 1937, "I got a big boot out of Herschel's sound but Lester I couldn't hear too well because he cocked his horn at an angle and the resonance of his horn went up into the canopy."[18] (Soon after this encounter, Warren accepted an offer to replace Caughey Roberts as lead alto saxophone.)

On occasion, Young played clarinet. At first he liked to use an old metal clarinet. Benny Goodman loved Young's playing, and at a jam session at the Black Cat early in 1937 he and Young are said to have exchanged instruments. Goodman was so entranced with Young's performance that he later had Young at his apartment and presented him with a wooden clarinet.[19] Sad-ly, this gift was stolen from Young's dressing room a few years later, and Young virtually dropped clarinet playing, although he could easily have replaced the instrument. (Young appeared in a *Down Beat* advertisement endorsing Martin Frères clarinets in April 1939.)

Young and vocalist Billie Holiday became close friends. Young said they first met when he was in New York with Henderson in 1934. Jo Jones confirms this, but John Hammond believes they met at the first recording session they did together, on January 25, 1937. Holiday, in her autobiography, remembered having met Young at an after-hours jam session. The varying accounts may reflect a lack of agreement as to what constitutes a "meeting." The two may have "met" in 1934, but it was certainly during 1937 that their friendship developed. Jo Jones, Buck Clayton, and Benny Morton, who participated in their recordings and knew them well, all reported that their relationship was a deep, platonic friendship, not a love affair.

Young, who was unhappy living at the Theresa Hotel in Harlem, moved in with Holiday and her mother. He called the older woman "Duchess" and referred to Billie, who was already known as "Lady," by the name "Lady Day." ("Day" was short for "Holiday.") "She was teaching me about the city, you know—which way to go, you know? Yeah—She's still my Lady Day," he said in 1959. Holiday responded by dubbing Young "the President"—"Pres" for short—because she felt "Lester was the world's greatest. I loved his music, and some of my favorite recordings are the ones with Lester's pretty solos. Lester sings with his horn; you listen to him and can almost hear the words." Young included some of his recordings with Holiday among his own personal favorites, such as "A Sailboat in the Moonlight," and "Back in Your Own Backyard." He once commented on the outstanding musical rapport he and Holiday enjoyed: "Sometime[s] I sit down and listen to [the old records] myself, and they sound like two of the same voices, if you don't be careful, you know—or the same mind or something like that."[20]

Another important relationship during this period was that between Young and his old friend Herschel Evans, who now played beside Young in the Basie saxophone section. The difference in their styles led to much talk of rivalry.

Herschel Evans was a Hawk [Coleman Hawkins] man. That was the difference between the way we played. He played well, but his man was Hawk like my man at the beginning was [Frankie] Trumbauer.

We were nice friends and things, but, I mean, there wasn't no bullshit or nothing. When we got up on the bandstand to play, like a duel (laughs), you know; and then other nights we'd get along nice. You know what I mean. But I mean, it's coming through his instrument, you dig?

Billie Holiday, who sang with the Basie band from March 1937 until February 1938, recalls:

Pres and Herschel Evans were forever thinking up ways of cutting the other one. You'd find them in the band room, hacking away at reeds, trying all kinds of new ones, anything to get ahead of the other one. Once Herschel asked Lester, "Why don't you play alto, man? You got an alto *tone.*" Lester tapped his head, "There's things going on up there, man," he told Herschel. "Some of you guys are all belly."[21]

But the rivalry was a friendly one, and was sorely missed by Young after Evans died of heart disease in February 1939. He became restless and at times he would reportedly attempt to leave the bandstand in the middle of a set.

A small white woman, an Italian-American named Mary who worked as a nurse, became Young's second wife by 1937. (Actually, the marriage was common-law, so did not become legal for a few years.) Lester and Mary moved into the Woodside Hotel in Harlem, where most of the Basie band was headquartered. Lester's brother Lee informs us that Lester was strictly monogamous, not interested even in prostitutes. "As far as women were concerned—when he was married to Mary, it was nothing but Mary and his horn." (On the other hand, Buddy Tate, who replaced Herschel Evans in the Basie band, says that Lester would flirt around when they were on tour.)

While with Basie, Lester discovered a third interest that would eventually rival his love for music and for Mary—getting high. He and Holiday would smoke marijuana in large quantities while in the recording studio, and he began to enjoy alcohol, too, especially a mixture of gin and sherry. Some said he preferred pot to women, and spread false rumors that he was gay. Young never indulged in hard drugs; he was repulsed by them and scared of needles.

Young also enjoyed gambling with his band mates while riding from one city to another on the band bus. But this was purely for fun and not a serious habit. Many of the musicians participated in the dice games to pass the time, and they report that Lester loved to play despite the fact that he usually lost. While in New York, the band entertained themselves by playing softball against other bands in Central Park. Lester surprised everyone by dropping his usual mischievous sense of humor to do an effective pitching job at these games.

Lester's life with Basie appeared to be happy and musically rewarding. This made it all the more surprising when he left the band in December 1940, shortly before a recording session that took place on Friday the thirteenth. The story usually told, and given in *Down Beat,* January 1, 1941, is that Young was superstitious and refused to play. (The next issue said Young was "fired." Mrs. Young refuted this in the March 1 issue.) But there were obviously much deeper reasons behind this split.

Young himself was of little help, since he generally refused to explain why he left Basie. On one occasion he did say that he got bored with rehearsals, which usually were three hours long, three times a week:

> In Basie's band there would always be someone who didn't know his part. Seems to me that if a musician can't read, he should say so, and then you help him. Or you give him his part before. But Basie wouldn't. I used to talk to him about it, but he had no eyes for it. You had to sit there and play it over and over and over again. Just sit in that chair. . . .

Even Young's fellow musicians have trouble elaborating on Young's reasons for leaving. Several do mention, however, that Young was not satisfied with the financial arrangement. John Hammond says Lester's wife Mary wanted him to make more too. Basie was becoming more and more the celebrity, while Young made only slighly more than all the other players, notwithstanding his popularity. (Basie made around $7,000 a year, Young and the best sidemen probably around $5,000.) After all, in the December 1, 1940 *Down Beat* he was voted the number-four tenor saxophonist in jazz. He also received no recognition for his contributions to the band's repertory. Many of the numbers were put together at rehearsals from ideas suggested by various members. Young's fellow saxophonists attest to the fact that he contributed many of the saxophone riffs played in those arrangements, yet his name rarely appeared in the credits. Young began to feel he would do better as a single, leading his own small band.

Personnel changes in the band disturbed Young, also. First there was the death of his friendly rival, Herschel Evans. Then, his good friend Shad Collins left at the end of 1939. Although Young never mentioned it, he may also have disliked the addition of altoist Tab Smith in May 1940, which changed the saxophone section from four to five pieces. Smith had originally been called in for a recording session to substitute for the ailing Earle Warren, and ended up staying.

Last but not least, the Basie band was embroiled in a battle with its agents at MCA, which precipitated Young's departure as well as that of Vic Dickenson in January 1941. Willard Alexander, the band's original agent at MCA, had left to join the William Morris Agency. His replacements had served the band very poorly, getting them work irregularly and at less than the best locations. Basie was particularly upset about the scarcity of live radio broadcasts. Basie appealed to the musicians' union to allow him to break his MCA contract and follow Alexander to the William Morris Agency, and MCA retaliated by sending the band on a grueling series of one-nighters, which forced them to travel as much as 500 miles per day. Basie, who had been recording and occasionally performing with Benny Goodman since February 1940, even threatened to leave his band and join Goodman permanently. Finally, MCA agreed to release Basie from his contract for $10,000, and the band returned to Willard Alexander who got them their first new job on January 3, 1941. The whole affair had been the last straw for Young, who was already involved in putting together a small group of his own.

The War Years (1941–1945)

On December 29, 1940, and January 12, 1941, Young participated in all-star jam sessions at New York's Village Vanguard. On January 26 he appeared in another one at Jimmy Ryan's. From February 27 through March 17, 1941, Young led a small band at Kelly's Stables in New York, with his friend Shad Collins on trumpet. But the group met with limited success and broke up after this engagement. In May, Young moved to Los Angeles to join his drummer brother Lee's band. The band also included another saxophonist, "Bumps" Myers, who served as an effective foil for Lester, much as Herschel Evans had. The other members were Arthur Twine, piano, Red Callendar, bass, Red Mack on trumpet, and Louis Smith on guitar. Despite the small size of the group, such important young composers as Billy Strayhorn, Dudley Brooks, and Gerald Wilson contributed to their repertoire. Lester and Mary bought a house in a black section of the city, and Mary stayed there most of the time through World War II. But Young often stayed alone at a boardinghouse, an indication that the relationship was in trouble.

Lee Young had become quite successful, having worked with Lionel Hampton, Fats Waller, and others. He was a good businessman, and was able to manage the band effectively. In this respect, he contrasted with Lester, who had been unable to make a success of his band with Shad Collins. "He didn't know how to do *anything* but play saxophone," said Lee. The band played at Billy Berg's Club Capri as part of a show that also included the Spirits of Rhythm and other acts. Unfortunately, union rules prevented Lester from playing regularly in Los Angeles until he had applied for a transfer from the New York union to the local one, so for the first few months he had to appear for a few numbers each set as a "guest artist." After a long tenure at the Capri, the Youngs continued to work regularly on the coast, managed by the William Morris Agency. (Red Callendar says that Lester and he also played with the "Phil Moore Four" at a club on Vine Street during this period.)

On February 24, 1942, the Youngs reopened at the Capri, this time as part of a joint venture with "Slim and Slam." Slim Gaillard played guitar and sang, and Slam Stewart played bass. Arthur Twine had died suddenly and was replaced by white pianist Jimmy Rowles, from Slim and Slam's group. Interracial groups were still unusual enough for this to be noted in *Down Beat.* In the spring of 1942, the Youngs and the entire show from the Capri moved to Billy Berg's new club in the Beverly Fairfax area, a much more luxurious place called the Trouville.

Rowles and the band called Lester "Uncle Bubba," no doubt picked up from Young's family in the area. Rowles conjured up the Young of that time with vivid detail: "Lester was unique. He was alone. He was quiet. He was unfailingly polite. He almost never got mad. If he was upset, he'd take a small whisk broom he kept in his top jacket pocket and sweep off his left shoulder. The only way to get to know him was to work with him. Otherwise, he'd just sit there playing cards or sipping, and if he did say something it stopped the traffic. I never saw him out of a suit, and he particularly liked double-breasted pin stripes. He also wore tab collars, small trouser cuffs, pointed shoes, and Cuban heels." Singer Sylvia Syms added, "He used cologne, and he always smelled divine."

According to Rowles, "Lester didn't have a big reputation with nonmusicians. The guys who would come to see Lester would be the guys in the traveling bands." Young's name virtually disappeared from the *Down Beat* polls after he left Basie. In the California band, he received second billing since Lee was the director. It was usually "Lee and Lester Young's Band," or a variation thereof. Nevertheless, Young declined to rejoin Basie when Basie called long distance with an offer in July 1942, as reported in *Down Beat.*

The Youngs moved to New York in September 1942 for a residency at Café Society Downtown, followed by other engagements. Clyde Hart replaced Jimmy Rowles on piano, and later Charles Thompson came in, dubbed "Sir" by Lester. When the Youngs received news that their father, who had long been ill, had died on February 6, 1943, at the age of sixty-seven, Lee went out to Los Angeles for the funeral and to help their stepmother, Sara. Sara was an invalid, having had her leg amputated some years before, and died, grief-stricken, only about two weeks after Willis Handy. Lee stayed in Los Angeles, Lester stayed in New York, and that was the end of their joint venture. (They did play together again at times, such as the 1946 "Jazz at the Philharmonic" concerts in Los Angeles. Lee eventually dropped out of performing to enter the production end of the record business. His son followed him into the business and Lee and family still live in the Los Angeles area.)

Lester guested at jam sessions at Minton's Playhouse, the Village Vanguard, and other Manhattan clubs. He showed great interest in the modern jazz or "bebop" style that was showcased at Minton's. In the spring of 1943 he worked with the Al Sears big band at the Renaissance Casino and Ballroom and went on a U.S.O. tour with them. Budd Johnson, who was also in the saxophone section, recalls that the tour took them through Texas and Arkansas, and that the band alternated with classical pianist Artur Rubinstein! Al Fisher, a fan who heard Lester with the band at an "Air Force base in Sheppard Field [*sic*] Texas," remembered it as "the high of the war for me" (letter to *Jazz Review,* July 1959). "When he stepped out in front with his pork-pie hat and dark glasses (no U.S.O. monkey suit for him), he blew the crackers, the hayseeds, and even we studiedly casual Easterners right out of our seat."

On June 15, 1943, *Down Beat* printed a letter from another fan, Lou Donati, who lamented the current state of Young's career. "If he were to rejoin Basie . . . he would be giving a lot of us a real break in the increase in his audience and in his activities." In October, Young tried working with Basie again at the Apollo Theatre in Harlem. He appeared with Dizzy Gillespie at the Onyx Club, then rejoined Basie for a longer term beginning in December. Don Byas had been fired for drinking and arguing with Basie, and drummer Jo Jones was sent, on behalf of Basie, to invite Young to return in place of Byas. Young showed up that night at the Lincoln Hotel (later known as the Washington—the band had been there since November 5). He quickly settled back in. He recorded with fellow Basie-ite Dicky Wells on December 21, recorded "Afternoon of a Basie-ite" on December 28, and appeared in several more fine small group sessions during 1944. In the *Down Beat* poll at the end of 1943, Young had already moved back up to fourth place.

Young felt at home with Basie and resumed his humorous antics. Trombonist Dicky Wells recalled those days:

It was at the Lincoln that Pres got his little bell. If somebody missed a note, or you were a new guy and goofed, you'd hear this bell going—"Ding-dong!" If Pres was blowing and goofed, somebody would reach over and ring his bell on him.

"Why, you . . . ," he'd say when he'd finished.[22]

At the beginning of 1944, the band went on a tour of the Northeast. It returned to New York City from March through May, including another stint at the Lincoln, then went on a cross-country tour, leading to an opening in Los Angeles on August 1. Young appeared on a few V-disc recordings and many radio broadcasts with the Basie band, and was featured with fellow saxophonist Illinois Jacquet and a small group in the film short *Jammin' the Blues,* made in August 1944. But the fun was soon to end. During this period the army had unsuccessfully attempted to draft Young, and Jacquet claims that Young "was actually cryin' in that film because he didn't want to go into the army. . . . To see Lester up there cryin' and playin' that slow blues was really a touching moment in my life."[23]

An FBI agent served induction papers to Young and Jo Jones at the Plantation Club in Los Angeles, while they were appearing with the Basie band. Milt Ebbins, Basie's personal manager, and Norman Granz, a producer who had been involved with the Trouville engagement and with *Jammin' the Blues,* appealed to the draft board. Besides, Young had developed a case of syphilis in the late 1930s that was becoming worse, and there was some evidence that he occasionally suffered epileptic seizures. But the draft board never wavered. Lee Young met his brother in Los Angeles and drove him to the induction center. At his interview, Lester admitted on a questionnaire that he smoked marijuana, perhaps hoping that this would be cause for rejection. But this too was ignored by army authorities. Young even showed up drunk for a spinal tap and was placed in a padded cell for more than a day. All notwithstanding, Young was inducted on September 30, 1944.

Young and Jo Jones were sent to Fort MacArthur in California for five weeks of basic training, then went to two other bases including Fort Ord. Jones stayed for a while at Ord, but Young quickly moved on to Fort McClellan in Alabama, where he was stationed as a private in the infantry beginning December 1. Ironically, that same month he finally reached first place in the *Down Beat* poll for top tenor saxophonist. (*Down Beat* also reported that Norman Granz wanted to get Young out of McClellan for an all-star concert on December 17 or 18, but it does not appear that Granz was successful.)

Young's army experience was traumatic. Troubles began almost immediately. Charlie Carpenter, Young's manager in later years, reported that his saxophone was confiscated and his hair ordered cut. There was an excellent jazz band at McClellan, recalls drummer Jerry Potter. He remembers among his fellow members another fine drummer, Chico Hamilton, as well as "lots of good players from Hamp's [Lionel Hampton's] band, and two terrific trumpet players." He places Jo Jones there for a while, too. But Young was not a member. Trombonist Jimmy Cheatham, who was stationed with Young, said that the warrant officer, "a short, flightish" black man with a background in college teaching, took a dislike to Young and refused to let him play in the band. Cheatham described how Young's fellow musicians helped him to by-pass this obstacle:

We would get him in sometimes, like for a rehearsal. And the guys in his company—a lot of them knew about him, they were trying to protect him—they would sneak him in. When they'd go out on their different training problems, they'd pass right by the band building and they'd just walk Lester Young right in there. And when they'd come back, he'd be ready and they'd walk him right back out. But no, he was never formally approved for the band.[24]

Lee Young feels that Lester may have been partially to blame for his situation. Lester wasn't the type to research his options, says Lee, and probably didn't even know to request a placement in the band. Jerry Potter found that Young was rather bitter, and didn't even want to play. Lester was deeply hurt that a popular white band, Glenn Miller's, could play as a unit for the army, whereas he and his Basie colleagues were drafted individually like ordinary civilians, and scattered around the country.

Potter describes Young as someone who "liked the booze" and stayed up until five o'clock in the morning. Lester was repeatedly placed on KP duty, where, some say, he tried to distill alcohol out of fermented food. Friends of Young, including several officers, began a move to have him discharged because of "maladjustment to the confines of the army." But a series of events defeated this effort, beginning when Young entered the hospital for minor rectal surgery on January 1, 1945. He had injured himself running an obstacle course, and was given pain-killing drugs while he recovered in the hospital. On January 24 he was sent back to active duty, but was being watched closely, because while in the hospital he had been diagnosed as a chronic user of drugs and alcohol. On February 1, he was arrested for possession of marijuana and barbiturates.

Lester's court-martial hearing convened on February 16. Several officers testified for the prosecution, basically recounting how they found the unlawful drugs. All agreed that Young had never denied that he used drugs. Researcher John McDonough continues the story:

The only witness for the defense was Pvt. Lester Young himself, who admitted virtually everything. He was a cooperative, if bewildered, witness on his own behalf. He was a man of music now caught in a rigid system of discipline he could not begin to understand—and the army was no less puzzled by him. Whether they were trying, the representatives of two cultures showed no mutual understanding.[25]

Young discussed the whole incident quite candidly, admitting that he had obtained the barbiturates—the same kind he had been given in the hospital—without a doctor's knowledge. He even disclosed that he didn't feel capable of coping with military service without drugs. Young's counsel, Major Glen Grimke, based his defense on the fact that Young was obviously unsuited for army life in the first place. Two psychological reports confirmed that he was unfit for soldiering. Nevertheless, after ninety minutes, Young was given the maximum sentence. He was dishonorably discharged from the army and sentenced to a year in the disciplinary barracks of Fort Gordon, Georgia.

While at Fort Gordon, Young seems to have been able to engage in musical pursuits. John McDonough reports:

> The court martial record says nothing about Young's ten months at Ft. Gordon. It is known, however, that he played music regularly while confined. Every Sunday, there was a dance for the noncoms on the base, and Lester would be let out to play. Fred Lacey, who became Young's regular guitarist in the postwar years, was also a prisoner there, and played in the little group. Sitting in most of the time on piano was Gil Evans, who was assigned to Oliver General Hospital ten miles away in Augusta. On his way to Ft. Gordon every Sunday, Evans would pick up a few bottles of whiskey and perhaps some other gifts, which he made sure found their way discreetly to Lester.

(Evans was later to become one of the most admired of jazz arrangers.) On December 1, 1945, Young was excused from the last few months of his sentence and granted a dishonorable discharge. His friend Norman Granz paid for his plane ticket back to Los Angeles and arranged for a recording contract with Philo Records (soon changed to Aladdin). At the first session (usually dated as October 1945, but it must have been in December) he recorded an original entitled "D.B. (Disciplinary Barracks) Blues." He described his army experience as "a nightmare, man, one mad nightmare."[26] But the public had not forgotten him this time. They voted him third place in the end of the year *Down Beat* poll, and eagerly awaited his new performances.

Postwar Years (1946–1959)

Early in 1946, Young signed a personal management contract with Norman Granz, who was now the producer of a series of all-star concerts called "Jazz at the Philharmonic," or "JATP" for short. Young's first appearances at these concerts, in Los Angeles in January and April, were released on records. Other musicians at these concerts included Coleman Hawkins, Dizzy Gillespie, and Charlie Parker. The group played in Chicago on May 14, then a series of concerts at Carnegie Hall, returning to Chicago on June 22. Young and other musicians on the tour stayed in New York while Granz tried to set up a trip to France for August. When the trip didn't materialize, the JATP tour went to California. Young went also, but seems to have gone home and not played on the remainder of the tour, which included concerts in San Francisco, Los Angeles, and elsewhere, ending in New York by November 23. This kind of itinerary was typical of a JATP all-star season. Young took 1947 and 1948 off from JATP, but soon returned, playing at least one JATP concert each season, if not the whole tour. He appeared in Granz's shows throughout the 1950s, long after Charlie Carpenter had become his personal manager.

Young's popularity and income soared during the later 1940s, to as high as $50,000 a year. He could command a fee of $500 a week for club engagements, and twice that for JATP tours. He ranked high in polls conducted by *Down Beat, Metronome,* and *Esquire,* winning Esquire Silver Awards in 1945 and 1947. In a poll conducted by Leonard Feather in 1956, jazz musicians voted Young "Greatest Tenor Saxophonist Ever." Most of the time, except when touring with JATP, Young appeared at jazz clubs with small groups of his own, usually including piano, bass, drums, and trumpet. He preferred to play with younger musicians of the new modern jazz or "bebop" generation. Members of his groups in the late 1940s and early 1950s included trumpeter Jesse Drakes; pianists John Lewis, Horace Silver, and Junior Mance; Aaron Bell, bass; and Roy Haynes, Connie Kay, and Jo Jones, drums. Young's group played at the opening of the club Birdland at the end of 1949 and frequently appeared there and at the Royal Roost when in New York. On February 21, 1951, the group was featured at Carnegie Hall. By the mid-1950s, Young was touring as a single, playing with local rhythm sections in each city.

Young joined several overseas tours with JATP beginning in March 1952, including a visit to London in March 1953; he also went to Europe with the "Birdland 1956" show. He guested with the Count Basie band many times in the 1950s, notably at the Newport Jazz Festival in July 1957.

Young had continued to write Mary while he was in the army, but their relationship ended soon afterward. In the late 1940s he married for the third time, with another small, quiet woman named Mary, but this one black. They settled into a house in the St. Albans section of Queens in New York

City. Young's first child, Lester Young, Jr., was born in 1947 (he is now Dr. Young, an educator in the New York City area), and a daughter, Yvette, was born in 1957. Bill Coss wrote in *Metronome* (October 1955) of a typical day Young spent "enjoying his lovely wife and sprouting son, his modest brick home, his mid-afternoon nap (he sleeps very few hours at a time) and the constant and simultaneous din of television set and record player." But this picture of family bliss was deceptive, for Young lived through it numbed by alcohol. He drank heavily, mostly gin, and still smoked marijuana frequently. His health was deteriorating, leading to hospitalization several times in the 1950s. Two of his musicians report occasions when Young suddenly fell down or had to lie down because he felt ill, and another incident was described in print as "a mild heart seizure."

Many writers have commented on Young's eccentric habits during his later years. (One, Alain Gerber of France, even suggested that he had become psychotic.) He would approach the bandstand with little, mincing steps at times. His speech, which had always been heavily loaded with personal slang words, became even more cryptic. "He calls whomever he's working for, a club owner, or a promoter, 'Pres,'" said George Wein. "Fellow musicians he addresses as 'Lady.'"[27] For example, Louis Bellson became "Lady" Bellson. But he continued to be reliable and punctual where performances were concerned.

Horace Silver, who played piano for Young during the early 1950s, made some sensitive observations:

If you were a member of his band and he opened up to you, he was beautiful. He'd keep you laughing all the time. . . . But he'd come off the bandstand and go right in the dressing room. He wouldn't go out till it was time to go on the bandstand again. If we were on the road he'd stay in his hotel room all day, and he'd either send out for food or get his food in a paper bag and come back and eat it in his room. . . . I was riding home from a gig one night in the car and . . . somehow I felt he felt dejected or something and he told me—he called everybody "Prez"—he said, "Well, Prez, I really don't think nobody really likes old Prez." That's the way he felt.[28]

White producer John Hammond experienced Young before the army as a taciturn, lackluster sort except when playing or listening to music. After Young's discharge, observed Hammond, he was even more suspicious and uncommunicative. But Young's behavior was a result of his discomfort around white people. He said that he "felt a draft" around certain "grey boys."[29]

Young had always been sensitive to racial prejudice—remember, he had left his father's band rather than tour the South—and became increasingly bitter. He spoke vehemently about the attitudes of white people in the interview taped in Paris just before he died:

Young: I'd have left here the other night if I had five hundred dollars. I just can't take that *bullshit,* you dig? It's all *bullshit,* and they want everybody who is a Negro to be a Uncle Tom or Uncle Remus or Uncle Sam and I can't make it.

Postif: Not here you know, not in France.

Young: Shi-i-it! Shit! Are you kiddin'? I've been here two weeks, I've been picking up on that. Well, I won't tell you what I know what [jumped off]. Seeing is believing and hearing is a bitch—that's a sound! Right here in Gay Paree. Maybe it wouldn't happen to you, y'dig? You're not a colored person like I am, y'dig? They're gonna take advantage of me.

But all I can do is tell you what happened. And I'm not gonna tell you *that* part of it. But it did happen. By somebody you wouldn't believe, [too]—great person. But it's the same way all over, y'dig. It's fight for your life, that's all. Until death do we part, you got it made.

Young was still haunted by memories of his childhood church where blacks could not be saved, and only the intervention of the Reverend John Gensel, a New York minister who had long been involved with the jazz community, convinced him that he, too, could be saved.

Young had been hospitalized at Bellevue for a few weeks in the winter of 1955 and came out relaxed and confident. But he needed hospital treatment again in 1957. His health was poor during the last American JATP tour that year (nevertheless, he sat in at local clubs along the way), and he appeared weak during his appearance on the CBS television show "The Sound of Jazz" in December 1957, which brought him back together with Basie and Billie Holiday. Soon after, he was again confined, at King's County Hospital, for a combination of ailments including malnutrition, alcoholism, and cirrhosis of the liver. By February 1958, he was ready to record and perform again. Norman Granz, who supervised most of Young's recordings during the 1950s, persuaded him to record on a metal clarinet for the first time in twenty years, but the results were very disappointing. Young could hardly control the instrument, and the released recordings contain several disturbing squeaks. In mid-February he was scheduled to play a weekend in Westbury.

In the spring of 1958 Young left his home and moved into the Alvin Hotel at Fifty-second Street and Broadway in Manhattan, across the street from Birdland, where he'd often played. He watched western movies in the theaters almost every afternoon, ate meals in a nearby cafeteria, and drank gin in the evening. Wearing his shorts and the porkpie hat that had become his trademark, he would sit by the window in his hotel room and watch the musicians arriving at Birdland while he drank gin. Often he would hold his saxophone and work the keys without blowing into it. He enjoyed listening to recordings of pop vocalists including Frank Sinatra and Jo Stafford. Gil Evans described the scene to Whitney Balliett:

He had a great big room at the Alvin, and when I'd go up to see him I'd find full plates of food everywhere. They'd been brought by friends, but he wouldn't eat. He just drank. . . . One of the reasons his drinking got so out of hand was his teeth. They were in terrible shape, and he was in constant pain. But he was still fussy about things like his hair. . . . It was amazing—a man more or less consciously killing himself, and he was still particular about his hair.

Jazz historian Marshall Stearns, who knew Young well, called in psychologist Luther Cloud to determine the causes of Young's depression. Dr. Cloud, along with several other persons close to Young in his last years, believed that Young's own fame and influence, ironically, had brought him unhappiness. So much of modern jazz was based on the innovations of Young, and so many of his ideas were played note for note by younger musicians, that he began to feel obsolete. Cloud remembers him commenting about the young saxophonists playing across the street at Birdland, "They're picking the bones while the body is still warm." A few years before, when Young was playing alternate sets at Birdland with Paul Quinichette—who sounded so much like Young that he was called "Vice-Pres"—he told his manager, Charlie Carpenter: "I don't know whether to play like me or like Lady Q, because he's playing so much like me." As Connie Kay, who played drums with Young for a while, summed it up, "Lester didn't feel he was getting the recognition he deserved and finally he got to the point where he didn't care whether he lived or died."[30]

The final year of Young's life was spent with a young woman named Elaine Swain, who cared for him and recorded his reminiscences in notebooks, to date unpublished. Swain and Dr. Cloud persuaded Young to eat, and diluted his gin with water. They fed him tranquilizers and vitamin pills, and eventually replaced his gin with wine. In a few months, Young had gained weight and was going outdoors again.

Young appeared at the Newport Jazz Festival in July 1958 with Jack Tea-garden and "Pee Wee" Russell, two outstanding jazzmen active since the 1920s. On August 27 Marshall Stearns and writer Nat Hentoff sponsored a birthday party and tribute for Young at Birdland, where he performed cred-itably. Several performances in Harlem followed, as well as one for Norman Granz at the Academy of Music in Brooklyn, and several weeks at the Five Spot club at the end of the year. He had greatly reduced his drinking and began visiting his family on occasion. (His last wife, Mary, still lives in the New York City area.)

Lester began making plans to rejuvenate his career. He wanted to leave his recording contract for Norman Granz, and *Down Beat* (October 2, 1958) reported that he had signed with United Artists. He expressed a desire to record with woodwinds and strings. He ordered a poster and other new pro-motional materials to be made up, and his manager began work to try to obtain more and better bookings.

Young accepted an offer to perform in Paris. This engagement at the Blue Note Club, which began in January 1959, was to be his last. Because the hotels would not allow him to cook in his room, he practically stopped eating altogether, and resumed drinking heavily. He became ill and weak, unable to join one of Norman Granz's JATP tours of Europe as he had planned. Ben Benjamin, owner of the Blue Note, said Young was "almost pathetic. He wanted to go home because he said he couldn't talk to a French doctor."[31] Granz helped him with airfare back to New York. Young cabled Elaine Swain on March 13 and arrived in New York the following day. But he had vomited blood during the flight and was in such pain that he had bitten through his lip.

Returning to his hotel room, Young continued drinking and still would not eat. His condition rapidly worsened, and he died at three A.M., March 15, 1959. He was buried in Evergreen Cemetery, Queens, New York. The im-mediate cause of death was heart failure, but Young had advanced cirrhosis of the liver, which was a major factor.

Young realized that drinking would eventually destroy him. In fact, Bobby Scott remembers that he had twice "referred to himself in the past tense and didn't seek to rectify the mistake." He pulled out of his slump toward the end. He was touring again, and at his last interview he spoke with vitality. But his reformation came too late. He was too addicted to alcohol to avoid it for long, and even if he had, he could not have repaired the serious damage already inflicted on his internal organs.

Recently Scott paid tribute to the late saxophonist:

He had the courage that makes for *self*. The quality of bravery that never asks dumb questions or looks for conspiracy in honest words. The great danger of *becoming* your musical expression was one to which Lester never succumbed. It set him apart from other musicians, made less by their inability to be something other than their music. No one who knew him would call him a "regular guy." Not ever. But he *could* be, if he so chose. That in itself broadens his humanity.

Young passed his humanity on to us in his music.

2

Lester Leaps In

Lester Young did indeed leap into the national jazz scene with his first recordings in 1936, which revealed a breathtakingly original and mature artist. He was already twenty-seven years old, relatively late for a major jazz musician to make his recording debut. Most of the greats—Louis Armstrong, Charlie Parker, Dizzy Gillespie, and the like—began recording before the age of twenty-five, often as early as twenty.

It is a shame that Young was discovered so late, because we are forever barred from hearing him develop his unique style over the preceding years. Unlike the other artists named above, we will never know what he sounded like before he came fully into his own, whether he developed gradually or suddenly, or whether he always sounded as he did on those first recordings. We do, at least, know something about his tastes in music, and we can compare his recorded style with recordings he may have heard during his formative years.

Young was a product of tradition, and worked within the traditions established by his predecessors, those we outlined in the preface. But even though he clearly accepted and built upon that foundation, his style was perceived as very new and different. In fact, his arrival into national prominence when he began touring and recording with Count Basie occasioned much controversy. One 1939 reviewer said Young's playing reminded him of the sound of "a table being dragged across the floor."[1] Critic Mike Levin referred to his saxophone tone as "cardboard" and said his playing of that instrument was less "tasteful and ideaful" than his clarinet playing.[2]

But a growing number of young musicians, black and white, idolized Young. Al Cohn was not alone when he said, "Prez was the reason I became a tenor saxophone player."[3] Charlie Parker reportedly memorized Young's solos on [*Oh*] *Lady Be Good* and *Shoe Shine Boy* (Take 1), and Dexter Gordon still quotes from these solos in his performances. Budd Johnson, a contemporary of Young who was already well established in the late 1930s, quickly adopted many of Young's stylistic qualities.

Young's style was controversial because it derived partly from a classically oriented approach used by certain white saxophone players of the 1920s rather than the rich, muscular style of the leading black tenor saxophonist, Coleman Hawkins. There were two issues at stake: it was heresy not to sound like Hawkins, and it seemed somehow improper for a major black artist to name white musicians as his influences.

Coleman Hawkins (1904–1969) was known as "the father of the tenor saxophone." Certainly not the first to play the instrument, he brought to it such a high level of technical mastery and creative authority that he reformed the vaudeville conception of the instrument that was then prevalent. Discerning musicians continue to find stimulating ideas in Hawkins's recordings. The same can be said of Young's records, but before Young, Hawkins was the unchallenged king. Hawkins played with a rich, guttural tone, a wide, fast vibrato, and a stunning command of his instrument. Raymond Horricks wrote: "With his way of poising a melodic line firmly upon a strong rhythmic pattern and his tendency to produce a dramatic turn of phrase, the Hawk's expression is essentially very direct and forceful." Yet, in a world where almost all of his peers were trying to follow in Hawkins's footsteps, Young managed to carve out a quite different path. Of course, Young knew of Hawkins and he always expressed admiration for the great master, but explained that he simply had never felt that approach was for him. In his youth, he rarely, if ever, listened to Hawkins. The best technical comparison of the two tenor players was written by Don Heckman for *Down Beat,* January 3, 1963. Heckman illustrates, with musical examples, differences in phrasing and structure. Benny Green summed it up well when he wrote, "Where Hawkins is profuse, Lester is pithy, where Hawkins is passionate, Lester is reflective."[4]

Lester's preference for the white school of saxophonists helps greatly to account for his arrival at a new approach. Many white players, in contrast to the Hawkins school, preferred the alto saxophone to the tenor and used a light tone and a slower vibrato. American virtuoso Rudy Wiedoft, a master of light classics, served as the model for Young's two favorite saxophonists, Jimmy Dorsey and Frankie Trumbauer. (Trumbauer played C-melody saxophone, which is slightly lower in range than the alto.) Both of these musicians occasionally composed semiclassical pieces in the Wiedoft manner, which displayed their ability to tongue rapidly and precisely while playing intricate lines. They also incorporated classical routines into their jazz solos. For example, in the second chorus of Dorsey's *I'm Just Wild About Harry*, recorded in 1930, he executes a very rapid pattern of eighth-note triplets involving arpeggios and chromatic scales.[5] Dorsey articulates every note clearly, using classical triple-tonguing. He repeats the pattern almost exactly in the second half of the chorus, beginning in measure 17, which confirms that he prepared it beforehand and was not improvising. (All measure numbers in this book are counted from the beginning of the solo chorus mentioned, in this case chorus two.)

Young recalled, "I had to make a decision between Frankie Trumbauer and Jimmy Dorsey—y'dig? I wasn't sure which way I wanted to go, y'dig? . . . The only people that was tellin' stories that I liked to hear were them . . . Ever hear him [Trumbauer] play *Singin' the Blues*? That tricked me right there, that's where I went." (Fellow saxophonist Eddie Barefield met Young in 1927 when the Young family band stayed in North Dakota for a while. He and Young used to order Trumbauer's records from a mail-order catalog, Barefield recalls.)[6] Trumbauer's light tone influenced Young's concept of tone. Young even said, "I tried to get the sound of a C-melody [saxophone] on a tenor."[7] He added, "I liked the way he slurred the notes."

Trumbauer's playing was notable for its structural sense. As Young put it, he "always told a little story. . . . He'd play the melody first and then after that he'd play around the melody." He produced an uncrowded flow of notes in a relaxed rhythm, balanced an upward gesture with a descending one, and generally gave an impression of poise and control rather than effort and abandon. Young, too, possessed these qualities. He communicated more intense emotions than Trumbauer, but always in a sensitive, tasteful manner, and his solos were elegantly constructed.

Young also expressed admiration for Trumbauer's musical partner, cornetist Bix Beiderbecke. In relation to this point, Beiderbecke expert Richard Sudhaldter pointed out (in the Time-Life Young box) that Young's own composition *Tickle Toe* ends with a phrase from Beiderbecke's solo on *When* (recorded March 12, 1928, with Paul Whiteman). Young's enthusiasm for Trumbauer and Beiderbecke, both white, was shared by many other black musicians. Louis Armstrong highly praised Beiderbecke, and the Fletcher Henderson Orchestra—which, incidentally, included Coleman Hawkins—made several recordings of *Singin' the Blues* in which the saxophone section re-created Trumbauer's solo.[8] According to Budd Johnson, "Everybody memorized that solo. . . . At that time, Frankie Trumbauer was the baddest cat around."[9]

The most detailed comparison of Trumbauer and Young comes from a 1982 thesis on Young by an English jazz musician, Bernard Cash. Cash compared Trumbauer's 1927 solo on *Way Down Yonder in New Orleans* with Young's of September 27, 1938, on the same song. He concluded that the two players were very alike in the lightness of sound and in the relative absence of vibrato. But he found that their improvising methods were quite distinct, Trumbauer's being characterized by frequent surprising leaps (like his colleague Beiderbecke) in contrast with Young's rather even melodic flow. Trumbauer's music was built in fairly predictable two-bar phrases, whereas Young's phrases were longer and of more varied lengths. From the point of view of harmony, however, Trumbauer revealed a sophisticated ear for his time in his use of ninths, elevenths, thirteenths, and of augmented arpeggios instead of dominant chords, all elements of Young's playing. In sum, "While Lester Young's own statement of Trumbauer's influence on him deserves to be taken seriously, this study shows that certainly Trumbauer's tone and lightness of approach were a direct influence, his harmonic ingenuity might well have been, but that his improvising technique was not only decidedly different but also less productive in a profound musical sense." It may be that at an early stage Young sounded much like his early idol, but by the time he began to record he had moved quite far away from that style.

When Young decided on Trumbauer he did not forsake Jimmy Dorsey entirely. Dorsey, a rougher and more aggressive stylist than Trumbauer, experimented with several of the striking effects possible on the saxophone through alternate fingerings and "honks"—effects that Young developed even further, as we will see.

Many critics have suggested that Bud Freeman, a tenor saxophonist active since the 1920s, was an influence on Young, but Young consistently denied this. Freeman was one of a group of white Chicago musicians who eschewed the sophisticated style employed by Trumbauer and others, preferring to follow such black New Orleans style performers as King Oliver and his Creole Jazz Band. Freeman's early work, with its fast vibrato, rough tone, and short, choppy phrases, bears little resemblance to Young's first performances. In 1933, Freeman wrote and recorded *The Eel,* a theme composed of looping arpeggios that is closer to the Young approach, but his improvised solo still reflects a quite different conception.[10] Young expressed admiration for Freeman's playing, but never indicated that he had heard Freeman during his formative years or that he had ever tried to emulate him. "I did like Bud Freeman very much," he said. "Nobody played like him. That's what knocked me out. I remember when he was with Benny Goodman [in 1938]."[11]

It is probable that trumpeter Louis Armstrong influenced Young. His innovations had such a pervasive impact on jazz during the 1920s and early 1930s that nobody could escape at least an indirect exposure to him. Only

Armstrong had a rhythmic drive and propulsive swing comparable to that of Young. Several of Young's specific rhythmic and melodic formulas could have been derived from Armstrong's recordings, especially the ones I label Formulas 1 and 2 (see chapter 4). For example, as early as 1924 Armstrong recorded a solo on *Shanghai Shuffle* in AABA form that uses Formula 2 in each of the A sections. During the B section or bridge of this solo, Armstrong swings powerfully by simply repeating one note while varying the rhythm and the vibrato, another technique that Young was to master. Young need not have absorbed these devices directly from Armstrong, since Armstrong drew upon the fund of musical ideas common among jazz players and he, in turn, became the major contributor to that fund. These ideas were in the air during Young's formative years, and were easily available on the recordings of Armstrong and others. It is also significant that Young worked with King Oliver, because Oliver had been the inspiration for Armstrong and the direct source of some of his melodic ideas. Young may, then, have gotten his Armstrong influence from the source as well as from Armstrong himself. Sadik Hakim and Bobby Scott, two pianists who knew Young in later years, said he owned and admired Armstrong's recordings. [12]

It is difficult, perhaps foolish, to attempt to pin down Young's sources with any more precision, since the evidence is so sparse. Moreover, one gets the very strong feeling that Young made much out of a little, taking some ideas he heard and developing each one into a whole family of ideas. Geniuses can do that. They are able to take existing ideas farther than anyone else could have dreamed. So it may be that the few sources we have identified for Young's playing, the works of Trumbauer, Beiderbecke, Dorsey, and Armstrong, were enough for him to work with.

Young's tastes for pleasure listening are revealing. Since such information comes from interviews after he became famous, it cannot directly help us to find more about his early influences. But it shows us what he looked for and enjoyed in the works of others. He especially liked vocalists, and not necessarily ones associated with jazz. For example, he several times expressed admiration for the recordings of Jo Stafford, Frank Sinatra, and Dick Haymes. This suggests that Young liked to hear songs delivered in a smooth style, with the lyrics clearly articulated, which makes sense in light of his own very smooth approach. (He also liked the more gutsy records of Kay Starr.) Lyrics were very important to him. "A musician should know the lyrics of the songs he plays," Young insisted. "A lot of musicians that play nowadays don't know the lyrics of the songs. That way they're just playing the changes [chords]. That's why I like records by singers when I'm listening at home."[13]

Interestingly, one does not find evidence that Young studied recordings of instrumentalists to get improvisational ideas, once he had learned the songs from vocal recordings. Probably he had so many ideas of his own that he had little interest in looking to others.

So, we are able to draw a few conclusions about the development of Young's music. He had very specific tastes at a very early age with respect to the music he wanted to emulate. He ignored Coleman Hawkins, concentrated on Dorsey and Trumbauer, and finally decided on the latter. He probably was quite aware of the music of Armstrong, and that influence may account for the fact that Young came out sounding much different from Trumbauer, much richer and harder swinging.

In contrast to his narrow selection of musical idols, Young had very broad interests for pleasure listening. He especially liked to hear popular songs delivered in a fairly straightforward and tasteful manner. But he was open to all kinds of music, as he told Leonard Feather after his "blindfold test" in *Down Beat,* November 2, 1951: "Just all music, all day and all night music. Just any kind of music you play for me, I melt with all of it."

3

"Everybody Plays the Blues"

In order to understand better the discussion of Young's musical style that follows, the reader needs to know more about the context in which he created that music. Young's repertoire and performance practices were shaped during his years of playing in the Southwest. Musicians in that region of the country improvised outstanding instrumental interpretations of the blues. "Everybody plays the blues,' Young said, "and *have* 'em too." Blues inflections were added to nonblues pieces also, such as the *I Got Rhythm* chord progression—"rhythm changes" in jazz jargon—which was a favorite among musicians and inspired many variations. While Young was a member of the Basie band in the late 1930s, about half of the pieces in the repertoire were thirty-two-bar AABA popular song forms—including several based on rhythm changes—played at moderate and fast tempos; one-fourth were twelve-bar blues; and the remainder were primarily thirty-two-bar forms other than AABA.

Basie featured Young on many driving medium and fast numbers, such as *One O'Clock Jump*, a blues, and *Jumpin' at the Woodside*, an AABA form. *Clap Hands, Here Comes Charlie,* probably the band's fastest arrangement, showcased Young's slyly understated method of generating excitement. One can imagine the screams of the audience when Young takes his first break. (A "break" is a two- or four-measure phrase during which the band drops out, leaving the soloist alone.) Young became known for this kind of playing.

Young was also a master of ballad playing, but the Basie band performed relatively few ballads (slow, lyrical songs, often in AABA form), and usually reserved them for vocalists. The instrumental ballad *Blue and Sentimental* (6/6/38) featured the other tenor saxophonist, Herschel Evans, although Young did play clarinet toward the end of this number. Young had little opportunity to play ballads in "live" performances during the 1930s, but he played many such songs in the recording studios with Billie Holiday. The Holiday sessions, many of which were actually led by pianist Teddy Wilson, united musicians who did not normally perform together to play songs they may have never heard before. Yet beautiful and classic recordings resulted. Young revealed a natural affinity for ballads on such Holiday recordings as *I Can't Get Started* (9/15/38). Significantly, after leaving Basie he chose to record two ballads in the first session under his own name (7/15/42), including a new version of *I Can't Get Started*.

When Lester began recording regularly with his own groups in the mid-1940s, he favored a repertoire of one-sixth ballads, one-third blues, one-third moderate- and fast-tempo AABA pieces (about one-fifth based on rhythm changes), and one-sixth other thirty-two-bar song forms. The tune types were the same, but the proportions differed from his Basie days in that there were more ballads and more blues.

Young composed very little of his own repertoire. It seems that there often exists a strong relationship between great jazz improvising and great jazz composing (written). Charlie Parker, John Coltrane, and Dizzy Gillespie excelled at both. But then Louis Armstrong did relatively little writing. Jazz writing requires a different kind of concentration than does improvising, and more patience. Young apparently did not have that patience. The few pieces he did compose are basically "riffs"—short rhythmic phrases played repeatedly over the changing harmonies of a blues or simple AABA progression. In AABA forms, the riff could not be used during the B section, because it usually had chords very different from those of the A section. Rather than write out another melody, Young usually left the B section open for himself or someone else to improvise.

While with Basie, Young composed *Tickle Toe*—the most intricate theme he ever recorded—and *Lester Leaps In.* Young was not a big band arranger, so Andy Gibson filled out *Tickle Toe* for the Basie band. Young received co-composer credit with Basie on *Taxi War Dance, Dickie's Dream, Rock-A-Bye Basie* (the last also with Shad Collins), *Nobody Knows,* and *Baby, Don't Tell on Me* (the last two with Jimmy Rushing added). It is unclear just what Young's contribution was to each of the coauthored titles. Perhaps he came up with the saxophone riffs used in most of them—that on *Nobody Knows* in particular sounds like a Young creation.[1] It is even possible that he named some of these pieces. As we discussed in chapter 1, several of Young's colleagues claim that many of the ideas the Basie band played were invented by Young but that he was not credited. Unfortunately, we can only guess which riffs he may have contributed.

Young's post-Basie output contained many original blues themes such as *Jumpin' with Symphony Sid, D.B. Blues* (actually a blues with a bridge, 12, 12, 8, and 12 measures), *Neenah,* and *Up 'N Adam,* as well as Rhythm variants such as *Sax-O-Re-Bop* and *Lester Leaps In,* which he re-recorded several times.[2]

Young preferred the tenor saxophone keys C and G major. Rhythm variants were usually in C. (Remember, I give all keys for the tenor saxophone, that is, one whole step above concert key, unless noted otherwise.) He fairly often played in E♭ and F, less often in D, A, and minor keys, and almost never in keys with more than three sharps.

Like his contemporaries, Young played exclusively in 4/4 meter. Throughout his career, his tempos tended to fall between ♩ = 172 and ♩ = 200, or "medium up-tempo." He rarely matched or exceeded the tempo of *Clap Hands, Here Comes Charlie,* ♩ = 284. Ballad tempos slowed down over the years; during the 1930s few went below ♩ = 100, while tempos of ♩ = 80 and even 65 (*These Foolish Things*) appeared at times after the war.

Arrangements varied depending on the size of the group. A typical Basie band up-tempo arrangement consisted of a four- or eight-bar introduction (possibly twelve bars on a blues), a theme played by the entire band, a series of solos accompanied by the rhythm section and brass or saxophone figures, and one or more choruses of climactic riffs by the entire band. The theme often did not reappear after its initial statement. Ballads featured much more writing for the band, a vocal, and one or two brief instrumental solos.

Young's small group recordings of the 1930s, in contrast, often used no written material aside from the given song and its chord progression. From the first chorus, each player would improvise. The records with Billie Holiday included a vocal chorus in the middle. Towards the end of the performance, the musicians might "trade fours"—take turns improvising for four measures while the chord progression continued underneath. Endings often consisted of a half or whole chorus of improvised polyphony, all the wind instruments improvising separate but compatible melodies.

During the middle 1940s the bebop generation established the practice of playing a theme in unison at the beginnings and endings of medium- and up-tempo pieces so that, unlike many 1930s performances, there was a literal recapitulation. Young used this format on most of his later small group recordings. After playing the theme in unison with a trumpet, he invariably took the first solo, followed by the other wind instruments ("horns" in jazz jargon), and then by the piano. Before the reprise of the theme, there might be a chorus or two of trading fours with the drummer—four bars of improvisation by Young, followed by four of drums, four of trumpet, four of drums, and a repeat of this sixteen-bar cycle beginning with Young again to comprise a thirty-two-bar chorus.

On recordings without other horns, Young followed the same format except that he took improvisatory liberties with the initial theme statement. He "poked" at the melody, wrote Whitney Balliett, "in an easy, one-finger manner, until he had reshaped it into a starker design that appeared, in spite of its rhythmic liberties, to skid along parallel to the beat, as a revised and improved shadow of the original tune."[3] The beginning of *Indiana* illustrates this procedure (see example 1). In example lb and all following examples, a note in parentheses is barely audible or "ghosted" on the recording. The symbol ⌐⌐ indicates that the note starts below pitch, then slides up to pitch by way of a short glissando, usually one to three half steps.

Example 1. *Indiana (Back Home Again in Indiana),* measures 1–7; initial theme
           statement

a. Original (transposed to tenor saxophone key)[4]

b. Young's improvisation (7/15/42), measures 1–7

All the main notes of the melody are in Young's version, but he has added passing tones and made several rhythmic changes.

On ballads, Young usually played one and a half choruses in the form of AABA'BA'. He often improvised quite freely from the beginning of a ballad. On *These Foolish Things,* one of his best-known and most emotionally powerful ballad performances, he creates a new melody based on the chord progression of the written song, with only fleeting references to the original as in measures twenty-one and twenty-two (see examples 2 and 3). Young's melody has its own logic (see example 2b). It begins with a repeated E, which is echoed by a repeated F at the beginning of the second measure. The third measure, and the second phrase, begins with a G, so that we have so far heard an ascent from E to G. The second phrase has an inverted arch shape. First it descends in two-note groups (third measure), then it ascends (fourth measure). Young saves a harmonic surprise for the end of the second phrase—the D♭ and A♭ are the flatted ninth and flatted thirteenth, respectively, of the underlying C dominant seventh chord.

In the transcription, I have attempted to reflect Young's rubato style of playing with arrows over the notes. An arrow pointing forward, $\vec{\uparrow}$, indicates that the note actually occurs slightly later than notated, while an arrow pointing back, $\overleftarrow{\uparrow}$, indicates a note that occurs slightly earlier than notated. Young used so much rubato in the 1940s and 1950s that I have only noted the more extreme instances of it in my transcriptions.

Example 2. *These Foolish Things (Remind Me of You)*, measures 1–4

a. Original

b. Young's improvisation (12/45)

Example 3. *These Foolish Things (Remind Me of You)*, measures 21–22

a. Original

b. Young's improvisation (12/45)

In contrast to *These Foolish Things*, the melody of *I Can't Get Started* is clearly discernible in Young's opening solo, as demonstrated by a comparison of my transcription with the published sheet music (see example 4). Young's most noticeable departure from the original song is his use of A♯ at the end of the second measure instead of A-natural, in order to anticipate the F♯ dominant seventh chord that begins the next measure. His accompanists have changed the last chord in the phrase from a C# minor to an E dominant seventh. The dominant seventh adds motion because of its drive to resolve a tonic.

Young sometimes emphasized longer and more important notes by intensifying the speed of his vibrato. The symbol ～ over a note indicates that it is played with a pronounced vibrato. If the symbol occurs slightly after the note, ρ͠ , this means that the note begins normally and the vibrato grows more intense at the point that the symbol appears. This type of terminal vibrato was employed by Louis Armstrong and became a standard jazz technique.

Example 4. *I Can't Get Started,* measures 1–4

a. Original

b. Young's improvisation (7/15/42)

With regard to instrumentation, Young's recordings through 1941 almost always included a rhythm section of guitar, piano, bass, and drums. Besides the rhythm section, the Basie band generally consisted of three or four trumpets, three trombones and four saxophones (incuding Young). Small group recordings of the 1930s usually featured a rhythm section and a combination of saxophone, trumpet, trombone, and clarinet. The clarinet fell out of favor as modern jazz began, partly because the tone of the clarinet could not compete with the variety and flexibility of the saxophone's tone, and because modern jazz is very demanding technically and the clarinet is a difficult instrument to play well. (The clarinet requires a tighter mouth position than the saxophone, and has many more finger positions that must be memorized.) The guitar remained very popular among jazz improvisers, but was no longer considered essential to a rhythm section, because modern jazz musicians wanted occasional chordal punctuations from either piano or guitar instead of the strumming on every beat that the guitar had provided during the Swing Era. The modern jazz accompaniment was sparser, lighter. As a result of these developments, almost all of Young's recordings from the late 1940s on feature him with piano, bass, and drums, often trumpet, and, on rare occasions, trombone.

Now that we have given the reader an orientation into Young's musical environment, we will look at some details of Young's music. We begin with the aspect of any music that first attracts a listener's attention—the sound itself. For the rest of this chapter we discuss Young's sound and the ways he manipulated it. The succeeding chapters analyze the notes he chose and the structures he created with them. We will constantly refer to the changes in Young's sound and style over the years. As stated in the preface, we find Young's work divisible into three main periods—1936 through 1942, 1943 through about 1950, and 1950 through 1959. These are his early, middle, and later style periods.

Tone

On his first recordings, Young articulated his notes very cleanly and played with a full, round tone. He gradually moved toward a softer tone and more legato articulation until, by 1939, he had developed the famous ethereal, feathery quality that inspired Stan Getz, Zoot Sims, and thousands of other musicians. Young said he liked *Taxi War Dance* from this period (recorded 3/19/39) because at one point he sounded "like a foghorn."[5] (He probably meant the soft low notes during the bridge of his opening solo, although he conceivably might have meant the high F# or the alternate fingerings that occur near the end of the recording.)

By 1941 his soft tone sounded dead and his playing had become very controlled—what years later would be called "cool." His music was beautiful and moving, although introverted. A heaviness had entered his sound, and vibrato, which he always had used sparingly, was sometimes not discernible at all.

Following a break from recording, which had begun after July 1942 (partly the result of a nationwide ban beginning on August 1, imposed by the musician's union as a tactic to win higher wages), Young returned to the studios in December 1943, with a thicker and darker sound. At times he affected a raspy sound in the upper register (e.g., *After Theatre Jump*, 3/22/44). On *Destination K.C.* (same date; both takes) he produced long, high, wailing "blue" notes. He played energetically again, especially on the sessions that reunited him with Count Basie, Nat "King" Cole, or drummer Jo Jones, his long-standing friends and his most sympathetic accompanists. Frequent "honks" and sudden contrasts in register abound during Young's recordings of 1943 and 1944.

After Young left the army in 1945, a dramatic pathos entered his work, making his ballad playing even more emotionally powerful than before. His tone retained the heaviness and richness of the period just before the army.

Young's tone began to change again during the early 1950s, becoming pathetic and fluffy. He produced a thin, squeezing sound in the upper register; his low notes often sounded weak and uncertain. The sound of air blowing into the saxophone became more and more apparent during the 1950s. He could barely produce a sound on several of the studio recordings from his last few years (incuding most of the ones with Harry Edison). But his playing from 1953 on varied greatly, and he still produced a full, strong sound on occasion, especially on live dates.

Young was consciously experimenting with tone colors throughout his career. The changes in his sound were intentional, except for those last recordings on which he was in poor health. He proudly told an interviewer shortly before his death, "I developed my saxophone to play it, make it sound just like a alto, make it sound like a tenor, make it sound like a *bass,* and everything, and I'm not through working on it yet."[6]

During his early period Young played a Conn saxophone,[7] and photos from this period show a metal mouthpiece. Most later photos show Young playing a black hard rubber mouthpiece, probably a Brilhart model. Young told Leonard Feather in 1950 that he was using plastic saxophone reeds, which is surprising in view of plastic's reputation.[8] Most musicians find that plastic reeds have great longevity but an inferior sound when compared with cane reeds. It is not known how long Young used them—conceivably only for a very short time.

Young also played clarinet on many recordings in 1938 and 1939, and briefly in 1958. Sadik Hakim, who toured with Young in 1947 (when he was still known as Argonne Thornton), remembers him playing clarinet several times that year also. Young produced a lovely, wistful tone on this instrument, and many musicians and critics rank him among the best jazz clarinetists. He owned a metal clarinet as well as wooden ones (see the biography chapter, "Count Basie Years"). Other than the obvious difference in sound, his style on clarinet was the same as on saxophone, and does not require a separate treatment.

Range and Register

The tenor saxophone has a range of two octaves and a fifth (the upper range may be extended by use of the overtone series) (see example 5). Young played mostly in the middle register of the saxophone, using the extreme ranges selectively. (This is not unusual. The highest notes on the saxophone are awkward because they must be played with the left palm, and the lowest notes must be played with the little finger of the left hand. It is also hard to obtain a full and controlled sound at the extremes.) He generally did not play the high F,[9] but did employ the lowest notes for honks. In this respect, as in so many others, Young contradicted Coleman Hawkins and his school of followers. They exploited the high register for exciting, screaming effects, and audiences responded enthusiastically. Young provoked equal enthusiasm through the opposite device—honking on the lowest notes (more on this later).

Example 5. The range of the tenor saxophone (sounds a major ninth lower)

Most of Young's recorded solos utilize a range of about two octaves, but this was affected by the key in which he was playing. For example, a solo in the key of Bb or Eb might extend down to the low Bb and up to the high Eb. The solos utilizing the widest range—two octaves plus a fourth or augmented fourth—are in Eb, such as *Honeysuckle Rose, Easy Does It,* and *After Theatre Jump.* Keys F and C utilize the next largest range, while the smallest occurs in D and G (both minor and major keys). The range of *Hello, Babe* (Master), in G major, is unusually narrow—only a twelfth.

High notes, like any notes, may be approached by a leap or by scale steps. In his early period Young usually approached the highest note of a solo by a leap of a third or more, often favoring a fourth, as in *Boogie Woogie* (high Ds in several places) and *Honeysuckle rose* (several high Ebs). Sometimes the leap was simply the top of an arpeggio, but usually Young treated the high note as an important goal of the solo and approached it in isolation. At times he played a long glissando up to the highest notes, as in *Shoe Shine Boy* (Take 1), measure 10 (see the next section, example 6b). He rarely approached the highest note of a solo by step. As far as its location, he might play the note anywhere during a chorus, and sometimes played it several times during a solo. From 1943, in such songs as *I Got Rhythm* and *After Theatre Jump,* most of the above still applied, except that the highest note occurred more frequently during the bridge than in any other part of an AABA chorus. This was one of many ways in which Young tended to isolate the bridge and emphasize its dissimilarity with the A sections during his middle and later periods.

Young's lowest note in solos from 1936 to 1941 was usually the bottom note of an arpeggio, as in *One O'Clock Jump,* measure 9, and *Jumpin' at the Woodside,* measure 21. It was rarely approached by an isolated leap —if so, it usually made a loud "honk") and almost never by step, and was likely to occur in any part of a chorus. In general, he did not treat lowest notes as structural goals; he did not emphasize them or build up to them as he did the high notes, except for the infrequent instances of "honks."

Between 1942 and about 1948, his lowest notes assumed more structural importance. He approached them most often by leap, often creating "honks," as in the second A of the second chorus of *After Theatre Jump.* Young's 1950s solos, such as *Just You, Just Me,* reveal a decline in his leaps to the lowest note as compared with the middle 1940s. It was only in the 1950s that Young reached the lowest note by step as often as by leap.

Glissandos

Young popularized, if not actually invented, many techniques that enlarged the expressive resources of jazz. One of these techniques was his use of long glissandos. Short glissandos originated in vocal music, and their frequent use by instrumentalists helped create the unique sound of jazz. Young, however, had a penchant for glissandos that traversed intervals of an octave, ninth, or more, and which served structural and not purely decorative functions. For example, in the second A section of *Shoe Shine Boy* (Take 1; see example 6b), in the last A of the third chorus of *I Got Rhythm,* and in the second chorus of *Jammin' with Lester* (1/46), the glissando is varied and developed just as a melodic or rhythmic motive would be. Young primarily played long glissandos at medium-fast and fast tempos.

During Young's early years, 1936 to about 1941, his glissandos almost always spanned an octave in the time of a quarter note. The goal of the glissando was usually a high note, among the so-called "palm keys" of the saxophone. In many cases the top note of the glissando was the highest note of the solo in which it occurred (although, if the highest note appeared more than once during the solo, it was not always reached by glissando).

The glissando allowed Young to negotiate large intervals without a complete break in the line, at the same time bringing attention to significant changes in register. Example 6 shows some typical glissandos from Young's early years. During this period he primarily used diatonic notes in glissandos. In my transcriptions a long wavy line,   ⌐⌐⌐   , appears over notes that are connected by glissando. Depending on the speed and accuracy with which the glissando is played, it is sometimes possible to write out the individual notes that make it up, as in examples 6a and 6c. In uncertain cases I give only accented pitches and omit any rhythmic notation.

Example 6. Glissandos from Young solos of 11/9/36

a. *Lady Be Good,* second chorus, measure 21

b. *Shoe Shine Boy* (Take 1), measures 9–10

c. *Shoe Shine Boy* (Take 2), second chorus, measure 13

Beginning in 1943, Young used glissandos more often; they traversed intervals as large as twelfths and thirteenths, and frequently occupied two or more beats. (One of the only comparable instances in the early works is the glissando in the sixth measure of the bridge of *Honeysuckle Rose,* which spans a twelfth in two beats.) Young played many chromatic notes in these glissandos to make them last longer. Glissandos served the same structural functions as before, but occurred with more predictability at beginnings of choruses and eight-bar sections, and especially during the bridge in AABA form. In part they were a respite from the pace of eighth notes required at fast tempos.

In the recordings of the 1950s fewer and shorter glissandos occur, part of a general tendency toward more circumscribed melodic lines. *Neenah* has more glissandos than most solos from this period, but none is over a sixth in range.

Honks

Young created great excitement by an occasional use of the "honk." This is a loud, ringing low note, usually the lowest note on the horn—B♭—or the C above it; however, a comparable effect is possible in the middle register. Normally one approaches the lowest register of the saxophone cautiously, using a controlled embouchure and a moderate air flow to minimize the contrast with the middle register. The honk is a conscious exploitation of that contrast. The player loosens his embouchure and speeds up his air flow. This device, like other Young trademarks, was used by Jimmy Dorsey, one of Young's early idols, on early recordings such as *Tiger Rag* (7/15/30),[10] but Young was the one who influenced hundreds of other jazz players to adopt it.

Young's earliest recorded honk occurs on the bridge of *Honeysuckle Rose* (1/21/37). Throughout the 1930s, he used this device infrequently and only on medium- or up-tempo pieces. Among other early solos, a honk occurs in *Easy Does It* (fourth measure of solo introduction), and middle-register honks—all on the note D—are found in *Honeysuckle Rose* (concert) and *Clap Hands, Here Comes Charlie.* In each of the latter cases, the honks end an eight-bar section and lead into several repeated Ds played in the usual manner. The broadcast version of *I Got Rhythm* from 6/30/37, where Young opens his solo with a thrilling effect by alternating low Cs with upper-register motives, is exceptional in his early period use of honks.

The year 1943 marked a turning point here, as with other aspects of Young's playing. During his middle period, which began that year, Young played honks much more frequently and even developed routines or formulas involving honks that recur in various solos (see chapter 4 on formulas). Variants of the formula given in example 7 appear at the beginning of both bridges and the second A of the second chorus of *After Theatre Jump,* and in many other pieces as well (see example 7. I use an exclamation point over the "honked" note, and an *X* over an alternate fingering. See next section).

Example 7. Honk formula from *I Got Rhythm* (12/21/43); Young's second solo, measures 25 and 26 of the second chorus

The essence of this formula is the prolongation of a note, or several notes, by splitting the note between two registers at once. The above is simply a C followed by a D*b*, but the octave jumps and the honks give it a striking character. Similarly, the beginning of the first bridge in *After Theatre Jump* prolongs a C; the second A2 is a chromatic ascent, B*b*-B-C; and the second bridge again prolongs C. (The entire solo appears in chapter 5.)

The arrangement of *Lester Leaps In* that Young used in the 1950s employed a similar idea, although the low notes are not necessarily honked (see example 8).

Example 8. Young's solo from *Lester Leaps In* (10/56), measures 9–10 of first chorus after theme

During the 1950s Young began to use honks as well as other expressive devices for increasingly bizarre effects. The third chorus of *Neenah* is a good example. Here he constructs the entire chorus out of brief fragments, ending with isolated honks at irregular time intervals.

Alternate Fingerings

Young, like Jimmy Dorsey before him, rapidly alternated the standard fingering of a note with its substitute fingering. This lent a subtle excitement to the simple device of pitch repetition, and Young used it almost exclusively at fast tempos. Several notes on the saxophone are playable through more than one fingering. The alternate fingerings, however, produce different tone-colors and sometimes are slightly out of tune. Saxophonists traditionally used alternate fingerings only in situations where they permitted more rapid execution, and the tone and pitch discrepancies were minimized as much as possible. For example, there are right-hand keys that enable one to trill between B and C and between F and F# much more quickly than would otherwise be possible, but these keys are awkward for most scale playing. There are also alternate fingerings which produce such coarse sounds that they would not normally be recommended under any circumstance, but Young particularly liked these and exploited them for shock value.

Young's favorite alternate fingering was based upon the use of overtones. He fingered a low C but, by adjusting his mouth position, produced its first overtone, the middle C of the saxophone. This middle C had a color different from that of one fingered the usual way, and often had a coarse edge because some of the low C tended to speak at the same time as its overtone (see figure 1; some performers add the octave key to facilitate the production of the overtone). Young uses this fingering during the introductory bars of his solo in *Jumpin' at the Woodside*, the ending eight measures of his solo on

Lester Leaps In (Take 1), the second chorus of the opening solo in *I Want to Be Happy,* and numerous other recordings.

Figure 1. Fingerings for middle C on the saxophone

a. Conventional middle-C fingering

b. Alternate middle-C fingering

Using the same overtone principle, Young produced alternate sounds for B♭, B natural, the middle C already noted, and D♭. For example, the Cs from *I Want to Be Happy* are followed by D♭s. He also uses these effects on *JATP Blues* (4/22/46). The equivalent effect on B♭ occurs during the second bridge of *Clap Hands, Here Comes Charlie.*

Middle D, E♭, and E natural are normally obtained through the use of overtones; the octave key helps them to speak. To find alternate fingerings for these, one has to look into the high register. By simply opening the appropriate palm keys for each note, but not depressing the octave key, one may produce the note in the middle register. These alternates tend to be flatter than their normally fingered counterparts. Especially for the E, it helps to open the high F key also. Young seemed to enjoy the difference in pitch as he alternated the standard fingering of middle E with its flatter version during the first bridge of *[New] Lester Leaps In* (August 1946). An alternate E♭ appears in the last eight measures of the second chorus of this recording. Young shows off the group of alternate fingerings we have discussed so far by descending from middle E♭ to B♭ at two points during a version of *Lester Leaps In* (9/17/49).

Young realized that the overtones beyond the octave could also be produced, with practice. This is easiest on the lowest note of the saxophone, the B*b*. Most jazz saxophonists today know about the possibilities of overtones, especially since John Coltrane's brilliant explorations of the 1960s, but classical musicians and a few jazz artists had known about them for many years. Significantly, Jimmy Dorsey produced overtones on a 1926 recording of *That's No Bargain.*[11] He fingered low B*b* and produced middle B*b*, followed by the next overtone, the F above it. Young plays the same overtones, with the F not sounding very clear, at the start of his tenth chorus on *Neenah* (8/4/51), and again, with the F sounding nicely, at the very end of his solo on *Indiana* (9/16/50).

Young usually played the alternate fingerings in rapid exchange with the conventional ones, using repetitive rhythms such as those shown in example 9. Young relied increasingly on these expressive devices over the years. Long strings of alternate fingerings occur during many of his up-tempo 1950s recordings, particularly those based on simple harmonic structures, such as blues, *Lester Leaps In,* and *Jumpin' at the Woodside.*

Example 9. Typical Young rhythms for alternate fingerings (x = alternate fingering)

Beginning in the late 1940s, Young sometimes used alternate fingering techniques to produce a "wah-wah" sound leading into certain notes. Closing the keys below certain notes will muffle the tone (usually slightly lowering the pitch, too), and quickly releasing these keys will produce a "wah" sound as they open again. Young often exaggerated this effect by using his mouth. For example, wah-wah As in the upper register were probably produced by closing and opening all the right-hand keys (including C), and may be heard in *Pres Returns, Lester Leaps In* (10/56), and leading into the third improvised chorus of *Jumpin' with Symphony Sid.* Closing all the right-hand keys also produces a wah-wah effect on high C (left middle finger), as heard on such recordings as *Neenah* (4/2/50) and *Jumpin' at the Woodside* (1/17/53). A comparable effect for upper register F may be achieved by depressing the C and D below it, and Young sometimes used this also.

During the 1950s Young introduced another alternate fingering, which he employed when playing a long A♭ followed by B♭. He used this on the blues in B♭, where the A♭ was a "blue" seventh (see next section). While fingering the A♭, he depressed some keys below it (D and C, or E and D—either pair works well), creating a choked sound and lowered pitch. He released those keys until the A♭ assumed its normal sound, using his lip to ensure a smooth connection. The open sound of the B♭ goal note that followed seemed very relaxed in comparison, as Young intended. This occurs on several versions of *Neenah* (1/20/51, 8/2/52); judging by the sound, Young may also have used this fingering on the first two notes of his solo on an earlier recording, *Pleasing Man Blues* (December 1945 or January 1946).

Dynamics and Expression

Young conformed to the standard practice of jazz musicians in adopting one basic dynamic level for each solo he played. He was sensitive, however, to subtle, dynamic variation between individual notes, which added to the interest of his music. Naturally, any note played with a honk or alternate fingering also created a change in volume. Young varied the volume during note repetitions by tightening and loosening his mouth. The effect resembled an alternate fingering in that he produced two different sounds on one pitch—an "um" sound when he tightened his mouth and an "aah" when he relaxed it. This effect, which is sometimes difficult to distinguish from alternate fingerings, appears on many recordings beginning in the late 1940s, such as *Lester Leaps In* (9/18/49), *Neenah* (4/2/50; also 8/4/51), *Jumpin' at the Woodside* (1/17/53, mainly during bridges), and others.

Young frequently accented longer and more important notes by leading into them with a short glissando from about a half step below. This differs from a grace note in that no separate pitch is heard. The effect appears frequently throughout Young's career on the highest note of a phrase and on the first note after a rest.

The distinctive "blue note" of jazz and other Afro-American music is an important coloration in Young's playing. He produced these notes with longer bends and dips on the saxophone in which he attacked the note on pitch, then lowered it, and sometimes returned to the original pitch. At times he simply played the lowered pitch and held it. As in other Afro-American music, the blue note occurs on the third and, to a lesser extent, the seventh degrees of the major scale in Young's output. Note the G-naturals in *[Oh] Lady Be Good* (key of A), the Gbs in *One O'Clock Jump* (key of Eb), F-naturals in *Boogie Woogie* (key of D), and Ebs in *I Got Rhythm* and *Lester Leaps In,* 10/56 version (both in C) (see example 10).

Example 10. Characteristic blue notes in Young solos

a. *Boogie Woogie* (11/9/36), measures 4–5; a blue note on the third scale degree, attacked and then dropping in pitch

b. *I Got Rhythm* (12/21/43), second solo, beginning of third chorus; a blue note on the third scale degree, pitch held constant

c. *[Oh] Lady Be Good* (11/9/36), measures 28–29; a blue note on the seventh scale degree, attacked and brought up in pitch. The curved line,   , shows the bending of the pitch and the arrow shows the point at which the pitch is raised.

Young used glissandos infrequently at the ends of notes, either downward ("falloffs") or upward ("doits"). He employed several falloffs in *One O'Clock Jump* and *Hello, Babe* (Alternate). Doits, even rarer, occur mostly in later solos such as *Lester Leaps In* (10/56).

He often connected notes one half step apart, up or down, by bending the pitch with his lip toward the second note at the same time that he moved his fingers. When the second note is lower, it sounds like "wa-ah." This was common at all tempos and during all periods. (For example, *Honeysuckle Rose,* the bridge; *Boogie Woogie,* second chorus; *After Theatre Jump,* beginning second chorus). The "wa-ah" sound is more noticeable after 1943 because of the thicker tone quality and contributes to the poignant, crying sound of many of the later recordings.

Certain expressive characteristics are found almost exclusively in Young's own work of the 1950s. These include "squeezed" notes—upper-register notes attacked below pitch and slowly "squeezed" up to pitch by tightening of the embouchure—and wide trills, or "shakes." An instance of the squeezed note occurs in *Destination Moon,* measure 12 of the second chorus; the wide trills, in *Jammin' with Lester* (1/46, second chorus) and *Sent for You Yesterday* (7/7/57). Young uses both devices on *Neenah* (February 22, 1950).

Summary

During his early period Young progressed from a full-bodied tone and clear articulation to a very soft tone and legato articulation. Toward the end of this period, he used very little vibrato and a somewhat heavier tone quality.

Young's repertoire of expressive devices included glissandos an octave in length that ended on high notes, sparing use of honks, a variety of alternate fingerings that he used to vary the tone quality of a repeated note (a device especially common in unaccompanied breaks), and many blue notes, short glissandos into high notes, and bent notes.

One is immediately struck by the darker, heavier tone and increased emotional depth of Young's middle-period work, when his style became increasingly dramatic, especially in ballads. He varied his tone and dynamics, used raspy sounds and wails. Melodic lines became progressively abstract in all respects.

Young used all the expressive devices of his early years. Honks and glissandos were much more frequent, and the latter took more time and covered greater intervals. He continued to use alternate fingerings, and now also used them to produce grace notes.

Young's playing during his last period was inconsistent, making it hard to generalize. Especially on live recordings, he usually produced a full, strong sound. In the studio, however, Young's tone during much of the early 1950s was fluffy and, at times, pathetic. He produced a thin, "squeezing" sound in the upper register, and low notes often failed to speak clearly. Toward the end of this period, one is often able to hear his airstream entering the horn before the note sounds.

Long glissandos are not as common during this period as in the 1940s, but honks and alternate fingerings are very prevalent, sometimes to the point of grotesqueness. In addition to the expressive devices used in earlier solos, he used wide trills or "shakes," and long bends and blue notes.

4

"I Try Not to Be a Repeater Pencil"

To many, jazz improvisation connotes a formless stream of notes related, if at all, only by chordal and rhythmic continuity. Jazz performers, however, could not produce coherent music without applying structural principles.

Improvisation is part of all music. Whenever someone performs a written piece, he must apply a limited amount of improvisation in order to interpret the tempo, dynamics, tone, articulation, and ornamental style, no matter how precisely the composer has notated his wishes.

Improvisation, in a fuller sense, is a compositional process. Bach and Mozart improvised several of their compositions in public before committing them to paper.[1] (Admittedly, they may have changed the pieces as they wrote them down. Written composition allows for numerous revisions and detailed planning that are not possible in an improvised performance.) The art musicians of India learn to improvise, using given materials, by following certain governing principles. This is also true in jazz, although the principles may not be as explicit.

We may state the task before the jazz musician as follows: Given some predetermined materials—usually a harmonic progression, chorus structure, tempo, and mood—and a knowledge of jazz styles, compose a coherent musical statement spontaneously. The musician prepares for his spontaneous effort by hundreds of prior attempts and by a thorough study of the given materials. Only then is he able to create at a high level while improvising.

As with any composition, we want to understand why the composer chooses the particular notes that he does, and why this phrase is followed by that phrase, and why he repeats this part over here. The answers may be of a sort different from that for written compositions. One must not look for classical forms—exposition, development and recapitulation, or even variations on a theme—in jazz recordings. Mainstream tonal jazz from the 1920s to the present is characterized by free-flowing melodies created to fit a repeating chord progression. The melodies do not necessarily relate to the theme of the piece. Competent solos follow principles of good melodic construction—clear phrasing, harmonically appropriate note choices, logical contours, and discreet use of angular leaps.[2] At this level of simple competence, formulas may comprise most of a solo. A formula—called a "lick" by jazz musicians—is a brief idea that is functional rather than compositional. It is, for example, a pattern that fits a particular chord, chord sequence, or cadence. Formulas recur in similar contexts regardless of the song. (In contrast, a motive is a short idea used compositionally, perhaps developed and varied, that cannot be transferred haphazardly from one song to another.) But every artist has his own repertoire of formulas. In fact much of the distinctive quality of any music, be it Beethoven or Indonesian gamelan music, may be accounted for by the uniqueness of its repertoire of formulas. At the fast pace required for improvisation, musicians need to have many formulas at their disposal. Nobody can come up with entirely new ideas constantly, since there is a necessary time lag in transferring new ideas to the instrument. We recognize formulas whenever we listen to a number of recordings by one artist and find ourselves saying, "He always does that right there!"

Solos composed mostly of formulas will never be ranked with the great solos of all time. When a musician depends upon formulas, he depends upon ideas that he has used before instead of challenging himself to create new ones. He's not pushing himself to his limit, and this can be heard in the result. The player's involvement may be heightened by a creative, nonliteral use of formulas, as found by Thomas Owens in his study of the music of Charlie Parker:

While specific [formulas] often recur in specific locations within groups of pieces, the precise forms that they take are varied by means of metric displacement, augmentation and diminution, addition and subtraction of notes, and altered phrasing and articulation. In addition, they are juxtaposed in many different ways and are often connected by newly invented melodic material. Thus, no two improvised choruses are alike.[3]

As Young put it, "I try not to be a repeater pencil. I'm always loosening spaces, and laying out to somewhere, and something like that."[4]

The greater the percentage of newly composed, nonformulaic ideas in a solo, the more exciting it will be for both player and listener (although it is probably impossible for more than a certain percentage of a solo to be new ideas). Such a solo has a feeling of discovery in it, an involvement with the present moment that is essential for a recording to be considered "classic." At this level of improvisation, the musician establishes connections among his melodies. Continuity between phrases is ensured through the use of related melodic material. Some soloists even utilize material from the preceding soloist. (Young does this on *One O'Clock Jump* of 11/3/37.) Motives are introduced, repeated, varied, and developed. A motive is a short idea that is developed by repetition, variation, and other means, as opposed to a formula that appears when needed, then disappears. An idea may be a formula or a motive, depending on how it is employed.

The advanced soloist carefully builds up the level of intensity through variation in dynamics, timbre, range, and note values. Surprises such as honks, novel sounds created by alternate fingerings, and harmonic dissonances keep the solo from becoming predictable. The improviser has, intuitively and unconsciously, created a structure as seamless and concise as any written composition. Advanced analytical techniques may reveal that the solo is built around a Schenkerian *urlinie*,[5] or by filling in implied intervals, or is based entirely on related motives or on a few intervals. All of these structural strategies appear in the solos that attest to Young's genius.

Since these concepts will be new to many readers, let us observe how they apply to a specific solo—the famous original recording of *Lester Leaps In* (9/5/39, Take 1). Even without counting measures on a first listening, we notice that the opening melody repeats, followed by a bridge for the rhythm section alone, and then a repeat of the opening riff. So we know this is an AABA form. (If need be, we can count it later to confirm that each chorus is thirty-two bars long.) Then we hear Lester for two choruses. His solo is stunning—full of life and creativity. During the second chorus of his solo, the rhythm section stops keeping time (this is called, appropriately, "stop-time"), just playing on the first beat of every other measure. At first Basie duets with Lester, but then he, too, drops out. They come back in for the bridge, making it easy for us to hear the form of the chorus. Lester has to carry the ball basically by himself, then. He seems to do so by becoming busier than in his first chorus, using noodling, climbing ideas, and long, long phrases.

In a second listening, we focus in on fine details. We notice that the opening of his solo echoes the theme. The second A section begins with a little bluesy motive, which he plays with for the first three measures. By the end of the bridge we begin to realize that he likes to end a phrase with a long arpeggio that descends from a high note, as in measures 4, 15, and 23. This gives a kind of consistency to the solo. The last A of the first chorus begins with three measures of playing with a simple motive, and ends very unresolved, leading into the next chorus.

The transcription that appears as example 11 will help the listener to follow these observations, but they should be attempted by ear first. With the notation at hand, one will notice that the beginning of the second chorus plays with a little motive of three half steps, and the second A develops the downward arpeggio idea, using it as a motive, balancing it with the slowly ascending figure of measures 13 and 14. The final eight measures begin with a motive based on the rhythmic and timbral variation of one note—the tonic (first) note of the key. The timbre is changed by opening and closing extra keys, so one hears the normal tone of the note alternating with a sort of honking sound. The whole phrase, measures 25 to 29, seems to be an elongated version of the theme's riff—notice that it ends the same way as the theme—and the timbral play adds an intensity to it. The last phrase is a descending line that employs the blue note and the half-step ideas heard several times during this solo. Compared with measures 9 through 14 of the first chorus, it contains many of the same notes but in condensed form. The entire last 8 measures make a remarkably appropriate conclusion, a sort of summing up, to the whole solo.

The recognition of formulas takes longer, because it requires a knowledge of a number of works by the same artist. Once one has such a knowledge, one will recognize that the little arpeggio figure that first appears at the end of measure 5, into measure 6, pervades Young's work. Even in this solo, it recurs in measures 6–7, 12–13 (a variation), 28–29, and, in the second chorus, measures 7–8, 15–16 (with the first note missing), and at the very end. Notice that it occurs at phrase endings—the sure mark of a formula is that it always serves the same function.

Many more observations could be made about this solo, and the reader may have made some already. But this discussion will suffice as an introduction to some of the elements we will be discussing. By listening regularly in the way we have just demonstrated, one will greatly enhance one's understanding of music. The reader will also remain constantly aware that, even though we must isolate structural elements in order to point them out and discuss them, in reality they are all interrelated parts of an organic whole.[6]

Example 11. *Lester Leaps In* (9/5/39), Take 1; complete improvisation in B♭ key

Formulas

Formulas are the building blocks of a style. All jazz artists practice formulas or licks regularly and in a variety of keys in order to develop a repertoire to use in improvisations. (This kind of practice improves one's ability to improvise more directly and efficiently than general technique such as scales and arpeggios, a fact that is important in jazz education.) Each person has a slightly different repertoire of formulas. Presumably, the repertoire of an innovative artist is highly original. Musicians wishing to play like Lester Young must begin by becoming facile at playing his formulas in several keys, and learning where best to use each one in solos. Now we will examine several formulas found frequently in Young's work.[7] The reader is reminded that the examples mentioned during the rest of this chapter are drawn from a sampling of Young's recorded work, listed after the preface, and that most are easily obtainable on LP.

I have arbitrarily numbered the formulas for easy reference. Formula 1 appears most frequently in solos before 1942, but is still found until 1945. After that, it becomes relatively scarce. Formula 1 outlines a tonic arpeggio, so it occurs over tonic chords (see example 12a. I have notated all formulas in the key of C). This formula may begin on any beat and occurs at phrase endings as well as during the middle of phrases.

Formula 1 appears several times during *Lester Leaps In* (Take 2), for example, measures 30–31 of the first chorus and measures 3, 6–7, and 13 of the second, and during *Honeysuckle Rose,* measures 6, 12, and 16–17. *One O'Clock Jump* ends with Formula 1, and is interesting for the way the preceding measures lead up to the ending formula. This is an instance in which a formula functions partly as a structural motive (see example 12b). Young's sense of structure was so well developed that he often tried to integrate his formulas with the rest of the solo, especially in his early years. We will see similar instances with other formulas.

Example 12. Formula 1

a. the basic formula

b. Formula 1 as it appears in *One O'Clock Jump* (7/7/37), measures 9–12

Formula 2 occurs most often in the middle 1940s, and is also found in many 1930s solos. It is paired with the tonic chord in most instances. This formula fills in chromatically the interval between the third and fifth scale degrees, beginning on an accented flat third for a blues effect (see example 13).

Example 13. Formula 2

Formula 2 occurs several times during both of Young's solos in *I Want to Be Happy,* and the bridge of *Jumpin' at the Woodside.* In the first three measures of his *Jumpin' at the Woodside* chorus, he leaps up to Formula 2 by first playing C-D*b*-E, then G-C-D*b*-E, and finally the formula G-C-D*b*-E-F-F#-G, which he plays broadly, with the notes very connected, to emphasize its importance as an achieved goal. On the bridge of *Honeysuckle Rose,* he plays Formula 2 and then toys with the flatted third, natural third, and fourth degrees to heighten the effect of chromaticism (see example 14). Wavy lines between notes indicate short glissandolike bends connecting the pitches.

Example 14. *Honeysuckle Rose* (1/21/37), measures 17–21

A descending version of Formula 2 occurs in some 1940s solos, such as *I Got Rhythm,* where it occurs several times (see example 15).

Example 15. *I Got Rhythm* (12/21/43), second solo, second chorus, measures 14–15; descending version of Formula 2

Formula 3 is very characteristic of Young's work through 1947. It appears in several forms, and is adaptable to a variety of chords. Its simplest form is the alternation of two notes a major second apart, Formula 3a (see example 16). Most often the two notes are the first and second scale degrees, although the sixth and seventh degrees occur in *I Got Rhythm* (Young's second solo, second chorus, measure 9). Formula 3a appears in *Clap Hands, Here Comes Charlie* during measure 18 of the first chorus and measures 3, 4, 5, and 15 of the second chorus. Young gives it a sequential treatment in measures 3, 4, and 5, transposing it up a whole step the third time (see example 17).

Example 16. Formula 3a

Example 17. *Clap Hands, Here Comes Charlie* (8/4/39), measures 3–5 of second
chorus; application of Formula 3a

In Formula 3b, the interval between the two notes is a minor third (see example 18). This usually occurs over the tonic chord, with the two notes being the fifth and third scale degrees. Formula 3b appears in *Shoe Shine Boy* (Take 1), measures 25 to 27, in alternation with Formula 3a, and in the fifth measure of the second chorus of this piece. It also appears several times in takes 2 and 3 of *Dickie's Dream*; since this piece is in the minor mode, the formula involves the first and third degrees of the scale in most of its appearances here.

Example 18. Formula 3b

The most common version of Formula 3 combines 3a and 3b. It is an alternation between a minor third and a major second, the minor third usually being a flatted blue third or seventh (see example 19). Young begins his second solo on *I Got Rhythm* with two statements of this formula, and he plays it in measures 9 and 10 of both takes of *Lester Leaps In*.

Example 19. Formula 3c

Formula 4 appears in several forms, all of which have in common an alternation between a constant upper note and a variable lower note, implying a progression of two-note chords. Sometimes the lower note descends chromatically; it may also move down or up to a chromatic neighbor pitch (i.e., a note one half step away) and then back to the original note. In the process, it may create momentary dissonance against the underlying chords. This formula most often involves the tonic as the upper note and the sixth, flat sixth, and fifth as the lower notes (see example 20).

Example 20. Formula 4

a. The basic formula

b. Chord progression implied by the formula

In measures 5 to 7 of the second chorus of *Honeysuckle Rose* (concert), the E*b* in the bottom voice of Formula 4 creates some dissonance as it passes from E-natural to D (see example 21). Formula 4 figures prominently in both takes of *Shoe Shine Boy;* in Take 1, measures 1 to 3, and in the second chorus, measures 9 to 13; in Take 2, measures 25 to 27, and in the second chorus, measures 27 to 29.[8] Further harmonic aspects of Formula 4 are discussed in the next section.

Example 21. *Honeysuckle Rose* (1/16/38, concert), second chorus, measures 5–7;
                   Formula 4 used as passing tone

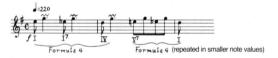

Formula 5 is a diatonic descending sequence utilizing thirds. The rhythms vary, but example 22 shows one frequent form (see example 22). This formula is characteristic, in both major and minor keys, of Young's solos from 1939 and 1940. For example, it appears in *Clap Hands, Here Comes Charlie* (beginning of second A section); the bridge of Take 3 of *Dickie's Dream; Dickie's Dream,* Take 2, (measures 4–5), and Take 1 (measures 6–7, 10, and 14).

Example 22. Formula 5

Formula 5 also occurs in *Twelfth Street Rag* (4/5/39), *Ad-Lib Blues* (10/28/40), *Charlie's Dream* (10/28/40, on the bridge), *Evenin'* (8/8/40), *Laughin' at Life* (6/7/40, Take A), and *Ebony Rhapsody* (2/20/40).

During this same time period one finds descents involving alternating fourths (see example 23). An attractive variation of this Formula 6 appears in *Jive at Five*, delicately played with a rhythmic lilt (see example 24). Formula 6 also occurs during the clarinet solo of *Texas Shuffle* (8/22/38) as well as the final ensembles of that recording, the second eight bars of *Hollywood Jump* (11/7/39), and the end of the *Blow Top* solo (5/31/40, Take B).

Example 23. Formula 6; descent with alternating fourths

Example 24. *Jive at Five* (2/2–4/39), measures 9–10; variant of Formula 6

(For discussion of other important formulas—a chromatic descent that usually involved triplets, and two formulas most characteristic of the later work, one utilizing honks, the other consisting of repetitions of one note—see, respectively, the sections entitled "Young's Treatment of Harmony," "Honks," and "Alternate Fingerings.")

Young's Treatment of Harmony

Young selected his formulas at any given point in a solo on the basis of the key and the underlying harmonic progression. The key and harmonic progression also control the selection for each individual note in a solo by limiting the number of appropriate choices.[9] I ask the reader to bear with me while I present some data that, despite their clinical nature, will provide an accurate picture of exactly which notes Young chose, and when. Such data cannot be replaced by general impressions.

About 25 percent of the notes in any given solo were the tonic, or first scale degree. The solos with the highest proportion of tonic notes were ones from the 1950s in which whole phrases were composed of rhythmic repetitions of the tonic note, such as *Just You, Just Me* and *Pres Returns*. In the latter solo, almost 60 percent of the notes were tonic notes. Among the pre-

1941 solos, *Lester Leaps In* (Take 1) had a similarly high percentage of tonic notes, mostly because of the repeated notes in the last eight bars.

While the ratio necessarily varied from solo to solo, the fifth scale degree was generally more important than the third. It figured most prominently in solos in minor mode, as in the three issued takes of *Dickie's Dream,* and in *The Modern Set.* Perhaps most interesting is that the sixth scale degree often appeared as frequently as any other. In *Tickle Toe* this simply reflected the large number of chords built on the sixth degree in the underlying harmony. In *One O'Clock Jump,* however, the whole first phrase is composed of repetitions of the sixth degree over a tonic chord. This use of the sixth to add coloration to a chord is characteristic of Young's playing throughout his career.

Another example is the D-minor arpeggio played over an F-major chord eight measures from the end of the *Jive at Five* solo. Young repeats the D-minor arpeggio over the changing chords, so it changes function. Over the F chord, the D is the sixth and the F and A are chord tones; over the G-minor chord, the D is the fifth, F the seventh, and A the ninth; and over the C-dominant-seventh chord, the D, F, and A are the ninth, eleventh, and thirteenth, respectively. I would not call A the sixth in this case, since it would clash with the seventh of the chord if placed in the same register (see example 25). This is a good example of Young's thinking horizontally, across several chords, rather than articulating each individual chord of the progression, which I will discuss further shortly. In the transcription I put parentheses around a note that is barely audible or "ghosted."

Example 25. *Jive at Five* (2/2–4/39), measures 24–27

Young was fond of adding the sixth to minor chords also. Notice, for example, the use of b-naturals over d-minor tonic chords in all takes of *Dickie's Dream.* This emphasis on the sixth was not unusual for the Swing Era. Added sixths are prominent in the melodies of many of the songs Young played, such as *Jumpin' at the Woodside* and *Honeysuckle Rose.* Young occasionally added ninths for coloration, especially after 1943. For example, ninths are prominent in *Neenah.* He used the major seventh as a melody note from 1942 on, especially in the master take of *Hello, Babe.* Another characteristic of Young's later work was the use of the blue third degree on other than blues songs, creating a tension between the major third in the accompanying chords and the lowered third in his melody line. This is the most apparent on *Lester Leaps In* (10/56), and also *I Got Rhythm* (see example 10b again).

Young frequently added coloration to the dominant-seventh chord at the end of the B section in AABA form. After having modulated into another key for the B part, the dominant-seventh chord of the original key appears in the last measure before the A section returns. Young highlighted this exciting point in the form harmonically. He liked to omit the root of the dominant-seventh chord and add a ninth and possibly eleventh, or else to use an augmented chord instead of the dominant seventh. The latter device appears at the end of the bridge on *Jumpin' at the Woodside*. Other members of the Basie band also substituted the augmented chord for the dominant seventh.

A study of the intervallic content of Young's music reveals a preference for scalar rather than arpeggiated melodies. Major seconds are the most frequent interval in Young's career taken as a whole. Major seconds up are more frequent before 1942, after which downward seconds predominate. Downward minor seconds are never common, but it is interesting to note that upward minor seconds are much more frequent after 1943. Before that year, the most minor seconds up are found in *Jumpin' at the Woodside,* mostly in the form of ascents from sharp second scale degree to third. This particular inflection is increasingly common beginning with *After Theatre Jump,* accounting partly for the increase in upward minor seconds. On songs where this simple inflection was not appropriate, the minor second occurred between the leading tone and the tonic, for example, on *These Foolish Things, Just You, Just Me,* and *The Modern Set.* Another reason for the increase in ascending half steps is their use in long chromatic glissandos. Solos after 1942, then, have more descending scales and more ascending half steps than those from Young's early period.

Minor and major thirds in both directions, which most often were part of arpeggios, were much more prominent in Young's intervallic vocabulary during his early years than in later periods. Major thirds were always less common, but particularly so in the later solos. The only exception to this rule was *East Does It,* an early-period solo, where the augmented arpeggios in the opening four bars accounted for a large number of upward major thirds.

Minor thirds, which are usually found descending, are the most frequent type of interval in the 1936 recordings, either second or third most frequent during 1937 to 1945, and after that quite rare. The minor third appeared outside arpeggios in certain solos. For example, it was the most common interval in *Tickle Toe* and in *Lester Leaps In* (10/56), most often appearing as an isolated interval; in the former, between the tonic and sixth (actually between minor third and tonic when one considers that the first 24 measures of this tune are in the relative minor), and in the latter, between a lowered or blue third and the tonic. In *Dickie's Dream* (all takes), *Honeysuckle Rose* (concert), and *Clap Hands, Here Comes Charlie,* the minor third occurred frequently as part of alternating figures (for example, Formula 3b, which occurs on scale degrees 5–3–5–3) as well as in arpeggios.

Intervals larger than a third were rare. Exceptions are *Boogie Woogie,* where fourths from the fifth up to the tonic are relatively frequent, and *Jive at Five,* where upward fourths appear between the third and sixth and other degrees as part of Formula 6 (see example 24 again).

Young played long chains of unisons, usually on the tonic but also on the sixth, lowered third, and other scale degrees, during all phases of his career, but only during the 1950s do these unisons at times comprise the bulk of a solo. As I noted in the preceding chapter, Young varied the timbre of repeated notes by using alternate fingerings. Coming between passages of long ascending and descending phrases, these repeated notes created tension as well as variety. Unisons clearly dominate the brief *One O'Clock Jump,* as well as the longer solos from *Clap Hands, Here Comes Charlie, Just You, Just Me, Pres Returns,* and *Lester Leaps In* (10/56). Many other 1950s solos contain a lot of this "one-noting," for example, *Neenah* and *One O'Clock Jump* (4/2/50), *Gigantic Blues* (1/12/56), and numerous versions of *Lester Leaps In* (1/6/51, 2/24/51, 3/17/51, 7/7/57, and others).

These data on intervals give a picture of the structure of Young's melodies and how they changed between one period and the next. During his early period, he favored scalar ascents and arpeggiated descents. A typical phrase from that period appears in example 26. In later years, after 1942 or 1943, he still used smaller intervals when ascending than when descending, but the ascents involved more semi-tones, and the descents were more scalar than arpeggiated. A typical phrase fitting this description appears in example 27. Long stretches of "one-noting," which served as plateaus between passages of ascents and descents, became more and more frequent in his later music. The reader must bear in mind that these generalizations apply not only to long ascents and descents as given in examples 26 and 27, but also to melodies composed of, say, two notes ascending, one descending, and one ascending.

The glissando that begins example 27 was not an unbroken chromatic scale; certain notes were omitted. Since not all the notes were distinguishable, I have written in some of the key ones over the wavy glissando symbol, without attempting to assign meaningful rhythmic values to them or to have them add up to a full measure. The glissando sign throughout the measure indicates that it lasts for all four beats.

Example 26. *Shoe Shine Boy* (11/9/36), second chorus, measures 22–24; early-period melody type

Example 27. *I Got Rhythm* (12/21/43), second solo, third chorus, measures 27–32; middle-period melody type

The nature of Young's melodies is in accord with common sense. He uses smaller note values when ascending; since he is working against "musical gravity," he must crawl and take longer to traverse a given interval than when descending. Young descends more quickly, using larger intervals as he is pulled along by "musical gravity." The occasional upward leap lends freshness to the melodic line. Young's melodies are in accord with the general principles of much Western music—a leap up is usually balanced by stepwise motion down. This does not necessarily hold true for arpeggios, which often occur in pairs, one ascending followed by one descending, in Young's early period.

Are there some principles of melodic motion that apply to most tonal music? Some studies of music from before the tonal system as we know it, such as Sarah Jane Manley Williams, *The Music of Guillaume de Machaut* (Ph.D. dissertation, Yale University, 1952), have reported a prevalence of descending scalar melodies, as I found in Young's middle period. A cursory look through the scores of Beethoven's piano sonatas suggests that chromatic scales usually ascend and diatonic scales descend. In contrast, a study of posttonal music, James Tenney's "The Chronological Development of Carl Ruggles' Melodic Style" (*Perspectives of New Music* 16, no. 1, 36–69), finds that ascents in this case are faster than descents—that is, leaps tend to occur upward, the opposite of Young's music. Is one type of melody more expected, more in accord with common sense than other types, as I have suggested in my discussion of Young? These are questions worth investigating, and Tenney's article suggests some useful techniques involving statistical analysis with computers. But they are questions we cannot answer now.

I mentioned earlier that Young thought in terms of the horizontal melodic line. The influential composer-theorist George Russell made the distinction in jazz between musicians who think horizontally, concentrating on the forward motion of the melodic line, and those who think vertically, articulating each individual chord as it passes by arpeggiating at least a few notes of each one. He pointed out that Young didn't articulate each chord in a progression. He restricted himself primarily to the tonic and dominant chords and their extensions and anticipated the other chords in a progression by playing a scalar melody that would fit over a series of chords.[10] Even when Young used arpeggiated melodies, he frequently chose an arpeggio that would fit over several chords (see example 25 again). This approach allowed Young considerable freedom in constructing his melodic lines, enabling him to concentrate on beauty and lyricism. Like many jazz performers of his generation, Young relied on his ear in choosing melodies to fit over the chord progression. If something sounded good, it didn't matter that it agreed or disagreed with a literal interpretation of the chords. Music theory, of which Young and his peers knew a little, could be a guide but was certainly not law.

Here again, we may contrast Young's work with that of Coleman Hawkins. Hawkins was the archetypal vertical player. He had a more solid grounding in music theory than most of his generation and was able to incorporate his knowledge into his playing. He not only arpeggiated the chords from the progression, but often inserted connecting arpeggios between chords that were not in the original progression. So he was relying not only on his ear but on a sophisticated knowledge of chords and progressions. In general, it is fair to say that vertically oriented musicmaking requires a greater knowledge of music theory than does horizontal playing.

The distinction between horizontal and vertical thinking is not absolute in practice. All jazz musicians use a mixture of the two approaches, but some are clearly more on one side than the other. Louis Armstrong was, like Young, primarily a horizontal thinker, which strengthens the possibility I discussed in chapter 2 that he may have been a formative influence on Young.

A simple example of Young's horizontal approach occurs at the beginning of *Honeysuckle Rose* (concert), where he plays a G-major scale over the ii and V^7 chords of G major. Since the ii and V^7 are diatonic chords, using no accidentals, the scale is an easy solution. Young begins the phrase by playing D and F# over the ii chord, an A-minor seventh. The D is heard as the eleventh and the F# as the thirteenth. Alternatively, one could say Young arpeggiates the V chord and ignores the ii chord (see example 28). The melody of *Shoe Shine Boy,* Take 2, at measure 11 is also drawn from the G-major scale, but the underlying chords include an E-dominant seventh (see example 29). Young intuitively perceived that the E^7 passes too quickly to create much dissonance, and that the whole progression reinforces G major. The clarity of his melodic line draws the listener's attention away from the underlying chords.

Example 28. *Honeysuckle Rose* (1/16/38, concert), measures 1–4

Example 29. *Shoe Shine Boy,* Take 2 (11/9/36), measures 11–12

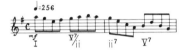

Before 1946, Young played melodies that clashed much more overtly with the underlying chords than in example 29 by using repetitive or sequential formulas. He used such formulas in places where the underlying harmony was static or composed of simple diatonic chords such as ii, V, and I. (Diatonic chords are those that only employ notes of the scale.) While he generally simplified complex chord progressions by finding a scalar melody to fit over them, he made moments of harmonic simplicity more exciting by adding these dissonant formulas to them. This is consistent with the horizontal approach, since a vertically oriented improviser theoretically would arpeggiate the simple progressions as he would the complex ones. One of Young's dissonant formulas works because it has such a strong character that the listener's attention is focused on it and not on the dissonance it creates. The repetitions or sequences engage the listener into trying to predict how the phrase will continue. The horizontal aspect remains foremost in the minds of player and listener.

One particularly striking dissonant formula is a descending chromatic sequence found in its basic form in *I Want to Be Happy* (see example 30). The rhythm varies in its other appearances, such as the last eight bars of the first chorus of *Clap Hands, Here Comes Charlie* and the second eight of *Jumpin' at the Woodside,* where Young prolongs the augmented fourth scale degree before finally releasing the tension at the end of the phrase in measure eleven.

Example 30. *I Want to Be Happy* (3 or 4/46), second solo, second chorus,
        measures 8–11; chromatic sequence descending from C to A

Honeysuckle Rose (concert) ends with a related descending sequence. It
was probably an improvisation rather than a formula, since it is not found
elsewhere in Young's work. In this sequence the intervals between the top
and bottom notes are varied much more than in example 30. The higher note
is held constant longer than the lower one so that they begin a minor third
apart and end a fourth apart, creating a great deal of dissonance in the process (see example 31). The final G is an anticipation of the G chord to follow
in the next measure.

Example 31. *Honeysuckle Rose* (1/16/38, concert), second chorus, measures 25–
        28; descending chromatic sequence

Young used another formula for chromatic ascents—a winding, twisting
sequence that appears in the second A section of the second chorus of *Clap
Hands, Here Comes Charlie,* as well as in *Ad-Lib Blues* (10/28/40) and *Jump,
Lester, Jump* (5/1/44). Notice the three-note underlined groupings, which
create a cross-rhythm against the quarter note beat (see example 32). This
sequence does not sound as dissonant as those in the preceding examples
because the third note of each grouping is accented by its being highest in
pitch and these notes are scale tones except for the B-natural. (Hawkins
used a very similar formula on "St. Louis Shuffle" in 1927.)

Example 32. *Clap Hands, Here Comes Charlie* (8/4/39), second chorus, measures
        9–10; ascending chromatic sequence

Young also played nonsequential dissonant formulas. In *Honeysuckle Rose*
he uses Formula 4, a repetitive pattern that alternates between a constant

upper note and a variable lower note, the lower note in this case descending chromatically from C to B♭. He reaches the B-natural while an F-dominant-seventh chord is being played by the rhythm section (see example 33). The listener's attention is drawn to the descending line and not to the dissonance it creates. As in the preceding example, there is a three-against-four cross-rhythm, this time in groupings of three beats each rather than three eighth notes.

Example 33. *Honeysuckle Rose* (1/21/37), measures 8–12; Formula 4 used to create dissonance (C♭ = B-natural)

Composer Peter Winkler offers another reason that the ear accepts dissonant formulas in cases such as the above. The B-natural could be the minor ninth of the V^7 chord, a B♭ chord, except that it arrives too late. Winkler calls this "syncopation on the level of harmonic rhythm." This adds to the momentum of the music since the listener must try to anticipate the next chord in order to accept the B-natural when it occurs.[11]

In the 1938 concert version of *Honeysuckle Rose,* Young makes this syncopation of harmonic rhythm explicit by first playing a pattern so as to coincide one way with the underlying chords and then displacing it (see example 34). The pattern appears in its original form in the first two measures of the excerpt shown. It is ear-catching because it implies a progression of V^7 to V diminished where one normally expects to hear ii^7 to V^7. This substitute progression seems to have been one of those that musicians passed around among themselves. Basie can be heard employing it later in this recording, behind Johnny Hodges, along with other substitutions (such as $♭VI^7$ to V^7 behind Buck Clayton). As early as 1932, clarinetist Pee Wee Russell played the pattern as one of his breaks on *Bugle Call Rag* (with Billy Banks, available on International Association of Jazz Record Collectors LP 4). The pattern is also interesting rhythmically, because it begins after an eighth rest in the first measure and is displaced in the second, beginning right on the beat (even Russell played it that way).

In the third measure, Young goes one step farther than his colleagues by reversing the pattern. He plays the diminished arpeggio first, then the dominant arpeggio. This creates extreme dissonance, albeit very briefly, between his line and his accompaniment. If his accompanists were playing the ii^7 to V^7 progression, this would clash fiercely with the ii^7 chord, but would resolve nicely over the V^7 chord. Even if they were playing the V^7 to V diminished progression, as they appear to be here (the fidelity does not favor them), this would conflict with both chords because it is in reverse order. The line straightens out prettily in the fourth measure. Clearly, Young is experimenting with syncopation of harmonic rhythm in this excerpt.

Example 34. *Honeysuckle Rose* (1/16/38, concert), second chorus, measures 9–12

These chromatic formulas begin to disappear after 1945. Chromaticism itself is more frequent, but, as I have pointed out, it appears in short inflections and in long glissandos rather than extended formulas. Individual dissonant notes such as appoggiaturas and upper chordal extensions continue to be prominent.

Writers on jazz often contrast Young with Coleman Hawkins in the treatment of harmony. Hawkins is cited as the harmonic innovator, while Young is considered the melodic genius who only uses the harmonic concepts standard in his day. The above discussion demonstrates that such a distinction between harmony and melody is misleading. Young's melodies were innovative partly because of the fresh ways in which they were related to the underlying chord progressions. He was no less concerned with harmony than Hawkins; he just chose a different approach.

Harmony and melody are interdependent and inseparable. Therefore, it makes more sense to speak of different approaches to melody, as George Russell suggested—vertical and horizontal. Hawkins was a master of vertical thinking, not only articulating the individual chords in a progression but implying passing chords and upper chordal extensions. Young thought more in terms of the horizontal line and developed his patterns and sequences in a logical manner even if they momentarily clashed with the underlying chord progression. Both approaches had precedents in the jazz tradition as far back as the 1920s, and both musicians took their approach farther then their contemporaries. At its most extreme Young's treatment of harmony was not at all standard for musicians of his generation. To hear his solo on *Jumpin' at the Woodside,* for example, in the context of the solos that precede and follow his is to hear something from a different, exotic musical world.

Rhythmic Organization

The eighth note was Young's basic unit of rhythmic activity at ♩ = about 140 and above. Shorter notes, primarily triplet eighths and sixteenths, occur mostly as ornaments. Louis Gottlieb, the author of several excellent analytical articles on jazz, observed that, "curiously, a good 75 percent of the small notes that he did use involve two pitches—F and G above middle C, concert pitch [high G and A on the tenor saxophone]—no matter what key the solo is in."[12] This is certainly true of the ornamental triplets, at least. Most ornamental triplets involve G–A–G, even though these represent different scale degrees depending on the key of the solo, for example 6–7–6 in *Neenah*, 2–3–2 on *These Foolish Things*, 1–2–1 on *Shoe Shine Boy* (Take 1) and *Hello Babe* (both takes), and 5–6–5 in *Lester Leaps In* (10/56), *I Got Rhythm*, *Jumpin' at the Woodside*, and *I Want to Be Happy* (first solo). Apparently Young's reason for choosing G–A–G was not related to the key of the piece. Probably this was a physically comfortable fingering for him.

For a short time at the end of his middle period, 1948 and 1949, Young played lines heavily ornamented with triplets. This was atypical for Young and probably the influence of bebop performers. This phase soon ended and Young returned to a direct, more sparsely ornamented style.

Young used values of a half note or more at endings and to a lesser extent, at beginnings of phrases. At tempos slower than ♩ = about 100, he preferred sixteenths and triplet eighths. A much greater variety in rhythms and durations exists at these tempos, especially on such songs as *These Foolish Things*. The alternation of triple and duple divisions of the beat provides added interest.

Pairs of eighth notes in jazz, whether written or improvised, are "swung," a sensation created partly by giving the two eighth notes unequal duration and accenting.[13] A jazz musician plays a pair of eighth notes approximately as ♩♪ (sometimes incorrectly transcribed as ♫), often with the second note lightly accented. Actual triplets are readily distinguishable from eighth notes at all tempos, largely because they are always played as written, whereas the value of eighth notes changes from performer to performer and from one tempo to another. At fast tempos Young's eighth notes are relatively even. This is also true in ballads, where one might expect a more exaggerated triplet feeling. Young also may interpret eighth notes differently within a solo. For example, he plays eighth notes in measures 19 and 20 of his *Easy Does It* solo relatively even in duration and accent, in contrast with the remainder of the solo. It seems that the long-short relationship between two eighth notes is more important to jazz musicians than the specific duration of each note.

Each eight-bar section of a thirty-two-bar chorus by Young was usually a self-contained and coherent unit. Most often, it was composed of two phrases. Young preferred to elongate the ending of the first of these phrases to make it five bars instead of four. During the years before 1947, he was as likely to divide an eight-measure section into five- and three-measure phrases as he was to use two four-measure phrases. Another characteristic of the prewar years was an occasional use of a three-measure phrase followed by a five-measure one, or even six measures followed by two.

Young also frequently invented unbroken eight-measure phrases. During the years with Basie, this was just as common as either four-four or five-three division. After 1941 the frequency of eight-measure phrases declined. An exception is the October 1956 version of *Lester Leaps In*; almost half of its eight-bar sections are not easily divisible into smaller phrases. (In fact, this piece and the others from this session bear remarkable similarity to Young's earlier works in tone, phrasing, and even melody.) An important change occurred in Young's work around 1947. After that year, most of his phrases in AABA choruses are predictably four measures long.

On twelve-bar blues solos, Young generally divided each chorus into three phrases, but frequently avoided the predictable four-bar units. Instead he phrased in five measures, four and three; or four, three, and five. He avoided pausing in measure eight, preferring to rest in measure seven, or, to a lesser degree, in measure nine. The first phrase was the most important, usually introducing a new and often striking melodic idea. At fast tempos, as on *Neenah,* the first phrase might continue for seven measures, with the remaining measures filled with simple formulas.

Young often began phrases with an anacrusis before the actual first measure of a section or chorus, but preferred to begin on the first beat of a section. He commonly rested for two beats or more between one section and the next.

The contours or curves of Young's melodic lines fell into certain types.[14] By far the most common, Contour Type 1, was that in which the first gesture was an ascent from the starting note to the highest pitch of the phrase. The line sometimes ascended gradually and at other times quite suddenly. After reaching this peak, the rest of the phrase descended. The lowest note often occurred very near the end of the phrase. In fact, it was sometimes part of a cadential formula. An ascent then led to the final note of the phrase, which could be higher, lower, or identical to the initial pitch. In some cases the highest note occurred twice in a phrase, once before the lowest note and once after its appearance (see figure 2). Sixty percent of Young's phrases during his early period had Contour Type 1, as did about 50 percent of his phrases during the middle and late periods. This held true for phrases of any length in blues solos, and for eight-bar sections in thirty-two-bar choruses regardless of how many phrases they comprised (as in the example 35). Contours were not consistent for individual phrases shorter than eight bars in solos based on thirty-two-bar song forms, so it would be more accurate to say that this contour type was most common for Young's blues phrases and for eight-bar sections, rather than phrases, in thirty-two-bar choruses. Perhaps this tells us that Young conceived of each eight-bar section as a whole, whereas he subdivided blues choruses in various ways.

Figure 2. Contour Type 1

a. The basic contour

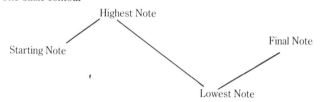

b. Contour Type 1 with the highest note appearing twice

A sample section having Contour Type 1 appears in example 35

Example 35. *Lester Leaps In,* Take 2 (9/5/39), second chorus, measures 1–8; an
       illustration of Contour Type 1

Throughout Young's career, two other contour types each appeared in approximately 10 percent of his blues phrases and eight-bar sections. Contour Type 2 was the same as Type 1 except that the lowest note was the last note of the phrase or section, identical with the final note (see figure 3). In Contour Type 3, the starting note was the highest note, followed by a descent to the lowest note, then an ascent to the final note. The highest note could reappear before the final note (see figure 4).

Figure 3. Contour Type 2

Figure 4. Contour Type 3

a. The basic contour

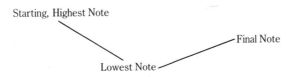

b. Contour Type 3 with the highest note reappearing after the lowest note

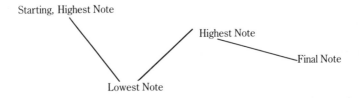

In Young's early period, almost all phrases conform to one of the three contour types given above. During the middle and later years, contours 1, 2, and 3 continue to predominate, but there is a greater variety of other contours and some are found in more substantial numbers. In particular, Contour Type 4, which is relatively uncommon during the early years, now comprises about 20 percent of the contours found in Young's phrases and sections. In this contour type, the initial gesture is a descent to the lowest note, after which the highest note appears. To conclude, there is a descent to the final note, which may be higher, lower, or identical to the starting note. The lowest note sometimes reappears after the highest note and before the final note (see figure 5). In the transcribed section given in example 36, the two notes in the fourth measure are played connected—therefore the wavy line indicating glissando. The pitch starts to rise at the point marked by the arrow. The second note is played with an accent and is not held for its full value. The sign, 𝆏 , indicates an accented note played short, while a normally accented note, 𝆏 , is held for its full value.

Figure 5. Contour Type 4

a. The basic contour

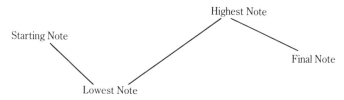

b. Contour Type 4 with the lowest note appearing twice

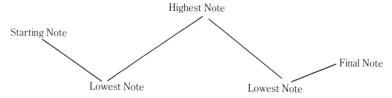

Example 36. *Destination Moon* (February 22, 1950), second chorus, measures 1–8; an illustration of Contour Type 4

Young's music, like all jazz, is characterized by ever-present syncopation. He usually played one or two syncopated notes per measure, creating a "push and pull" with the beats (see example 37). Example 37 begins with two measures of rhythmic relaxation, with accents on the first and third beats. Tension begins with the strong accents on the fourth beat of the second measure and between beats three and four in the third measure.

Example 37. *Hello Babe,* Master (12/21/43), measures 1–3; syncopation

Young usually did not play off the beat for as long as a measure during his early years; the extreme tension this created was part of his style after 1945. An exception occurs in *One O'Clock Jump* (see example 38). The fall-offs after each note in this example were usually part of this rhythmic figure; for example, see also *Jive at Five* (measures 15–16, 30–31).

Example 38. *One O'Clock Jump* (7/7/37), measures 5–7; playing off the beat

Certain syncopated figures dominated Young's recorded career.[15] They are defined by the note values and by their relationship to the bar line, which I have indicated in each case. For example, the figure ♫♩♩ (the last note is of variable length in this and other figures) practically defines the rhythm of his *Easy Does It* solo. This figure frequently occurs at phrase endings, for example, in *I Want to Be Happy* (first solo). A related figure, |♫♩♩ , appears at phrase endings in *Lester Leaps In* (Take 1). The figure |♪♩ ♪ prevails in solos from 1936, but also appears in the other periods—for example, hear *Just You, Just Me.* It also appears before the barline as ♪♩ ♪♩♩ . Another frequently played rhythm, especially at phrase endings, is |♩. ♪♩ | (hear *Lester Leaps In,* Take 1).

Honeysuckle Rose, Clap Hands, Here Comes Charlie, and other early solos abound in |♩. ♪ and ♩. ♪ | . These figures seem even more characteristic of the 1950s, as in the final chorus of *Just You, Just Me* and the October 1956 version of *Lester Leaps In.* The reverse figure, |♪ ♩ , frequently occurs at phrase endings in middle and later solos beginning with *I Got Rhythm.* In that solo it usually has an upward melodic interval, while in several 1950s solos, such as *Neenah,* it moves downward. Starting on the third beat of the measure— ♪ ♩. | —it appears in various places in all periods (see example 39).

Example 39. *Dickie's Dream,* Take 1 (9/5/39), measures 4–8; Young's use of the rhythmic figure ♪ ♩. |

As suggested by the above listing of rhythmic figures, Young accented any part of the measure. He usually accented by use of a higher pitch and longer duration; sometimes a short glissando led into an accented note. He accented through the use of dynamics more frequently in ballads than in other songs.

In his early period, Young was fond of three-against-four cross-rhythms, which he would repeat two to four times consecutively. Longer cross-rhythmic passages would create stronger tensions than was characteristic of his early style. Cross-rhythms operate at the rhythmic level of the eighth note or the quarter note (see example 40). Young stated a melodic idea of either three beats or three half beats in length and either varied or repeated it.

Example 40. Three-against-four cross-rhythms

a. [*Oh*] *Lady Be Good* (11/9/36), second chorus, measures 26–29; Eighth-note level

Each unit is three eighth notes long.

b. *Shoe Shine Boy,* Take 1 (11/9/36), second chorus, measures 9–12; an unusually long instance of three-against-four cross-rhythm at the quarter-note level

Each unit is three quarter notes long.

Other examples of this cross-rhythm appear in examples 32 and 33, in measures 17 to 19 of [*Oh*] *Lady Be Good,* measures 9 to 11 of *Honeysuckle*

Rose (concert), and the bridge of *Jumpin' at the Woodside*. Young generally did not use more complex cross-rhythms, such as five against four or two and a half against four.

Young's early work is rhythmically direct and swinging, partly because he returns to accenting beats one and three after any digression. This directness gradually evolved into a more abstract use of rhythm. His later solos exhibit much use of rubato, of quarter-note triplets, of a free mixing of duple and triple division of the beat, and, perhaps most significantly, of lagging slightly behind the beat. This lagging was so characteristic that I have only noted extreme cases on the transcriptions. The famous Aladdin sessions of 1945 to 1948 exemplify Young's rhythmic abstractness. For instance, Young would never have played the passage of example 41 during the 1930s. (This example is also related to formula 4 in that the high D remains constant while the B descends through a passing tone B*b* to A.)

Example 41. *Jumpin' with Symphony Sid* (2/18/47), second solo, second chorus, measures 1–2 with anacrusis

As younger musicians began to imitate his early style, Young was progressing to other rhythmic concepts. As a result, one can hear flowing, even rhythms on the late-1940s recordings of the youthful Al Cohn, Zoot Sims, and Allan Eager, whereas Young's own work had become complex and unpredictable.

Long-Range Structural Connections

As we continue to delve into the secrets of Young's music, it is time now to see how he developed his melodies. Most of Young's solos—and this is increasingly true in his later works—contain moments in which he takes a brief idea, uses it as a motive, and develops it. Frequently, he repeats the motive once or twice with little variation and then uses it as the beginning of the next phrase by adding notes to it. These passages have an organic form in which one section grows from the preceding one. This is particularly effective at the beginnings of solos, as in *After Theatre Jump* (see example 42). Motives a' and a" are variants of the initial motive a.

Example 42. *After Theatre Jump* (3/22/44), measures 1–5; motives used in an organic structure

Other instances of this organic development of motives are measures 4 to 6 of the second chorus of *Shoe Shine Boy,* Take 2; the opening measures of *Boogie Woogie* and *Jumpin' at the Woodside*; the second eight measures of *Dickie's Dream,* Take 3; the final eight bars of *Dickie's Dream,* Take 1; the second A of the second chorus of *Lester Leaps In,* Take 1; measures 25 to 28 of the first solo on *I Want to Be Happy*; the beginning of the second solo on *Jumpin' with Symphony Sid*; the second bridge of *Destination Moon*; the beginning of the second chorus of *Neenah*; and throughout such pieces as [*Oh*] *Lady Be Good* and *Easy Does It,* both of which I will discuss later.

The last eight measures of *Shoe Shine Boy,* Take 2, introduce another motivic technique. The note values in the initial motive became shorter with each variation (see example 43). The last eight measures of *Jumpin' at the Woodside* are similar in structure.

Example 43. *Shoe Shine Boy,* Take 2 (11/9/36), second chorus, measures 25–27

Occasionally Young structures an entire chorus around one motive. This is especially common in 1950s solos based on the blues, such as *Pres Returns, Encore* (March 1950), *One O'Clock Jump* (April 2, 1950), *Up 'N Adam* (1/20/51), and *Gigantic Blues* (1/12/56). Of course, the motives in some of these cases are simple blues riffs. A more subtly structured chorus is Young's 1940 *Easy Does It* solo. The upward arpeggios in the introductory four bars are clearly variations of one idea. This idea appears in a more basic form during the first measure of the solo proper. I call this motive c; its defining characteristics are the ascending contour and pentatonic melody type. The preceding measures are more complex rhythmically and harmonically, which is why I see them, in retrospect, as variations of c and not the other way around (see example 44).

Example 44. *Easy Does It* (3/20/40); motivic content

a. First two measures of introduction

b. Measure 1 of solo chorus; motive c in its basic form

Variants of motive c comprise much of the remaining material of the solo. The second measure of the solo proper leads directly into an organic extension of the motive, ending in a related figure, c'. Another variant of c follows this at measure 5 (see example 45).

Example 45. *Easy Does It* (3/20/40), measures 3–5

A form of motive c" leads into the bridge of *Easy Does It,* followed by another variant of c. This phrase ends in ascending and descending versions of c (see example 46). The last two measures of the bridge are also related to A, as is the second measure of the following A section. This final section is dominated by repeated attempts to move upward from the note G, which finally succeed in the last four measures (see example 47).

Example 46. *Easy Does It* (3/20/40), measures 11–14; ascending and descending versions of motive c

Example 47. *Easy Does It* (3/20/40), measures 17–22; repeated attempts to move away from the note G (circled)

The second A section of *Jive at Five* contains some fascinating motivic structuring. Its first two measures develop organically from the end of the preceding section. The second two measures are a variant of the first two; the rhythms are clearly related, but the contour is quite different (see example 48).

Example 48. *Jive at Five* (2/2–4/39), measures 7–12; motivic structure

By this point, the reader has seen and heard ample evidence of Young's ability to build phrases out of motives that are both logical and beautiful. In practice, these phrases were not isolated moments. Young masterfully combined them into whole choruses and longer solos so that they seemed inevitable in the light of what preceded them. Young was acutely aware of pacing. He began his solos authoritatively, then saved his fastest or most striking ideas for later on. For example, the way he enters *Honeysuckle Rose* (1937) captures the listeners's attention; his honking at the end of the bridge creates the climax of the solo.

In longer solos, Young carefully built toward climaxes of technical and emotional intensity rather than aproaching each chorus as a separate entity. Musicologist and jazz authority Lawrence Gushee writes that "although the welding of two choruses into a whole may seem a modest achievement by today's standards, it was not at all usual in 1936." Louis Armstrong was Young's greatest precursor in this. Gushee suggests that Young may have had the following plan, probably unconsciously, when taking two-chorus solos in AABA form: first, play an idea that will catch the attention and establish the change from ensemble to soloist. At the beginning of the second chorus, introduce more technically demanding, flamboyant ideas, climaxing in the second eight bars of that chorus. During the last eight measures, withdraw again into the ensemble by playing more naive or well-known ideas.[16] We can follow this plan clearly in both takes of *Shoe Shine Boy,* analyzed by Gushee, and *Lady Be Good,* where the increase in dynamic level and technical display during the first sixteen measures of the second chorus are very effectively underscored by the rhythm section. In both *Honeysuckle Rose* (concert) and *Clap Hands, Here Comes Charlie,* Young reserves striking harmonic ideas for the climactic second eight bars of the second chorus (see examples 32 and 34 again). Among the later solos, *After Theatre Jump* seems to follow the plan, climaxing in the same location with the honking formula (see example 7 again).

One-chorus solos were generally too short to adhere to this scenario—more often, they stayed at one basic level—but two solos, *Jumpin' at the Woodside* and *Honeysuckle Rose,* do build in intensity toward the bridge, then wind down again. Solos longer than two choruses often reach a peak about three-quarters of the way through, as in the four-chorus solo ending *I Got Rhythm.* More often there is simply a gradual increase of intensity followed by a shorter decline, without the peak occurring at any predictable point.

The plan does not appear on many of the later small group recordings on which Young took two solos, one at the beginning and one at the end. Frequently he ended the first solo at a high level of intensity and began the second solo at that same level. Furthermore, since the second solo ended the recording, he built in intensity instead of tapering off as in the two-chorus plan. *I Want To Be Happy* and *Pres Returns* are good illustrations of this structure.

Pres Returns, a blues, also illustrates Young's tendency to focus on the beginning of each blues chorus, starting each one with a more intense idea than the preceding one. This seems to have been his structural plan in blues solos of more than one chorus, an appropriate one since blues choruses are only twelve measures long and there is not much time to build within each chorus as in the two-chorus AABA plan.

In this chapter we have seen that Lester Young, though he notated very little music, was indeed a great composer. He had a repertoire of simple formulas that he used creatively to keep them from becoming boring. He introduced motives from which he developed phrases. Finally, he designed his phrases with the layout of the whole solo in mind, shaping a beginning, middle, and end. Every Lester Young improvisation is a satisfying and self-sufficient composition.

Summary

Contour Type 1 was the most common during the early period. This means that the highest note of a phrase was usually reached before the lowest note; the latter often occurred just before the final note. Young favored the sound of an added sixth over many chords, and was quite conventional in many of his harmonic implications, but he created striking dissonances in the course of long chromatic ascents or descents and was not afraid to lean on the lowered fifth.

Young's melodic lines most often ascended scalewise and descended in arpeggios. He frequently invented unbroken eight-bar phrases, or divided the eight bars unevenly, for example, five and three. He liked long, flowing eighth-note lines.

Rhythmically, solos from this period are very direct. A few beats of syncopation would be balanced by on-the-beat accents. Young would set up and repeat three-beat or one-and-a-half-beat ideas to create cross-rhythms for as long as five or six measures.

As in all jazz improvisation, a good percentage of Young's work utilized formulas from his personal repertoire. But this did not prohibit him from creating solos with exceptional structural coherence. He would frequently develop a whole phrase out of one motive, adding a few notes to it each time, or connect each phrase with the preceding one by reusing material. He was always aware of the total length of his solos instead of just thinking chorus by chorus or phrase by phrase. This is illustrated by the fact that, regardless of length, most of his solos begin energetically, build to a peak of complexity somewhere past the middle, and wind down again near the end.

During Young's middle years, Contour Type 1 was still most frequent, but not so dominating as in the early solos. A greater variety of contours is found. On the other hand, uneven phrase lengths are rarer; four-bar phrases are the rule.

More harmonic tension is introduced by the use of ninths, major sevenths, and blue thirds against major chords. He tended to ascend in semitones and descend scalewise. Increasingly long stretches of "one-noting" were plateaus between the more active passages.

Young's middle work is rhythmically very complex. Long passages of off-the-beat playing are common, as well as abstract, rubato rhythms that are nonnotatable. There was a pervasive tendency to lag behind the beat. Toward the end of this period, Young temporarily showed the influence of bebop by inventing long lines overcrowded with triplets. But these lines seemed forced and contained more filler material than is characteristic of most of Young's work.

Structurally, Young's solos were perhaps not as concise as those from the early years, but they had other strengths. There was a tendency to isolate bridges from A sections in AABA-form solos. Each type of section would have its corresponding type of material. Formulas were used more frequently and more literally, that is, with little variation. Young spent increasingly longer periods of time developing his motives, but would balance these passages with shocking contrasts. He still had a superior sense of pacing, managing to hold longer and longer solos together through a careful building up of intensity.

In most respects Young's late works are similar to those of the middle period—perhaps too much so, for there is a heavy reliance on previously recorded versions of songs. Some whole solos are composed from a small number of formulas and from quotations of previous recordings. In general, these solos also contain fewer small-note values, and are sometimes quite straightforward rhythmically in their even flow of eighth notes.

5

"That's Modern, Dig?"

Throughout this analysis so far we have noticed that Young's style changed from one period to the next in many respects. The particular analytic process we have used divides Young's music into its component parts, such as tone, phrasing, formulas, and so on. We have looked at each part separately and commented on its development over the years. The chapter summaries have, I hope, aided the reader in putting these separate parts back together somewhat and getting an overall impression of each period.

Of course, Young's music does not exist in separate parts in reality. All of the elements we have examined are part of an organic whole, and they are interrelated and interdependent. In their combined state, these elements also create new elements, as atoms combine to form molecules. These new resultant elements are so subtle that there may be no words to describe them, no way to separate them out and study them in isolation. In short, the whole is more than the sum of its parts.

That is why it is important for us at this point to examine some of Young's organic whole solos. By doing so we will be able to synthesize our separate observations into the context of a unified reality. The reader is urged to obtain the recordings themselves in order to experience these beautiful works rather than simply reading about them.

The three solos analyzed in this chapter represent Young's finest achievements during each period of his style. They are readily available on LPs, as indicated in the Catalog of Recorded Works.

An Early-Style Solo:
[*Oh*] *Lady Be Good* (11/9/36)

The fresh, bright tone quality, clean articulation, and precise rhythms mark this as an early-style solo. It comprises two thirty-two-bar AABA-form choruses. This solo, often cited as one of Young's greatest, exemplifies the organic type of structuring discussed earlier; see example 49 for a complete transcription.

Example 49. [*Oh*] *Lady Be Good* (11/9/36); complete improvisation in B♭ key

The initial three-note motive, e, reappears at the start of a longer phrase in measure 2. This phrase, an ascent to the high A and descent by dominant-seventh arpeggio built on A, is a formula, 7, that Young uses over tonic chords throughout this piece. It is a formula and not a motive because it is never followed by a development of the whole phrase and because Young plays it wherever it conveniently fits and maintains the melodic flow. Formula 7 appears also in measure 9 of the first chorus, and in measures 6 and 7, 14 and 15, and 30 to 31 of the second chorus. The last two notes of measure 3 become the motivic basis of measures 4 through 7. The two-note motive, f, is developed through variations in rhythm and in the interval between the two notes. On another level, this is also an instance of Formula 4; in this case the lower note descends chromatically from F# to E, while the top A remains constant.

The relationship of measure 7 to the preceding ones is primarily rhythmic (compare to measure 5). The change from tightly alternating notes to a relatively expansive upward arpeggio is surprising. The upward direction and ending on the sixth scale degree create irresolution, which propels the solo into the next section.

Young repeats the sixth for continuity, then introduces motive g in measure 9. Measure 10 is a variant of this, having a similar rhythm and descending contour. The tonic note at the beginning of measure 11 is both the ending of the preceding motive and the beginning of a couple of variations on the tonic arpeggio, the second of which extends into measure 13. Measure 14 provides a contrast with its sweeping arc, but is still related to the preceding measure by the prominence of D and F#. Measure 15 introduces a new motive, h, which accents the third beat of the measure. This motive carries through the next measure into the first measure of the bridge, linking the bridge to the preceding A section. Measure 16 is a response to measure 15 using basically the same rhythm, and measure 17, the beginning of the bridge, is the simplest and most conclusive version of motive h.

The rest of the bridge is composed of three versions of a new motive, i. The short glissando into the initial high note is not merely an ornament, but an essential part of this motive, as seen in the successive variants. The last one, in measures 22 and 23, is the shortest and most conclusive; as in measures 14 to 16 above, Young seems to prefer to end a series of variations with a feeling of finality. The last variation of i leads to repetitions of the note E, which begin the next section, the first four measures of which grow organically from these repetitions of E combined with a short motive, j. Motive j is the same as the first three notes of Formula 7 but this is its first appearance in isolation. It therefore serves as a good introduction to the long variation of Formula 7 that appears in measures 28 through 31. All the notes of Formula 7 are here—E, F#, and A ascending, followed by G-natural, E, C#, A, and F# descending—but there are several intervening notes and greatly changed rhythms. The G-natural, in measure 28, appears over an uncharacteristic chord and takes on the sound of a blue note, which Young exploits with an expressive bend. Interestingly, measure 30 is identical to measure 10.

The pickup to the second chorus circles around the note C#, which remains prominent during the first four measures of this chorus (circled in example 49). Following Young's plan for two-chorus AABA solos, he introduces shorter note values and more technical patterns. Measures 1 to 4 of the second chorus are variants of motive k, defined by a rhythm and a downward contour. Each variant is lower than its predecessor. After a short climb up, the phrase ends in measures 6 and 7 with Formula 7.

Measures 8 through 16 of the second chorus are clearly the climax of the piece, in accord with Young's two-chorus plan. He achieves this by shorter note values and heightened volume and vibrato. The rhythm section effectively complements Young. Jo Jones drums more forcefully, and pianist Count Basie begins to play the chords on every beat in guitar style instead of leaving spaces. This phrase is also a wonderful instance of organic structuring. Young repeats a simple turn around the tonic at shorter and shorter intervals until its velocity launches a series of arpeggios. The phrase ends with Formula 7.

A downward arpeggio, motive l, varied through rhythmic displacement, is the basis of the first three measures of the bridge, measures 17 through 19. The second note from the top of the arpeggio descends from F# to E. The tension between sixths and ninths, F# and B in this case, and their somewhat more relaxed counterparts, fifths and octaves, E and A, has been prominent throughout the solo so far. In several places we have heard F# as the sixth of a tonic chord or ninth of a dominant chord. Over a longer time span, F# descended to E during measures 4 to 7 of the first chorus. An F# appoggiatura resolved to E between measures 5 and 6 of the second chorus, and B resolved to A in measures 18 and 22 of the first bridge.

Measure 19 employs motive h as a formula, since it is purely functional here and not developed. It was also used as a formula between measures 3 and 4 of the second chorus. One of its defining features is the expressive bend connecting D and C#. A glissando up to the highest note of the solo in measure 21 leads the way for several more arpeggiated figures, mostly downward and ending on a low E in measure 24.

The last A section basically begins with the same E an octave higher; it is approached by a suspension of the F# above it. Similarly, the next measure begins with a high B, which resolves to an A. This reappearance of the F#-E and B–A relationship prepares the way for Young's next move, a brilliant structural tactic. In measures 26 through 28 he employs a formulaic routine that consists of filling in the intervals from F# to E in both the upper and lower registers and B to A in the lower register. This routine is a commonplace ragtime-style formula using three-against-four cross-rhythms (three-note groups are underlined in example 40). This formula, for example, forms the basis of *12th Street Rag* (a familiar pop song, not a rag). In accord with Young's two-chorus AABA plan, he is playing familiar ideas with which to end his solo. But, at the same time, his selection of this routine at this particular moment dramatizes the F#–E and B–A relationship, in a sense summarizing and resolving a major concern of the solo.

Measure 29 is a variant of 25—the F# to E again. The solo ends with Formula 7. This is a solo so well formed, so self-contained that each phrase seems inevitable. Young develops and explores each motive at its first appearance and unifies the solo by bringing some motives and formulas back later. He saves his most intense moments for the second chorus, and uses the last eight measures to tie it all together. Perhaps even more important than its structural conciseness, this is a beautiful solo, full of singing melodies and provocative rhythms.

A Middle-Style Solo:
After Theatre Jump (3/22/44)

Young employs a tone quality here that is much richer and heavier than on [*Oh*] *Lady Be Good*. The rhythms seem correspondingly lazier, a bit purposely dragging. I have only indicated extreme cases of such rhythmic freedom on the transcription, given as example 50.

Few of Young's solos are as tightly structured as [*Oh*] *Lady Be Good*, especially after 1942, but many of his middle-period solos have compensating strengths. *After Theatre Jump*, for example, has more melodic surprises than [*Oh*] *Lady Be Good*, great emotional intensity, and still manages to be well structured from the motivic point of view.

After Theatre Jump begins with an instance of organic structuring; motive n, used in each of the first four measures, is extended to create a longer phrase beginning in measure 5. We recognize variant n″ because it is Formula 2, here used motivically. The blue notes heighten the emotional impact of the otherwise formulaic cadence, again utilizing Formula 1.

The second eight bars begin with a melodic idea centering around Eb and C in measures 9 through 11 (circled). Measure 12 is a surprise, with its change in register and raspy tone. It begins a phrase that is basically a descent from the high Bb to the lower one in measure 15 (circled). The caden-

Example 50. *After Theatre Jump* (3/22/44); complete improvisation in Bb key

tial formula comes early—in measures 14 and 15—but then is repeated in order to end the phrase in the expected place, lending interest to this passage. The formula used here is the same as in measures 6 and 7, Formula 1.

Unlike [*Oh*] *Lady Be Good* and many of Young's earlier solos, there is no attempt to connect the bridge to the preceding section. Even when there is no pause before the bridge in Young solos from 1943 and after, the musical material of the bridge is often distinct from the A sections of an AABA chorus. This does not necessarily indicate a weakness in form, but rather a different concept, in which the bridge provides important contrast. This bridge begins with the striking motive o, involving tritones, which basically prolongs the low C in measures 17 and 18. This is followed by a series of two-note motives ascending, p, the last of which is extended into a descent, all of which prolongs the note D. (The D is circled in measures 19 and 20.) The remainder of the bridge is more lyrical, comprising two phrases somewhat similar in rhythm and contour, measures 20 to 22 and 22 to 25, the second of which is extended to lead directly into the next section.

The on-the-beat rhythm of measure 25 immediately relates it to the beginnings of the other A sections so far and distinguishes it from the bridge. Measures 27 and 28 are clearly related to each other as variants of motive q, and the remaining measures of this chorus are variants of one motive, r. The upward climb in measure 32 leads into the second chorus.

The second chorus begins with a new and more expressive motive, s, a downward bend between two notes, which is varied rhythmically and melodically throughout the first six measures of the chorus. The first A section ends with the same cadence observed in the first two sections of the solo, using Formula 1 in measure 7.

The following section, with its striking honks and chromatic ascent from low B♭ to C, is the climax of the solo, in accord with Young's two-chorus AABA plan. This is one version of the honk formula discussed earlier and shown in example 7. The last four measures of this section utilize the same cadential formula noted above. In fact, measures 14 and 15 of this chorus are almost identical to measures 6 and 5—in that order—of chorus one.

The bridge illustrates another characteristic of Young's work from 1943 on—the tendency to structure bridges similarly from chorus to chorus. It begins with two variants of the motive o that began the first bridge, and then ascends with wide leaps as in the first bridge. Following that is a chromatic glissando and bend up to a high D, a descent to a lower D (circled), and an unusual and long glissando using a type of blues scale that appears in measure 24 and ushers in the last eight bars.

After the excitement of the bridge, the beginning of the last A section is notable for rhythmic and melodic simplicity, again in accord with Young's two-chorus plan. Measures 25 through 29 are based on a simple two-note motive, t. It first appears in the lower register in measure 25, then an octave up. A turn is added between the two notes beginning in measure 27. Motive t is reversed so that it ascends in measure 29, followed by one final variant in which the top note is played twice; alternatively, all of measure 29 could be seen as an expansion of t. The solo ends with the cadential Formula 1 and then several reiterations of the tonic.

A Late-Style Solo:
Pres Returns (1/13/56), Second Solo

Young's tone here, no longer powerful as on *After Theatre Jump,* is tender and emotion-laden, as of a man giving his emotional and technical all. Like most of his 1950s work, this solo demonstrates no great fluency on the instrument, but the notes are so well chosen and the melodies so attractive that one does not wish for anything else.

The recording, in twelve-bar blues form, opens with a Young solo that builds effectively, followed by some beautiful piano playing by Teddy Wilson. Then Young picks up where he left off with five blues choruses, each more intense than the last, excitingly accompanied by the rhythm section with his old friend Jo Jones on drums. It is no accident that Jones played drums on all three of the recordings that I've chosen to illustrate Young at his best. Young always seemed to be inspired by Jones's presence. In *Pres Returns,* he expands upon an earlier blues in the same key, with the same bass and drums—*Undercover Girl Blues* (1/16/51).

Young employs different structural tactics on a blues such as this than he would on thirty-two-bar forms. Typically, each chorus begins with a very distinctive idea, which may be developed organically for the rest of the chorus. The opening idea of each chorus is more intense than that of the preceding chorus. Finally, there are several concluding choruses of "riffs"—sheer rhythmic intensity. See example 51 for my transcription.

The solo begins with a quotation, likely a conscious one, of the motive, u, that opened Young's first recorded blues solo, *Boogie Woogie* (11/9/36). Motive u is repeated in measure 2, then again in measure 3, with an extension that ends the phrase with an upward gesture between measures 4 and 5. Measures 4 to 6 are an F# minor arpeggio (superimposed on a D-dominant-seventh chord played by the rhythm section, ignoring the seventh, thus actually the chord D–F#–A–C# without the root), first in another upward gesture and then gently downward in three-note groups. The chorus ends with the highest upward climb yet in measure 8 followed by another gradual, looping descent through measure 12. Notice the little formula with the flat seventh, appearing in measure 10 for the second time—we first heard it in measure 3. This proliferates in the rest of the solo. I call it Formula 8 (see example 52).

The second chorus begins back in the upper register with two pairs of balanced measures—measure 2 answers measure 1, and 4 answers 3, the latter response a bit more emphatic, as it reaches the highest note heard thus far, high E. The opening of the next phrase, measure 5, uses a variation of the |♩ ♫ ♫ ♩ | rhythm just heard in measures 1 and 3. Its ending, motive x, is taken up to lead off another phrase in measure 7, whose final A–F#, motive y, is repeated and followed by a highly vocalistic moan. This chorus does not end descending as did the first, but stays in the upper register, a sign of the building momentum.

Example 51. *Pres Returns* (1/13/56), second improvisation, complete in B♭ key

Example 52. Formula 8

The third chorus begins with two balanced "question-answer" phrases built around Formula 8, which is heard on G as in example 51 and also transposed to the tonic, A. Again, measure 2 answers 1, and 4 answers 3. The third phrase, beginning in measure 6, is a simplified variant of Formula 8—remove the triplet and you have a minor third. This third gradually descends from A–F# to G–E, the two levels at which Formula A was heard in the preceding phrase. The ending motive z of measure 9 is echoed in measure 11, after another appearance of Formula 8. Another variant of z is the pickup to the fourth chorus. (Note that z resembles x.)

The note A, which has become more and more prominent in each chorus, now becomes the focus of some powerful "riffing" by Young. As he builds in intensity he becomes more direct, hammering away at the tonic with a few simple rhythms to create tremendous drive. The balanced phrases are easy to hear—two measures each—and myriad repeated As in measures 10 and 11 of chorus four lead into the final chorus and some more two-measure riffing, with Jo Jones filling in the spaces on drums. Chorus IV evokes "Lester Leaps In," which combines with z in the final chorus.

Typically of Young's late work, a few formulas are much used during this solo, yet it is far from boring. For all the apparent differences between Young's late and early work, some things remain constant—an exceptional sense of structure, revealed in the logical flow of ideas within each chorus and the careful building from chorus to chorus, and an ability to create unforgettable melodies.

6

Pres Returns

Author and researcher Jan Evensmo wrote, "The evaluation of Lester Young's music over his whole recording career of 20 years is one of the most argued and unsettled points in jazz criticism." Now that we have examined the music at some length, it is time to review the critical controversy.

Many jazz writers have flatly rejected Young's later work. Usually they take World War II as their cutoff point, assuming that the changes in Young's style were a direct result of his disturbing army experiences. Don Heckman wrote in *Down Beat,* 1963, that "Young's truly productive period ended with his induction into the army in 1944." Steve Voce, in liner notes to Zim ZL-1000, speaks of "a sad, almost empty echo of a giant in decline." Bernard Cash chose to omit Young's postwar recordings from inclusion in his thesis on the music, attributing what he sees as a marked drop in quality and creativity to Young's alcohol problem. These writers see the alcohol problem, in turn, as the result of Young's army tenure.

For these writers, as for many fans of the early Young, the problem is largely just that the style changed. Many people who loved the early style simply could not accept that Young would change in any direction. For example, both Cash and Heckman specify Young's rhythmic approach as a major factor in the deterioration of his music. Heckman complains that "in the postwar recordings Young's notes frequently are played under or well behind the beat." It is hard to imagine that someone who had not heard the early Young would necessarily see why this should be considered a defect. Both writers also criticize Young's tone. Raymond Horricks, in his book on the Basie bands, referred to Young's bored posture. He felt that Young had lost interest towards the end and tended to rely on repetition of the phrases and devices that elicited the loudest audience response. All of these writers re-

veal their bias when they speak of "those few recordings where Lester recalls the style of his youth."
Some of the cynics do admit to some value in the later work. Whitney Balliett found that Young's rendition of "I Didn't Know What Time It Was," from January 1956, contained "tantalizing" variations. Martin Williams agreed that the later Young was a tired man, but found there were "compensations" in the depth of his ballad playing and in "the profoundly ironic, melancholy joy" he brought to the blues.[1] These authors come close to realizing the greatest key to the appreciation of Young's late work, the fact that Young's style had changed and needed to be evaluated on different terms than the early works. One cannot understand the late records if one is constantly looking for echoes of the early ones, and constantly comparing with the early ones.

We have seen in the past few chapters that Young's style changed in objectively demonstrable ways. It was not a question of a general lack of energy, or of an inability to play in the early style. Young was growing older, developing as a person, and naturally he had to develop as a musician. His rhythmic approach did change after 1942, becoming more independent from the beat—which is not necessarily worse or better than his earlier approach! One finds different contour types after 1942 than before, and differences in phrase lengths and interval preferences. One finds more extroverted expressive devices after 1942, and increased harmonic tension. These devices were not cheap effects, nor is there any reason to think that Young adopted them merely to please audiences. Young's tone quality changed obviously after 1942 and again around 1950. His music around 1950 evolved in other respects also, enough so that we have set the works of the 1950s in their own style period.

Admittedly, it is difficult to listen to Young's late works with a new ear. The early solos are beautiful and refreshing, and they establish a certain aesthetic. It requires an effort for the listener to listen to other solos by Young without having the same aesthetic standards and expectations. It would probably be much easier if one did not know the later works were by the same person, for then one could listen to them on their terms. Interestingly, I find in teaching jazz history that the novice Pres listener does not immediately hear any superiority of the early works over the late ones, at least among today's college students. I play and discuss representative recordings from each period with my students and solicit their opinions. Invariably I have found that about an equal number favor each period. Some find [Oh] Lady Be Good of 1936 to be their idea of perfection—others find it too subtle and dated and prefer the aggressive excitement of After Theatre Jump from

1944. And there are always a few, usually not so many as for the other two periods, who identify most readily with the direct, uncomplicated beauty of *Pres Returns* from 1956. Would that experienced listeners could approach these solos with such open-mindedness!

One suspects, in fact, that the detractors of Young's later years may not be listening very hard at all. Looking for an explanation for Young's style changes, they have seized upon his army experiences. But they have become so committed to this answer that they have closed their ears to the music, which clearly began to change before Young entered the army. Our analysis of Young's recordings shows a fairly consistent style through 1942. In 1943 we hear the deeper tone, behind the beat rhythm, and other indications of the new style. That style is not any different on Young's first recordings immediately after leaving the service.

Most writers also fail to notice that Young's style changed again around 1950. True, we find that the changes are not as marked as between 1942 and 1943, but they are there to be heard, and indicate that Young's style was also changing five years after the army, which would be a highly delayed reaction.

This is not to say that Young's army sufferings did not leave an effect on him. They must have, but that effect did not translate so literally to the music as the critics would have us believe. His music gradually changed over the next decade as a result of many different factors, and had begun to change before the army. It is a very inexact type of psychology that attributes everything about a person to one experience. One must always remember that the same events will have different effects upon different people. Other people may have had the same kind of army experiences as did Young, and come out relatively unscarred, or perhaps more scarred than he did. And we don't really know just how he was affected by all that transpired—we are just guessing. It seems certain that Young hated the army, but whether he continued to brood about it for the rest of his life is certainly open to question.

Then, of course, there are artists who continue to produce works of joy despite personal suffering, which brings to question the whole idea that one can always tell about an artist's personal life from his work. It may be possible, but the connection may not be obvious or direct. In order to perform a really sophisticated psychological analysis of Young's music, we must begin by obtaining an accurate picture of the music itself, as we have done in this book. Then we must obtain as much information as possible about Young's personal affairs and state of mind, especially his social life, because one's relations with people are the main factor in psychological development. Last,

we should look to events that happened to Young, and attempt to recon-
struct how he was affected by these events. The army experience should be
brought in after the background is known, not as a substitute for a thorough
researching. Once we understand Young's psychology better, we can try to
relate it to the music, bearing in mind that the music has tremendous power
in 1944 as well as 1946, and moments of great joy right until the end. Any
explanation will have to take these musical facts into account. It is conceiv-
able that one may find direct corellations between Young's psychology and
his music, but it is equally likely that one will discover that he was personally
unhappy at times that his music sounds fresh and positive.

Perhaps the most important fact that the critics need to know is that
Young was aware of the changes in his style and indicated that he was in
control of them. As he told Postif in the last interview, "I get all kind of insults
about, (mimicking) 'You don't play like you played when you were with Count
Basie.' . . . They get all trapped up, they go, '*Goddamn,* I never heard him
play like this!' That's the way I *want* things, that's modern, dig? Fuck what
you played back in forty-nine, what the fuck you gonna play *today*—you dig?"

He continued (as we quoted in chapter 3), "I've developed my saxophone
to play it, make it sound just like a alto, make it sound like a tenor, make it
sound like a *bass,* and everything, and I'm not through working on it yet."
These comments indicate, first of all, a very understandable desire to move
on artistically. Second, they specifically address the burning question of
Young's tone, and here, too, he explains that he was consciously experimenting. When he first began recording, many people insisted his tone was
too small, calling it an "alto" tone. Young responded that he wanted a light
sound and that he was influenced by Frank Trumbauer, who played the C-
melody saxophone, which sounds between a tenor and an alto. As his tone
deepened over the years, Young occasionally spoke of using different reeds
to obtain the sound he was looking for.

In the light of Young's own words, it makes no sense to suggest that his
style changed only because he was emotionally depressed or because he was
no longer able to play in his early style, or some other such apology. Young
wanted to change. Besides, most of the 1940s and many of the 1950s works
are so strong and definite in character that one can hear no mistake or lack
of ability behind them. There are a few recordings that we may assume do
not represent Young's total artistic control, and these are from the 1950s,
among them some from 1953 and the clarinet session of 1958, on which he
clearly is not in good physical health. He sounds out of breath, and occasionally misses a note or squeaks. But there are plenty of recordings that show
him in control, especially if we include the growing number of live records

from the 1950s, and these are the ones from which to judge his artistic intentions.

Since the late 1950s, a growing number of jazz commentators have spoken out in favor of Young's last works, each finding a different virtue in this music. Henry Woodfin came out strongly in the July 1959 issue of *Jazz Review,* saying that "Young's finest works were made after he left Basie," beginning in 1943—the beginning of his second style period. He analyzed two versions of "These Foolish Things," one from 1945 and one from 1952, as examples of Young's best work, and even—unusual among jazz critics— points out that the 1950s version is in a slightly different style, especially in terms of the sound, which is "thicker and heavier" and contains "a slightly more perceptible use of vibrato." Woodfin ended by chiding other writers for casually accepting the established opinion without listening to the recorded evidence. Nat Hentoff concurred, writing on the back of an LP, *The Lester Young Story* (Verve 8308), "It seems inconceivable to me that somebody as totally in love with music as Lester could ever stop trying new ways of expression." He cited trumpeter Art Farmer as a witness on Young's behalf, and pianist Dick Katz, who noted "Lester became less symmetrically melodic in the later years. He began to be interested in how much variety one could get out of a few notes. He'd play one note or a three to four note phrase and play with it, vary it rhythmically, as [Sonny] Rollins now does." Katz was referring to the increased use of motivic playing that we find in Young's last period.

Michael Wells (*Jazz Monthly,* June 1966) wrote that Young's playing "'mellowed' rather than deteriorated, forsaking its most ambitious heights yet retaining most of its distinctive charm." The respected writer Dan Morgenstern eloquently defended Young in 1974 liner notes (Onyx 218), saying that his music, while it "sometimes speaks of pain and suffering," nevertheless, "often speaks with such power and conviction, humor and love—even joy— that it is quite impossible to accept the gloom-and-doom reporters' picture." Gary Giddins *(Village Voice,* June 12, 1978) even defended those few painful recordings with some interesting insights: "It's as though he distilled the work of a lifetime into the smallest number of notes—some ordered into cursory, oddly resolved arpeggios, others into finely turned sighs and grunts—required to sustain a musical statement. However weakened his sound, his solos conscientiously avoid clichés and despair."

As the above quotations reveal, a number of careful and respected listeners have found Young's later work meaningful. Perhaps the reader would do best to adopt an attitude of curiosity. The reader may or may not ever prefer the later work to the earlier, but at least he or she can try to understand it and recognize it for what it is, rather than see it as a departure from the "true" Pres. Young changed his style mindfully and the judgments of a great artist are not to be lightly discounted. Admittedly, there are some 1950s recordings on which Young is clearly not in total physical control of his work, but these are exceptional. It is only fair to ignore these in our investigation into Young's post-Basie work.

Young's importance to jazz has not diminished in the least. His sensitivity to tone color, his swing, his lyricism, are still echoing in the works of numerous musicians. Among the white performers he inspired were Stan Getz, Zoot Sims, Herbie Steward, Allan Eager, Al Cohn, Brew Moore, Jimmy Giuffre, Bill Perkins, Art Pepper, Paul Desmond, Bud Shank, Lennie Niehaus, Jack Montrose, and the entire school of Lennie Tristano, which included Lee Konitz, Warne Marsh, Ted Brown, and others. But, contrary to an old cliché found in some jazz journalism, his influence was equally strong in the black world. He not only launched the musical careers of Illinois Jacquet, Gene Ammons, Wardell Grey, and Paul Quinichette, but laid essential groundwork for some of the most important of all jazz saxophonists—Dexter Gordon, Sonny Rollins, and John Coltrane. (Some would add, with justification, Ornette Coleman to this list.)

Of all Young's disciples, Charlie Parker had the most profound impact on jazz. The relationship between Young's music and that of Parker has been explored by Bernard Cash in his Master's thesis for the University of Hull, England, 1982. By comparing Parker solos with Young's, Cash demonstrates that Parker utilized some of the same formulas as Young in his formative years. Even in mature Parker one can find many rhythmic devices that derive from Young. Parker's rhythmic accenting and use of rests, in fact his whole way of unifying a solo, recall the works of his original model. While Cash is quick to point out aspects of Parker's originality, he clearly establishes the source of Parker's style in that of Young.

Since about 1970 there seems to have been a renewal of interest in Young's music. The Kool Jazz Festival in New York presented a "Salute to Prez" in 1982. Columbia Records reissued all of its Lester Young holdings in five volumes of LPs. Verve restored to print many of Young's recordings made for Norman Granz in the 1940s and 1950s. Over ten LPs released on various labels in the 1970s were comprised totally of material never before released. So we are now able to enjoy not only Pres classics that have long been unavailable, but exciting concert performances never before heard outside a small circle of collectors.

It is a blessing to have all of this music by Young. And with each new release or reissue, we acquire a better understanding of his style and the way it developed over the years. Every serious jazz listener—in fact, every music listener—owes it to himself or herself to spend some time getting to know Young's music. This task brings rewards with it that extend beyond the subject of study. There is much to learn from Young—how to construct a flowing, well-ordered melodic line, how to build up a solo over several choruses. Because his impact was so great, understanding his music helps one to understand much of jazz since his time. But even if Young had not been such a great influence, his music would be worth studying just for itself. Lester Young may have become an unhappy person, but he did not leave us unhappiness. He left us music that demonstrates how to express intense feelings with taste, maturity, and, at times, serenity. He left us a recorded legacy full of profound and beautiful sounds.

Notes and References

Chapter 1

1. All Bobby Scott quotations are from his article "The House in the Heart," *Jazzletter* 3, no. 2 (September 1983); Barney Kessel from his "Guitar Journal" column in *Guitar Player,* January 1979, 22.

2. All quotations of John Lewis, Sylvia Syms, most of Jimmy Rowles, and one of Gil Evans derive from "Pres," by Whitney Balliett, in *Jelly Roll, Jabbo, and Fats* (New York, 1983), 119–28.

3. Douglas Henry Daniels was kind enough to share with me some of his research on Young's ancestors from his book in progress on Young's life. Some of the family lived in Natalbany, Louisiana, as well, and Lee Young faintly recalls seeing his grandmother (not known which one) at a general store she ran there. Other material in this chapter comes from interviews conducted by John McDonough in 1980. I owe him thanks for permission to draw from them. I have added a great deal of material from my telephone interviews with Lee Young on February 17, 1983, and July 29, 1984. Yet more information came from Lee's interview at the Institute of Jazz Studies, Oral History Project.

4. Most of Young's words in this chapter were transcribed by this writer from a tape of the interview with François Postif made around February 18, 1959. The interview was published several times (see Selected Bibliography) but my transcriptions are the first to be accurate as well as unedited. Mumbled and unclear words are bracketed. Other Young quotations are juxtaposed with the Postif interview, taken from "Here's Pres!," by Leonard Feather (*Melody Maker,* July 15, 1950) and "Pres Talks About Himself, Copycats," by Pat Harris (*Down Beat,* May 6, 1949). They may be recognized by the much more formal, edited language.

5. Boots and Sport remained New Orleans citizens except for their tours with the Youngs. A rare photo of the Young family band appears on page 21 of Linda Dahl, *Stormy Weather: The Music and Lives Of A Century Of Jazzwomen* (New York: Pantheon Books, 1984). Another appears on page 4 of the booklet with Time-Life Records STL J-13, in which Lester appears to be playing a C-melody saxophone!

6. Ralph Ellison, *Shadow and Act* (New York: The New American Library, Inc., 1966), 231, 206. Ellison recalls the year as 1929. Judging from the musicians he names, it could have been anywhere between 1929 and 1932.

7. Leonard Feather, *From Satchmo to Miles* (New York, 1972), 119.

8. Stanley Dance, *The World of Earl Hines* (New York: Scribner's, 1977), 208.

9. Don Gazzaway, "Conversations with Buster Smith," *Jazz Review,* December 1959, 22. Smith says they received the Beckley offer while in "Martinsville," but I find no such town in standard atlases. There is a Martinsburg, but then Buddy Tate recalled Young mentioning Bluefield, which is much closer to Beckley (interview with Phil Schaap).

10. Nat Hentoff, "Pres," *Down Beat,* March 7, 1956, 9. On the same page, Young says he played with King Oliver after the Bostonians, which would have been 1930 or 1931, and that he worked regularly with him for one or two years. Subsequent researchers have disproved this statement by uncovering details of Young's whereabouts after Bronson, but there still remains some controversy over the exact date and length of Young's stay with Oliver. John Hammond and John Chilton, both highly reputable sources, agree with the 1933 estimate I have used. Trombonist Clyde Bernhardt said Young was with Oliver in 1932, and presented a photograph in *Storyville,* no. 46, 147. But Bernhardt left Oliver before Young joined and had no proof of the date of his photograph, which appears to be of Art Bronson's sax section, not Oliver's. Unfortunately the veteran researchers Walter Allen and Brian Rust did not address this question in their book *King Joe Oliver* (London: Sidgwick & Jackson, 1958, 2d ed.), although they mention in passing on page 30 the probability of 1932 as the year of Young's tenure with the band. Also see Harold S. Kaye in the Selected Bibliography.

11. In the liner notes to *The Lester Young Story, Volume 1* (Columbia CG 33502), Jo Jones states that he remembers the date, December 18.

12. Nat Shapiro and Nat Hentoff, eds., *Hear Me Talkin' to Ya* (New York, 1966), 292.

13. John Hammond, "Lester Young," *Jazz,* no. 3 (Summer 1959):182; "George Dixon," in *An Autobiography of Black Jazz* by Dempsey J. Travis (Chicago: Urban Research Institute, 1983), 295–97. Dixon also confirms that Young went directly to Detroit—Hammond and Walter Allen (see *Hendersonia,* 292–96) thought he went to New York first.

14. Liner notes of *The Lester Young Story, Volume 1,* Columbia CG 33502.

15. Sally Placksin, *American Women in Jazz* (New York: Wideview Books, 1982), 206–8; Irma Young on pages 66–67.

16. Recently the October 9 date usually given for these recordings has come under serious question. John McDonough raised the issue in *Down Beat,* September 1981, 65. Hammond, Young, and Jo Jones all said they made these records during the tenure at the Grand Terrace, which only began November 7 (or November 6 according to Hammond in *Down Beat,* November 1936). Jo Jones, however, also claimed the date of the session was his birthday, October 8, which casts doubt on his reliability. Also, it is possible that since Basie was in Chicago in September, he stayed through October 9. But it is not certain that Young was back from California by then. Perhaps the most definitive evidence for a redating comes from Harry Schröder, who sent me the Vocalion matrix numbers and showed that the Jones-Smith numbers fall between those for a session from October 28 (Harry "Freddie" Shayne) and one from

November 16 (Louis Prima), strongly suggesting November 9 as the date for Jones-Smith.

17. Ralph Gleason, *Celebrating the Duke, and Louis, Bessie, Billie, Bird, Carmen, Miles, Dizzy, and Other Heroes* (New York: Dell Publishing Co., 1975), 84–85.

18. Stanley Dance, liner notes to MCA-4050; Ellison, *Shadow and Act,* 206; Powell quotation from Nat Hentoff, "Lester Young," in *The Jazz Makers,* ed. Nat Shapiro and Nat Hentoff (New York: Rinehart & Co., 1957; reprinted Da Capo Press), 254; Ross Russell, *Jazz Style in Kansas City and the Southwest* (Berkeley: University of California Press, 1971), 154; "Earl [*sic*] Warren before Basie," *Coda* 8, no. 1 (April–May 1967):15.

19. This version of the clarinet story was researched by Loren Schoenberg and differs from that usually given by John Hammond and others, who omit the exchange of instruments and say that Goodman gave Young his clarinet on the spot. This version appears to be more authentic.

20. Billie Holiday and William Dufty, *Lady Sings the Blues* (New York: Doubleday & Company, 1956; Lancer Books, 1965), chapter 6, 58–59. Ross Russell believes Young was called "Pres" while still in Kansas City. See Russell, *Jazz Style in Kansas City,* 154–55. I transcribed Young's words from a tape of him talking with Chris Albertson on August 26, 1958. Incorrectly transcribed in Stanley Dance, *The World of Count Basie* (New York, 1980), 30.

21. Shapiro and Hentoff, *Hear Me Talkin',* 310.

22. Dicky Wells, *The Night People* (Boston: Crescendo, 1971), pp. 62–63.

23. Illinois Jacquet interview with Ron Della Chiesa, WGBH-FM, Boston, January 4, 1980. Norman Granz reports preparing a later film with Young, but the only known film plans did not include him. In any case, no footage has survived.

24. Owen D. Coyle, "Moving On," *Mississippi Rag,* April 1977, 1; Jerry Potter interview with the author, 1983.

25. This and the next quotation from John McDonough, "The Court Martial of Lester Young," *Down Beat,* January 1981, 17–18. In the next quotation, I omitted a reference to Gil Evans as a Sergeant because Evans denied this.

26. Allan Morrison, "'You Got to Be Original, Man,'" in Art Hodes and Chadwick Hansen, eds., *Selections from the Gutter* (Berkeley: University of California Press, 1977), 228.

27. Hentoff, "Lester Young," 257. The Gerber article, "Le President Etait-Il Fou?" appeared in *Les Cahiers Du Jazz,* no. 15 (1967). The seizure was mentioned by Dan Morgenstern in "Lester Leaps In" (*Jazz,* March 1963); Sadik Hakim, talking to Phil Schaap on April 9, 1976, and Norman Simmons, interviewed by me in 1984, each mentioned one other incident.

28. Michael Ullman, *Jazz Lives: Portraits in Words and Pictures* (Washington, D.C., 1980), 84–85.

29. Hammond, "Recollections," *Jazz and Blues Monthly* 3, no. 5 (August 1973):9. Also Hammond, "Lester Young," 181, 184.

30. Whitney Balliett, *Ecstasy at the Onion* (New York: Bobbs Merrill, 1971), p. 174.

31. Robert Perlongo, "Portrait of Pres," *Metronome,* May 1959, 41.

Chapter 2

1. *Swing,* November 1939, quoted in Eugene Kramer, record review, *Coda,* February 1972, 15.

2. Quoted in George Hoefer, "Early Prez," *Down Beat,* March 1, 1962, 18.

3. Ibid.

4. Raymond Horricks, *Count Basie and His Orchestra* (London, 1957; reprinted 1971), p. 109; Benny Green, *The Reluctant Art* (New York, 1963; reprinted Plainview, N.Y., 1975), 97–98.

5. Recorded July 15, 1930, and available on *The Early Duke Ellington,* Everest Archive of Folk and Jazz Music FS-221.

6. "Eddie Barefield's Many Worlds," by Frank Driggs, *Jazz Review,* July 1960, 18–22. *Singin' the Blues* was recorded February 4, 1927, and is available on *The Bix Beiderbecke Story, Volume II—Bix and Tram,* Columbia CL 845.

7. Nat Hentoff, "Pres," *Down Beat,* March 7, 1956, 9.

8. These were made in 1930–1931. One version is on *The Complete Fletcher Henderson,* RCA AXM2–5507.

9. Budd Johnson as told to Michael Zwerin, "Dues Paid," *Down Beat,* February 8, 1968, p. 19.

10. *The Eel* is on *Swing Street,* Columbia Special Products CSP JSN-6042.

11. Hentoff, "Pres," 9.

12. *Shanghai Shuffle* was recorded October 10–13, 1924, and was reissued on *The Fletcher Henderson Story: A Study in Frustration,* Columbia C4L–19, and more recently on *The Henderson Pathés,* Fountain (English) FJ-112. Sadik Hakim (formerly Argonne Thornton) was interviewed by Phil Schaap, April 9, 1976.

13. Hentoff, "Pres," 10.

Chapter 3

1. Martin Williams points out that Young can even be heard leading the saxophones on *Nobody Knows.* See Martin Williams, *The Jazz Tradition* (New York: Oxford University Press, 1983), 133.

2. In the interview with Schaap, Sadik Hakim states that he improvised the theme of *Jumpin' with Symphony Sid* at the recording session, and it became credited to Young when the record was released. Savoy Records mistakenly attributes *Up 'N Adam* to one "D. Rose" in the credits on the label of the recording *Pres Lives!* Savoy SJL 1109.

3. Balliett, *Dinosaurs in the Morning* (New York, 1962), 35. Reprint available from Greenwood Press.

4. On the LP reissue Phoenix LP5 and others, all the pieces from this session, including this one and *I Can't Get Started* (Example 4b of this chapter), have been transferred too fast, so that they sound approximately one half step too high. *Started* sounds in the correct key on the Time-Life box. Of course my transcriptions reflect

the correct keys. *Indiana* was published in G, but jazz musicians play it in A flat (B flat for tenor saxophone).

5. Leonard Feather, "Here's Pres!" *Melody Maker,* July 15, 1950, p. 3. Young was referring to Take 1, not the then unreleased Take 2.

6. Transcribed from a tape of the 1959 interview with François Postif.

7. This instrument is now on display at the Rutgers Institute of Jazz Studies, with a handwritten note by Young identifying it.

8. Feather, "Here's Pres!"

9. An exception occurs near the end of *Taxi War Dance* (3/19/39, both takes), where he even uses a high F#.

10. *Tiger Rag* is available on *The Early Duke Ellington,* Everest Archive of Folk and Jazz Music FS-221.

11. This recording was made with "The Red Heads" in December 1926 and is available on *Red Nichols/1925–28,* Fountain DFJ-110.

Chapter 4

1. For example, see Hans David, *J. S. Bach's Musical Offering* (New York, G. Schirmer, 1945), 110).

2. See also David Baker's method book, *Jazz Improvisation: A Comprehensive Method of Study for All Players* (Chicago: Maher Publications, 1969), chapters 12 and 13, for guidelines to constructing melodies.

3. *Charlie Parker: Techniques of Improvisation,* Ph.D. diss., University of California, Los Angeles, 1974, ix. I have substituted the word "formulas" for "motives" in the first sentence because Owens consistently uses the latter word to refer to what I call formulas.

4. Transcribed from a tape of the 1959 interview with François Postif.

5. See Owens, *Charlie Parker,* chapters 13, 14, and 15, for Schenkerian analysis of Charlie Parker solos. For an introduction to Schenkerian analysis read Allen Forte, "Schenker's Conception of Musical Structure," *Journal of Music Theory* 3, no. 1 (1959): 1–30.

6. The preceding analysis of *Lester Leaps In* appears in a chapter I wrote for *The Smithsonian History of Jazz* (Washington, D.C.: Smithsonian Institution Press, in press).

7. A number of Young's formulas were familiar to me from years of listening to his recordings, and I discovered more during the process of transcribing the sample solos. A computer program designed by George Stalker produced a thorough catalog of three and four-note patterns found in the sample. Not all of these could be described as formulas, but many formulas were included. This provided me with accurate frequency counts for each formula, and also suggested a number of formulas that might otherwise have gone unnoticed. I made an index, using the editing mode of the computer, of all the most common patterns, which enabled me to find the solos in which they occurred. Then I examined the transcribed solos to see which of these

patterns were formulas, what their function was, and during what years they were most often found.

8. Musicologist Lawrence Gushee has written a study of several Young versions of *Shoe Shine Boy* that discusses formulas and other structural aspects. See Lawrence Gushee, "Lester Young's *Shoe Shine Boy*," in *Report of the Twelfth Congress of the International Musicological Society, Berkeley 1977*. ed. Daniel Heartz and Bonnie Wade (Kassel, Germany: Barenreiter, 1981).

9. To complement the results of conventional melodic-harmonic analysis, I asked George Stalker to design a computer program to count the frequencies of every pitch of every solo. Results were given in terms of absolute frequency, relative frequency, absolute frequency times duration, and relative frequency of pitches weighted by duration. My analysis was based primarily on the relative frequencies weighted by durations, since this is more meaningful than the simple frequencies. It is of interest to note, however, that both measures usually agreed on the most prominent pitches; those pitches had higher relative frequencies when weighted. Since the selection of pitches is largely determined by the underlying harmonies, I reexamined my transcriptions in order to understand better why certain pitches predominated.

10. George Russell, *The Lydian Chromatic Concept of Tonal Organization for Improvisation* (New York: Concept Publishing Co., 1959), xviii–xxiii.

11. Peter K. Winkler, "Toward a Theory of Popular Harmony," *In Theory Only* 4, no. 2 (May–June 1978):11–18.

12. Louis Gottlieb, "Why So Sad, Pres?," *Jazz*, no. 3 (Summer 1959):194.

13. Among the many writings on this subject are Winthrop Sargeant, *Jazz, Hot and Hybrid*, 3d ed. (New York: Da Capo Press, 1975), chapter 5; Andre Hodeir, *Jazz: Its Evolution and Essence* (New York: Grove Press, 1956), chapter 12; Frank Tirro, "The Silent Theme Tradition in Jazz," *Musical Quarterly* 53, no. 3 (July 1967):334.

14. Following the procedure described in chapter 4 of Jeff Titon's *Early Down Home Blues: A Musical and Cultural Analysis* (Urbana: University of Ilinois Press, 1977), I made contour diagrams for every solo in my sample, indicating the relationship among the starting, final, highest, and lowest notes (respectively labeled S, F, H, and L) of each phrase. I defined a phrase as a musical thought between two and eight measures in length, usually marked off by rests at either end. Where the highest or lowest note occurred more than once, I included this in the contour. After all contours were diagrammed, I grouped them into families according to logical relationships.

15. Several of these syncopated figures are typical of the era, but not in the same combinations and frequencies as in Young's music. See Sargeant, *Jazz, Hot and Hybrid*, chapter 6, for discussion of common rhythms in early jazz.

16. Gushee, "Lester Young's *Shoe Shine Boy*."

Chapter 6

1. The Balliett article referred to is from *Dinosaurs in the Morning,* the Williams from *The Jazz Tradition.* Heckman, Cash, and other publications mentioned in this chapter without complete citations may be located in the Selected Bibliography.

Bibliography

Primary Sources

1. Books and parts of books

Dance, Stanley. "Lester 'Prez' Young." In *The World of Count Basie*. New York: Charles Scribner's Sons, 1980, pp. 28–33. Young's 1958 interview with Chris Albertson, with a few words wrongly transcribed.

Morrison, Allan. "'You Got to Be Original, Man.'" In *Selections from the Gutter: Jazz Portraits from "The Jazz Record."* Berkeley: University of California Press, 1977, pp. 225–28. Reprint of a July 1947 interview.

Postif, François. "Lester Young: Paris, 1959." In *Jazz Panorama*. Edited by Martin Williams. New York: Crowell-Collier Press, 1963; reprint ed. New York: Da Capo Press, Inc., 1979, pp. 139–44. Young's last interview, the most informal and revealing of all, but highly edited. More complete version, with French translation, in *Jazz Hot* 362 (June 1979) and 363 (Summer 1979). Originally in *Jazz Hot* 142 (1959), *Jazz Review* (September, 1959), then *Kulchur* (Autumn, 1962), the last two with a short discography by Erik Weidemann. See also Tape Recordings.

2. Articles

Brooks, Michael. Liner notes to *The Lester Young Story*, Volumes 1 and 5, Columbia CG 33502 and C2 34849. Include statements by Young, Jo Jones, Buddy Tate, and Count Basie.

Coss, Bill. "JATP's Chief Executive: The President." *Metronome*, October 1955, p. 25. Interview.

Feather, Leonard. "Here's Pres!" *Melody Maker*, July 15, 1950, p. 3. Interview.

———. "Pres Digs Every Kind of Music." *Down Beat*, November 2, 1951, p. 13. "Blindfold Test" interview.

Harris, Pat. "Pres Talks About Himself, Copycats." *Down Beat*, May 6, 1949, p. 15. Interview.

Hentoff, Nat. "Pres." *Down Beat*, March 7, 1956, pp. 9–11. Interview.

3. Tape recordings

Young, Lester. Interview with Chris Albertson. Probably August 26, 1958.
————. Interview with François Postif. Ca. February 18, 1959.

4. Music

Here are listed transcribed solos published with little or no text. For books, articles, and theses that include transcribed solos, see under Secondary Sources the entries by Byrnside, Gottlieb, Gushee, Heckman, Kamien, Newsom, Porter, and Winkler.

Cash, Bernard. *Prez/Lester Young.* 49 Main Street, Carnaby, North Humberside, England: Great Jazz Solos Revisited, Ltd., 1980. Twenty-five transcribed solos in B♭ tenor saxophone key.

Cole, John. "Lady and Her Man." *Down Beat,* April 8, 1975, pp. 42–43. Transcription of Young's obbligato behind Billie Holiday from *Me, Myself and I* (6/15/37).

Dexter, Dave. *The Jazz Story: From the '90s to the '60s.* Englewood Cliffs, N.J.: Prentice-Hall, Inc., 1964, p. xii. Reprint of Young solo "Hi Heckler," originally published in 1944 (not transcribed from any known recording).

Feather, Leonard. *The Book of Jazz: From Then till Now.* Revised ed. New York: Dell Publishing Co., 1976, p. 254. Transcription, with analysis, of *The Opener* (9/17/49).

Lee, Edward. *Jazz: An Introduction.* London: Kahn & Averill, 1972, p. 169. Transcription and brief discussion of Young's solo on *Salute to Fats* (4/18/44, Take 1).

Mehegan, John. *Jazz Rhythm and the Improvised Line: Jazz Improvisation II.* New York: Watson-Guptill Publications, 1962, pp. 94–95. Transcription of Young's *Just You, Just Me* solo (12/28/43).

Russo, Bill, and Lifton, Lloyd. "Jazz Off the Record." *Down Beat,* January 13, 1950, p. 12. Transcription of *Dickie's Dream* (9/5/39, Take 1), with brief commentary.

————. "Jazz Off the Record." *Down Beat,* July 28, 1950, p. 20. Transcription of *Just You, Just Me* (12/28/43), with brief commentary.

————, and Mulvihill, Jerry. "Jazz Off the Record." *Down Beat,* May 4, 1955, p. 6. Transcription of *Jive at Five* (2/2–4/39), with brief commentary.

"Some Great Reed Solos." *Down Beat,* May 25, 1961, p. 48. Transcription of *Undercover Girl Blues* (January 16, 1951).

(NOTE: *Toward Jazz,* by Andre Modeir, presents a transcribed excerpt from *These Foolish Things* (12/45), with discussion. New York: Grove Press, 1962; reprint ed. New York: Da Capo Press, Inc., 1976, pp. 191–195. Also, the group Prez Conference has recorded and published several arrangements of Young's solos.)

Secondary Sources

1. Books and parts of books

Allen, Walter C. *Hendersonia: The Music of Fletcher Henderson and His Musicians.* Highland Park, N.J.: By the author, 1973. A monumental research effort, which includes information about Young and Basie, especially pp. 292–96,
341–42.

Balliett, Whitney. "The President." In *Dinosaurs in the Morning.* New York: J. B.
Lippincott, 1962, pp. 33–37. A review comparing Young's early and late styles.
————. "Pres." In *Jelly Roll, Jabbo and Fats: 19 Portraits in Jazz.* New York: Oxford
University Press, 1983, pp. 119–28. Originally in *New Yorker,* February 23,
1981, this portrait includes new interviews with his colleagues.

Berendt, Joachim. *The New Jazz Book: A History and Guide.* Translated by Dan
Morgenstern. New York: Hill & Wang, 1962. See "Coleman Hawkins and Lester Young," pp. 53–61, and "The Dialectic of Modern Jazz: Bird Contra Pres,"
pp. 269–74.

Blesh, Rudi. "The Pres." In *Eight Lives in Jazz/Combo: U.S.A.* New York: Hayden
Book Company, Inc., 1971, pp. 85–110. Biographical article with original material about Young's last years.

Burkhardt, Werner, and Gerth, Joachim. *Lester Young—Ein Portrait.* Wetzlar,
Germany: Pegasus-Verlag, 1959. A 60-page portrait in German.

Byrnside, Ronald. "The Performer as Creator: Jazz Improvisation." In *Contemporary Music and Music Cultures.* Edited by Charles Hamm, Bruno Nettl, and
Ronald Byrnside. Englewood Cliffs, N.J.: Prentice-Hall, Inc., 1975, pp. 223–
51. This excellent article includes a transcription of part of Young's solo from
Taking a Chance on Love (1/13/56), with analysis.

Chilton, John. *Billie's Blues: Billie Holiday's Story 1933–1959.* Foreword by Buck
Clayton. New York: Stein & Day, 1975. The index will guide the reader to
discussions of the relationship between Holiday and Young.

Coker, Jerry. "Lester Young (1909–1959)." In *Listening to Jazz.* Englewood Cliffs,
N.J.: Prentice-Hall, Inc., 1978, pp. 95–103. Includes analysis of Young's solo
on *Lester Leaps In* (9/5/39, Take 1), but weak in other areas.

Connor, D. Russell, and Hicks, Warren W. *B.G. On the Record: A Bio-Discog-
raphy of Benny Goodman.* New Rochelle: Arlington House, 1969. Includes all
details on recordings featuring Goodman and Young together. New edition
planned.

Driggs, Franklin S. "Kansas City and the Southwest." In *Jazz: New Perspectives
on the History of Jazz.* Edited by Nat Hentoff and Albert J. McCarthy. New
York: Rinehart, 1959; Da Capo Press, 1975, pp. 190–230. An important early
attempt to chronicle the bands of this region where Young spent much time in
his early years.

Evensmo, Jan. *The Tenor Saxophone and Clarinet of Lester Young, 1936–1949.* 2d ed. Jazz Solography Series, vol. 13. Oslo, Norway: Jan Evensmo, 1983. This invaluable pamphlet gives the number of measures of every Young solo from this period and a critical appraisal as part of a fairly thorough listing of recordings, through 1949.

Feather, Leonard "Prez." In *From Satchmo to Miles.* New York: Stein & Day, 1972, pp. 115–27. Biographical article.

Franchini, Vittorio. *Lester Young.* Milan: Ricordi, 1961. In Italian, ninety-six pages.

Green, Benny. "Lester Young." In *The Reluctant Art: The Growth of Jazz.* New York: Horizon Press, Inc., 1963; reprint ed. Plainview, N.Y.: Books for Libraries Press, 1975, pp. 91–118. Thoughtful discussion of Young's style and influence.

Gushee, Larry. "Lester Young's *Shoe Shine Boy.*" In *Report of the Twelfth Congress of the International Musicological Society, Berkeley 1977.* Edited by Daniel Heartz and Bonnie Wade. Kassel, Germany: Barenreiter, 1981. Includes transcriptions of Young solos on several 1930s versions of *Shoe Shine Boy.* Gushee discusses and applies a variety of analytical approaches that illuminate Young's art, and suggests some implications for the study of jazz in general.

Hammond, John, with **Irving Townsend.** *John Hammond on Record: An Autobiography.* New York: Ridge Press, 1977. Contains reminiscences of Young in his Basie days.

Hentoff, Nat. "Lester Young." In *The Jazz Makers.* Edited by Nat Shapiro and Nat Hentoff. New York: Rinehart, 1957; reprint ed. Westport: Greenwood Press, Inc., 1975 pp. 243–75. Detailed biographical article with many quotations from interviews with Young and his friends.

Holiday, Billie, with **William Dufty.** *Lady Sings the Blues.* New York: Doubleday & Company, Inc., 1956. Of questionable factual accuracy, but valuable for Holiday's impressions of Young and his music.

Horricks, Raymond. "Lester Young." In *Count Basie and His Orchestra: Its Music and Its Musicians.* New York: Citadel Press, 1957; reprint ed. Westport: Negro Universities Press, 1971, pp. 104–18. Discussion of Young's musical career but strongly biased against his 1950s recordings.

James, Burnett. "Lester Young." In *Essays on Jazz.* London: Sidgwick & Jackson, 1961, pp. 61–79. Sensitive discussion of the positive qualities in Young's middle and late-period recordings.

Jepsen, Jorgen Grunnet. *A Discography of Lester Young.* Copenhagen: Karl Emil Knudsen, 1968. Once excellent but now outdated.

Kamien, Roger. *Music: An Appreciation.* New York: McGraw-Hill, 1976, pp. 492–96. Brief discussion and partial transcription of [*Oh*] *Lady Be Good* (11/9/36).

Lyttleton, Humphrey. "Lester Young." In *The Best of Jazz II: Enter the Giants, 1931–1944.* New York: Taplinger Publishing Co., 1983. Includes detailed analysis of [*Oh*] *Lady Be Good* (11/9/36).

Newsom, Jon. "Jazz: Aspects of Melodic Improvisation." In *Music in the Modern*

Age. Vol. 5 of *A History of Western Music.* Edited by F. W. Sternfeld. New
York: Praeger Publishers, 1973, pp. 395–406. This good introduction to the
study of improvisation includes a transcription of *Song of the Islands* (8/4/39)
and an excerpt from *Shoe Shine Boy* (11/9/36, Take 1), with analysis.

Russell, Ross. "Bebop. IV–The Parent Style and Lester Young." In *The Art of Jazz:
Essays on the Nature and Development of Jazz.* Edited by Martin Williams. New
York: Oxford University Press, 1959; reprint ed. New York: Da Capo Press,
1979, pp. 207–13. Discussion of Young's contribution to modern jazz.

———. "Lester Young." In *Jazz Style in Kansas City and the Southwest.* Berkeley:
University of California Press, 1971, pp. 147–62. Primarily biographical.

Scherman, Bo, and Hällström, Carl A. *A Discography of Count Basie, 1929–
1950.* Copenhagen: Karl Emil Knudsen, n.d. Once excellent but now outdated.
Revision scheduled for 1985.

Sears, Richard S. *V-Discs: A History and Discography.* Westport: Greenwood
Press, 1980. Includes detailed report on Basie and Young V-discs.

Shapiro, Nat, and Hentoff, Nat, eds. *Hear Me Talkin' to Ya: The Story of Jazz as
Told by the Men Who Made It.* New York: Rinehart & Company, 1955; Dover
Publications, 1966. A compilation of interviews with jazz musicians, including
Young and many of his contemporaries.

Ullman, Michael. *Jazz Lives: Portraits in Words and Pictures.* Washington, D.C.:
New Republic Books, 1980. The interviews with Horace Silver (pp. 79–88) and
Tommy Flanagan (pp. 111–21) contain revealing comments on Young in the
1950s.

Wells, Dicky, as told to Stanley Dance. *The Night People: Reminiscences of a
Jazzman.* Introduction by Count Basie. Boston: Crescendo Publishing Company, 1971. Wells shares several memories of Young with Basie.

Williams, Martin. *Where's The Melody?: A Listener's Introduction to Jazz.* New
York: Minerva Press, 1966, pp. 42–43. Analytical comments on the Young solo
Jive at Five (2/2–4/39).

———. "Count Basie and Lester Young," in *The Jazz Tradition.* New York: Oxford
University Press, 1970; revised ed. 1983, pp. 122–34. Contains an outstanding
analytical discussion of early Young.

2. Articles

Bakker, Dick. "Count Basie: Vocalion-Okeh's, 1936–1942." *Micrography* 44 (May
1977):5–6. A listing.

Bernhardt, Clyde, to Laurie Wright. "Ladies and Gentlemen—The King." *Storyville,* no. 46 (April–May 1973):146–48. Memories of the King Oliver band
during the period in which Young was a member and a rare photo of Young
around that time. This article is a compilation of reminiscences by Bernhardt
and others.

Bishop, A. J. "Lester Young: An Appreciation." *Jazz Journal,* June 1956, pp. 3–4.

Colomby, Graham. "Jo Jones Speaks Out." *Jazz Journal* 25, no. 12 (December 1972):6–8. Interview with Jo Jones about Lester Young and other topics.

Coyle, Owen D. "Moving On." *Mississippi Rag,* April 1977, pp. 1–2. Interview with Jimmy Cheatham about Young's army experience.

Daniels, Douglas Henry. "History, Racism, and Jazz: The Case of Lester Young." *Jazzforschung* 16 (1984), 87–103.

Gottlieb, Louis. "Why So Sad, Pres?" *Jazz: A Quarterly of American Music.* Edited by Ralph Gleason, no. 3 (Summer 1959):185–96. Includes transcribed excerpts from several Young solos of the 1930s, and insightful analysis.

Hammond, John. "Lester Young." *Jazz: A Quarterly of American Music.* Edited by Ralph Gleason, no. 3 (Summer 1959):181–84. Reminiscences.

———. "Recollections." Part 1 of "Two Views of Lester Young." *Jazz and Blues Monthly* 3, no. 5 (August 1973):8–10.

Heckman, Don. "Pres and Hawk: Saxophone Fountainheads." *Down Beat,* January 3, 1963, pp. 20–22. Incudes transcriptions and discussion of Young's solos on *Broadway* (11/19/40, Take 1) and *Poundcake* (5/19/39).

Hentoff, Nat. Liner notes to *The Lester Young Story,* Verve 8308. Defends Young's later style, with comments by musicians.

Hoefer, George. "Early Prez." *Down Beat,* March 1, 1962, pp. 18–19, 43. Discussion of Young's early career, with selected discography.

Kaye, Harold S. "Francis 'Doc' Whitby." *Storyville* 110 (December 1983–January 1984):50–65. Research on this contemporary of Young has important bearing on Young's early career.

Kessel, Barney. "Guitar Journal: Remembering Lester Young" and "Guitar Journal: Lester Young, Part II." In *Guitar Player,* December 1978, p. 14, and January 1979, pp. 22, 97.

Kramer, Eugene. Review of *The Alternative Lester* (Tax LP m-8000). In *Coda* 10, no. 5 (January–February 1972): 15. Gives interesting background information.

Lambert, Eddie "The Alternative Lester Young." In *Jazz Journal* 26, no. 2 (February 1973):22–24. Informative review of Tax m-8000.

———. "Count Basie—The V-Discs." *Jazz Journal* 26, no. 1 (January 1977):6–8. Identifies the V-discs that contain solos by Young, and gives background information and discographical data.

Lee, Edwy B. "Reconsiderations 2." *Jazz Review* 1, no. 2 (December 1958):43. Brief comparison of Young and Coleman Hawkins.

"Lester Laid to Rest." *Down Beat,* April 30, 1959, p. 10.

McDonough, John. "Lester Young." In booklet with Time-Life Records STL J13 (Alexandria, Virginia, 1980). Well-researched biography with rare photographs.

Morgenstern, Dan. "Lester Leaps In." *Jazz,* March 1963, pp. 12–13, 25; reprinted in *Down Beat,* April 3, 1969, pp. 19–20. Touching, honest report of Young's last birthday party, held at the Birdland nightclub, August 27, 1958. It originally apeared in slightly different form in *Jazz Journal,* August 1958, and Young told its author he liked it.

————. "Lester Young Discography, Part I." In *Down Beat: Music '71*. Chicago: Maher Publications, 1972, pp. 74–83. Updating of Jepsen.

————. "Lester Young Discography, Part II." In *Down Beat: Music '73*. Chicago: Maher Publications, 1974, pp. 49–54.

————. Liner notes to *Prez in Europe*, Onyx 218; 1974. Eloquent appreciation of Young's late style.

Perlongo, Robert A. "Portrait of Pres." *Metronome*, May 1959, pp. 17–19, 40–41. Moving memorial. Revised version in *Coda* 199 (1984).

Porter, Bob. "Hall of Fame—Special Report." In *International Association of Jazz Record Collectors Journal* 11, no. 4 (Fall 1978):25–26. Review of Hall of Fame LPs, giving information not found on the LPs.

Porter, Lewis. "Lester Leaps In: The Early Style of Lester Young." *Black Perspective in Music* 9, no. 1 (Spring 1981):3–24. Analysis with musical examples, and photographs.

————. Review of *Lester Young* (Time-Life STL-J13). *Black Perspective in Music* 9, no. 1 (Spring 1981):107–8.

Reisner, Robert. "The Last, Sad Days of Lester Willis Young." *Down Beat*, April 30, 1959, p. 11.

Rusch, Bob. "Jesse Drakes: Interview." *Cadence* 10, no. 3 (March 1984):15–21. Drakes knew Young well.

Schröder, Harry. "Lester Young 1946–1957." *Micrography* 41 (May 1976): 21–23.

————. "Lester Young 1937–1942." *Micrography* 42 (October 1976):21–22.

————. "Lester Young 1943–1944." *Micrography* 44 (May 1977):19.

————. "Lester Young 1946–1958 (Revision)." *Micrography* 48 (September 1978):16–18.

————. "Lester Young 1937–1942 (Revision)." *Micrography* 51 (July 1979):18–20. These entries list "live" recordings issued on LPs, giving all LP numbers.

Scott, Bobby. "The House in the Heart." *Jazzletter* 3, no. 2 (September 1983). A lovingly written reminiscence of Young. (Gene Lees, *Jazzletter*, P.O. Box 240, Ojai, California 93023.)

Sudhalter, Richard M. "Notes on the Music." In booklet with Time-Life Records STL J13 (Alexandria, Virginia, 1980). These notes incorporate perceptive analysis and biographical detail.

Ulanov, Barry. "The Four Men Who Made Modern Jazz." In *Jazz 1950: The Metronome Yearbook*. Edited by Barry Ulanov and George Simon. New York: Metronome, 1950, pp. 19–22. Discusses Young's importance in the development of modern jazz.

————. *Down Beat*, May 18, 1955, pp. 34–35. Untitled review of Young performances at Carnegie Hall and at Birdland; Ulanov implores fans not to take Young for granted.

Wells, Michael J. "Pres and Bop—The 'Live' Evidence." *Jazz Monthly* 12, no. 4 (June 1966):15–17. Perceptive comments about the LPs on the Charlie Parker label. His dates, however, have since been discredited.

Winkler, Peter K. "Toward a Theory of Popular Harmony." *In Theory Only* 4, no.

2 (May–June 1978):3–26. This novel and well-reasoned attempt to discover the general principles behind popular music harmony includes a detailed transcription and analysis of Young's solo on *Roseland Shuffle* (1/21/37).

Woodfin, H. A. "Reconsiderations." *Jazz Review,* July 1959, pp. 30–31. An appreciation of Young's late work.

Zwicky, Theo. "Lloyd Hunter's Serenaders and the Territory Bands—2." *Storyville* 36 (August 1, 1971):207–13. Much original research comprises this detailed listing of the personnel of many bands that never recorded. Young's name appears several times between 1928 and 1933.

3. Encyclopedias and collections

Bruyninckx, Walter. *60 Years of Recorded Jazz, 1917–1977.* Mechelen, Belgium: By the author, 1978–1983. The only discography that attempts to cover the entire international recorded legacy of jazz, as well as blues and gospel artists. A massive project with much information on studio, "live," and unissued recordings, but also contains some errors, self-contradictions, and omissions. It is published unbound in boxed sections.

Chilton, John. *Who's Who of Jazz: Storyville to Swing Street.* 2d ed. Chicago: Time-Life Records, 1978. Standard, authoritative biographical dictionary, now available only through Time-Life Records.

Feather, Leonard. *The New Edition of the Encyclopedia of Jazz.* New York: Bonanza Books, 1960. Biographical dictionary with critical commentary, poll results, articles, and indexes.

Jepsen, Jorgen Grunnet. *Jazz Records 1942–1962.* 11 volumes. Copenhagen: Karl Emil Knudsen, 1963–1970. Standard discography for the period. Revision planned but delayed by misfortunes.

McCarthy, Albert. *Big Band Jazz.* New York: G. P. Putnam's Sons, 1974. Indispensable guide written in narrative style to the careers, personnel, and recordings of all major and many minor bands.

McCarthy, Albert; Morgan, Alun; Oliver, Paul; and **Harrison, Max.** "Lester Young (1909–1959)." In *Jazz On Record: A Critical Guide to the First Fifty Years, 1917–1967.* London: Hanover Books, 1968, pp. 315–17. Overview of his recorded work.

Merriam, Alan P., with **Robert J. Benford.** *A Bibliography of Jazz.* Philadelphia: The American Folklore Society, 1954; reprint ed. New York: Da Capo Press, 1976. Includes thousands of periodical articles.

Porter, Lewis. "Lester Young." In *The New Grove Dictionary of Music in the United States.* London: Macmillan Publishers, 1986. Biography and some musical examples.

Rust, Brian. Jazz Records 1897–1942. 5th ed., partial revision of 4th. 2 vols. 66 Fairview Drive, Chigwell, Essex IG7 6HS, England: Storyville Publications, 1983. Standard discography, although weak on broadcasts and unissued recordings. The publisher also produces *Storyville* magazine.

Williams, Martin. "Lester Young." In *The New Grove Dictionary of Music and Musicians*. London: Macmillan Publishers, 1980.

4. Theses

Cash, Bernard. "An Analysis of the Improvisation Technique of Lester Willis Young 1936–1942." Master's thesis, University of Hull, England, 1982. Includes comparison of Young with Trumbauer and with Parker, with music examples, and nineteen transcribed solos (all available in Cash's book—see under Music).

Owens, Thomas. "Charlie Parker: Techniques of Improvisation." Ph.D. diss., University of California, Los Angeles, 1974, pp. 36–42. Chapter 4, "Early Period," includes Young formulas that were adopted by Parker. The thesis contains an extensive catalog and discussion of Parker's formulas, a discography, and a vast collection of transcribed solos. Available through Xerox University Microfilms, 300 North Zeeb Road, Ann Arbor, Michigan 48106.

Porter, Lewis. "The Jazz Improvisations of Lester Young." Master's thesis, Tufts University, 1979. Includes the thirty-four transcribed solos listed after the preface of the present book.

Catalog of Recorded Works

This catalog includes all commercial recordings on which Young appeared either as sideman or leader, all broadcast and concert recordings issued on "bootlegs," and all unissued titles known to exist in private collections. On some titles he solos, while on others he merely plays in the ensemble. In short, all of Young's recorded works are listed. Some doubtful items are mentioned as such, but not unsupported rumors; nor have I included titles performed at concerts or broadcasts that do not survive in any form. Young's taped interviews are included, and titles that derive from filmed performances are so indicated (see May 29, 1938; August 1944; December 16, 1954; probably November 1956; December 8, 1957; September 25, 1958).

Under the name of the recording group appears the date and location of the recording, the original label of issue for studio recordings, and the source and site of "live" recordings. Sessions known only by the month or year are placed at the end of the respective month or year. The titles recorded at the session are then given, in the order recorded (so far as is known). Titles marked "Inc." stop in progress but usually contain some improvisation; more details are given for particularly short or long ones. Titles marked "(Theme)," often unlisted on LP liners, are short theme statements that are nevertheless complete as intended. Longer performances of themes that include improvised solos are listed as regular titles and marked "Inc." where applicable (for example, at ends of broadcasts).

Next to each title, I provide the label and issue number of an LP on which it may be found (except for titles listed as unissued, or issued on 78 rpm only). Since titles may be available on more than one LP, I have favored LPs that are most available in America and that are most comprehensive. Many are imports (so noted when they might be confused with American issues). The titles of the LPs are indexed following this Catalog, in the Selected Discography, except for a few late additions.

Personnel listings, matrix numbers, and older LP issues may be found in the standard discographies of Rust, Bruyninckx, and Jepsen. But these sources have some incorrect dates and are missing many titles, some of which have been added to the recent Evensmo work, which omits LP issues for the most part but identifies which titles contain solos by Young. The present listing benefits from the latest research, with the help of the collector-specialists mentioned in the Acknowledgments. There are many new dates that differ from those on LP liners and other sources. For most I have provided some data; for all the reader may trust these are not typographical errors. My technique also involves comparing all dates and locations with Young's Chronology as reported by *Down Beat* and other publications of his day. This Catalog went to press in November 1984. If any readers can provide additions or corrections, I will be most grateful. Please write to Professor Lewis Porter, Music Department, Tufts University, Medford, Massachusetts 02155.

There is some speculation that Young may have recorded before 1936. Jo Jones says that a performer named Clarrie Cammell played him an aluminum disk of Young around 1930, but this is unconfirmed. Clarence Williams once said he used Young while he was in New York with Fletcher Henderson in 1934. Tom Lord discusses this matter on page 360 of *Clarence Williams* (Essex, England: Storyville Publications, 1976). If Young indeed recorded with Williams he must be one of the unidentified alto saxophonists on the session of June 28, 1934. In any event, there are no alto solos, so it becomes a moot point. We begin, then, in 1936:

Jones-Smith Incorporated

Possibly October 9, but probably November 9, 1936; Chicago; Vocalion

Shoe Shine Boy (Shoe Shine Swing) (Take 1) (Columbia CG 33502)
Shoe Shine Boy (Shoe Shine Swing) (Take 2) (Columbia CG 33502)
Evenin' (Columbia CG 33502)
Boogie Woogie (Columbia CG 33502)
[Oh] Lady Be Good (Columbia CG 33502)

(NOTE: See note 16 of chapter 1 about this date. Two takes were reportedly made of the last three items but they do not seem to survive.)

Count Basie and His Orchestra

January 21, 1937; New York City; Decca

Honeysuckle Rose (MCA 2-4050)
Pennies from Heaven (MCA 2-4108)
Swingin' at the Daisy Chain (MCA 2-4050)
Roseland Shuffle (Shoe Shine Swing) (MCA 2-4050)

Teddy Wilson and His Orchestra

January 25, 1937; New York City; Brunswick

He Ain't Got Rhythm (Columbia CG 33502)
This Year's Kisses (Columbia CG 33502)
Why Was I Born? (Columbia CG 33502)
I Must Have That Man (Columbia CG 33502)

Count Basie and His Orchestra

February 8, 1937, February 10, 1937, and February 12, 1937; Pittsburgh;
Broadcasts, Hotel William Penn

[Oh] Lady Be Good (Jazz Archives JA-16)
[Oh] Lady Be Good (different version) (Jazz Archives JA-16)
Roseland Shuffle (Shoe Shine Swing) (Jazz Archives JA-16)
Moten Swing (sign-off theme) (Jazz Archives JA-16)
St. Louis Blues into *Moten Swing* (sign-off theme) (Jazz Archives JA-16)
Moten Swing (opening theme) (Jazz Archives JA-16)
King Porter Stomp (Jazz Archives JA-16)
I'll Always Be in Love with You (Jazz Archives JA-16)
You Do the Darndest Things Baby (Jazz Archives JA-16)
Swingin' at the Daisy Chain (Jazz Archives JA-16)
Yeah Man (Inc.; ending cut off) (Jazz Archives-16)
Riffin' (LP falsely says "Rug Cutters Swing") (Jazz Archives JA-16)
Tattersfield Stomp (Jazz Archives JA-16)
Magnolias in the Moonlight (Unissued)
Moten Swing (opening theme) (Unissued)
Moten Swing (opening, different version) (Unissued)
Margie (Inc.) (Unissued)
Swing Brother Swing (Unissued)
You Do the Darndest Things Baby (different version) (Unissued)
I Cried for You (Inc.) (Unissued)

Count Basie and His Orchestra

March 26, 1937; New York City; Decca

Exactly Like You (MCA 2-4108)
Boo Hoo (MCA 2-4108)
The Glory of Love (MCA 2-4108)
Boogie Woogie (I May Be Wrong) (MCA 2-4050)

Teddy Wilson and His Orchestra

May 11, 1937; New York City; Brunswick

Sun Showers (Columbia CG 33502)
Yours and Mine (Columbia CG 33502)
I'll Get By (Take 1) (French CBS 66274)
I'll Get By (Take 2) (Columbia PG 32127)
Mean to Me (Take 1) (Columbia CG 33502)
Mean to Me (Take 2) (Columbia CG 33502)

Teddy Wilson and His Orchestra

June 1, 1937; New York City; Brunswick

Foolin' Myself (Columbia CG 33502)
Easy Living (Columbia CG 33502)
I'll Never Be the Same (Columbia CG 33502)
I've Found a New Baby (Take 1) (Columbia CG 33502)
I've Found a New Baby (Take 3) (Columbia CG 33502)

Billie Holiday and Her Orchestra

June 15, 1937; New York City; Vocalion

Me, Myself and I (Take 1) (Columbia CG 33502)
Me, Myself and I (Take 2) (Columbia CG 33502)
A Sailboat in the Moonlight (Columbia CG 33502)
Born to Love (Columbia CG 33502)
Without Your Love (Take 1) (Columbia CG 33502)
Without Your Love (Take 2) (Columbia CG 33502)

Count Basie and His Orchestra

June 30, 1937; New York City; Broadcast, Savoy Ballroom

Moten Swing (Theme) (Phontastic NOST 7639)
Shout and Feel It (Phontastic NOST 7639)
The You and Me That Used to Be (Phontastic NOST 7639)
The Count Steps In (Phontastic NOST 7639)
They Can't Take That Away from Me (Phontastic NOST 7639)
I'll Always Be in Love with You (Phontastic NOST 7639)
When My Dreamboat Comes Home (Phontastic NOST 7639)
Swing, Brother, Swing (Phontastic NOST 7639)
Bugle Blues (Phontastic NOST 7639)
I Got Rhythm (Phontastic NOST 7639)
Moten Swing (Theme) (Phontastic NOST 7639)

Count Basie and His Orchestra

July 7, 1937; New York City; Decca

Smarty (You Know It All) (MCA 2-4108)
One O'Clock Jump (MCA 2-4050)
Listen My Children and You Shall Hear (MCA 2-4108)
John's Idea (MCA 2-4050)

(NOTE: Reportedly, recordings of the band from the Ritz-Carlton Hotel of Boston in July 1937 were destroyed in a fire.)

Count Basie and His Orchestra

August 9, 1937; New York City; Decca

Good Morning Blues (Take A) (MCA 2-4108)
Good Morning Blues (Take B) (French MCA 510.167-510.170)
Our Love Was Meant to Be (MCA 2-4108)
Time Out (MCA 2-4050)
Topsy (MCA 2-4050)

Billie Holiday and Her Orchestra

September 13, 1937; New York City; Vocalion

Getting Some Fun Out of Life (Columbia JG 34837)
Who Wants Love? (Columbia JG 34837)
Trav'lin' All Alone (Columbia JG 34837)
He's Funny That Way (Columbia JG 34837)

Count Basie and His Orchestra

October 13, 1937; New York City; Decca

I Keep Remembering (Someone I Should Forget) (MCA 2-4108)
Out the Window (MCA 2-4050)
Don't You Miss Your Baby (MCA 2-4108)
Let Me Dream (French MCA 510.167-510.170)

Count Basie and His Orchestra

November 3, 1937; Cedar Grove, New Jersey; Broadcast, Meadowbrook Lounge

Moten Swing (Theme) (Phontastic NOST 7640)
One O'Clock Jump (Phontastic NOST 7640)
I Can't Get Started (Phontastic NOST 7640)
Study in Brown (Phontastic NOST 7640)
I Want Rhythm in my Nursery Rhymes (Phontastic NOST 7640)

John's Idea (Phontastic NOST 7640)
Good Morning Blues (Phontastic NOST 7640)
Dinah (Phontastic NOST 7640)

Count Basie and His Orchestra

January 3, 1938; New York City; Decca

Georgianna (MCA 2-4108)
Blues in the Dark (MCA 2-4050)

Teddy Wilson and His Orchestra

January 6, 1938; New York City; Brunswick/Columbia

My First Impression of You (Take 3) (Columbia JG 34837)
My First Impression of You (Take 4) (Columbia JG 34837)
When You're Smiling (Take 3) (Columbia JG 34837)
When You're Smiling (Take 4) (Columbia JG 34837)
I Can't Believe That You're in Love with Me (Take 3) (Columbia JG 34837)
I Can't Believe That You're in Love with Me (Take 4) (Columbia JG 34837)
If Dreams Come True (Take 1) (Columbia JG 34837)
If Dreams Come True (Take 2) (Columbia JG 34837)

Billie Holiday and Her Orchestra

January 12, 1938; New York City; Vocalion
(NOTE: The LP says 1/27/38, but a note in Brian Rust's discography explains that
the later date was not a recording session but a "dubbing" date.)

Now They Call It Swing (Take 1) (Columbia JG 34837)
Now They Call It Swing (Take 2) (Columbia JG 34837)
On the Sentimental Side (Take 1) (Columbia PG 32121)
On the Sentimental Side (Take 2) (Two Flats Disc T-5006)
Back in Your Own Backyard (Take 1) (Columbia JG 34837)
Back in Your Own Backyard (Take 2) (Columbia JG 34837)
When a Woman Loves a Man (Columbia JG 34837)

Benny Goodman Jam Session

January 16, 1938; New York City; Concert, Carnegie Hall

Honeysuckle Rose (Columbia JG 34837) (Young's solo only; longer version on
    Columbia OSL-160)

Count Basie and His Orchestra

February 16, 1938; New York City; Decca

Sent for You Yesterday (And Here You Come Today) (MCA 2-4050)
Every Tub (MCA 2-4050)
Now Will You Be Good (MCA 2-4108)
Swinging the Blues (MCA 2-4050)

Benny Goodman and His Orchestra

March 9, 1938; New York City; Victor

Please Be Kind (Take 1) (RCA AXM2-5557)
Please Be Kind (Take 2) (RCA LPM-6702)
Ti-Pi-Tin (RCA AXM2-5557)
Ooooh-Oh-Boom! (RCA AXM2-5557)
Always and Always (RCA AXM2-5557)
Make Believe (RCA AXM2-5557)
The Blue Room (Take 1) (RCA AXM2-5557)
The Blue Room (Take 2) (French RCA 731.092)

Count Basie and His Orchestra

May 29, 1938; New York City; Broadcast, Randall's Island, "Swing Carnival"
(NOTE: A silent film clip from this concert appeared in a newsreel.)

(Unknown titles) (Unissued)

Members of Basie Band

June 3, 1938; New York City; Private studio session
(NOTE: Originally reported to be from the 12/24/39 concert; this date from the
acetates.)

Mortgage Stomp (Phontastic NOST 7639)
Don't Be That Way (Phontastic NOST 7639)
Blues with Helen (The Blues) (Phontastic NOST 7639)
Song of the Wanderer (Phontastic NOST 7639)
Allez Oop (labeled "Mortgage Stomp" on a Vanguard LP) (Phontastic NOST 7639)

(NOTE: Young does not appear on *I Ain't Got Nobody.*)

Count Basie and His Orchestra

June 6, 1938; New York City; Decca

Mama Don't Want No Peas An' Rice An' Coconut Oil (MCA 2-4108)
Blue and Sentimental (MCA 2-4050)
Doggin' Around (MCA 2-4050)

Count Basie and His Orchestra

July 9, 1938; New York City; CBS and BBC Broadcast, "America Dances," Location unknown

One O'Clock Jump (Theme) (Fanfare 18-118)
Every Tub (Fanfare 18-118)
Song of the Wanderer (Fanfare 18-118)
Flat Foot Floogie (Fanfare 18-118)
[Oh] Lady Be Good (Fanfare 18-118)
Boogie Woogie Blues (Fanfare 18-118)
One O'Clock Jump (different version) (Fanfare 18-118)
I Let a Song Go Out of My Heart (Fanfare 18-118)
One O'Clock Jump (Theme) (Fanfare 18-118)

Count Basie and His Orchestra

July 23, 1938; New York City; Broadcast, Famous Door

Time Out (Unissued)
If I Could Be with You (One Hour Tonight) (Unissued)
Jumpin' at the Woodside (Unissued)
I Hadn't Anyone till You (Unissued)
King Porter Stomp (with Harry James) (IAJRC LP-14)
[Oh] Lady Be Good (Jazz Panorama LP-2)
Everybody Loves My Baby (Inc.) (Unissued)

Count Basie and His Orchestra

August 9, 1938; New York City; Broadcast, Famous Door

One O'Clock Jump (Theme) (Jazz Archives JA-41)
King Porter Stomp (Jazz Archives JA-41)
I've Got a Date with a Dream (Inc.) (Unissued)
[Oh] Lady Be Good (Inc.) (Unissued)

Count Basie and His Orchestra

August 12, 1938; New York City; Broadcast, Famous Door

I Haven't Changed a Thing (Jazz Archives JA-41)

Count Basie and His Orchestra

August 22, 1938; New York City; Decca

Stop Beatin' 'Round the Mulberry Bush (Take A) (Decca 78 rpm only)
Stop Beatin' 'Round the Mulberry Bush (Take B) (MCA 2-4108)

London Bridge Is Falling Down (MCA 2-4108)
Texas Shuffle (MCA 2-4050)
Jumpin' at the Woodside (MCA 2-4050)

Count Basie and His Orchestra

August 23, 1938; New York City; Broadcast Famous Door

Yeah Man (Jazz Panorama LP-23)
John's Idea (Jazz Panorama LP-23)
Melody in F (Jazz Panorama LP-23)
Must We Just Be Friends (Inc.) (Unissued)

Count Basie and His Orchestra

August 24, 1938; New York City; Broadcast, Famous Door

Nagasaki (Jazz Archives JA-41)
Doggin' Around (Jazz Archives JA-41)
One O'Clock Jump (Theme) (Jazz Panorama LP 23)

Count Basie and His Orchestra

September 6, 1938; New York City; Broadcast, Famous Door

Indiana (Jazz Archives JA-41)
Out The Window (Inc.) (Jazz Archives JA-41)

Count Basie and His Orchestra

September 13, 1938; New York City; Broadcast, Famous Door

Ta-Ta (Jazz Archives JA-41)
Indiana (Inc.; the LP gives wrong date for this one) (Jazz Archives JA-41)
Love of My Life (Jazz Archives JA-41)
John's Idea (Inc.) (Jazz Archives JA-41)

Billie Holiday and Her Orchestra

September 15, 1938; New York City; Vocalion

The Very Thought of You (Columbia JG 34837)
I Can't Get Started (Take 1) (Columbia JG 34837)
I Can't Get Started (Take 2) (Columbia JG 34837)
I've Got a Date with a Dream (Take 1) (Columbia JG 34837)
I've Got a Date with a Dream (Take 2) (Columbia JG 34837)
You Can't Be Mine (And Somebody Else's Too) (Columbia JG 34837)

Count Basie and His Orchestra

September 24, 1938; New York City; Broadcast, possibly from Famous Door

Margie (Unissued)
This Time It's Real (Unissued)

Kansas City Six

September 27, 1938; New York City; Commodore
(NOTE: Other dates have been offered, and the session may even be from June
1938, based on personnel.)

Way Down Yonder in New Orleans (Take 1) (Commodore XFL 14937)
Way Down Yonder in New Orleans (Take 2) (Commodore XFL 14937)
Countless Blues (Take 1) (Commodore XFL 14937)
Countless Blues (Take 2) (Commodore XFL 14937)
Them There Eyes (Take 1) (Commodore XFL 14937)
Them There Eyes (Take 2) (Commodore XFL 14937)
I Want a Little Girl (Take 1) (Commodore XFL 14937)
I Want a Little Girl (Take 2) (Commodore XFL 14937)
Pagin' the Devil (Take 1) (Commodore XFL 14937)
Pagin' the Devil (Take 2) (Commodore XFL 14937)

Count Basie and His Orchestra

October 9, 1938; New York City; Broadcast, Famous Door

Yeah Man (Jazz Archives JA-41)

Teddy Wilson and His Orchestra

October 31, 1938; New York City; Brunswick

Everybody's Laughing (Columbia JG 34840)
Here It Is Tomorrow Again (Columbia JG 34840)

Teddy Wilson and His Orchestra

November 9, 1938; New York City; Brunswick

Say It with a Kiss (Columbia JG 34840)
April in My Heart (Take 1) (Raretone 24011)
April in My Heart (Take 2) (CBS-Sony (Japan) YBPC1/SOPH 61-70)
I'll Never Fail You (Raretone 24011)
They Say (Take 1) (Two Flats Disc T-5006)
They Say (Take 2) (Columbia PG 32127)

Count Basie All Stars with Benny Goodman Orchestra

November 15, 1938; New York City; Broadcast

[*Oh*] *Lady Be Good* (Unissued)

Count Basie and His Orchestra

November 16, 1938; New York City; Decca

Dark Rapture (MCA 2-4108)
Shorty George (MCA 2-4050)
The Blues I Like to Hear (MCA 2-4108)
Do You Wanna Jump, Children? (MCA 2-4108)
Panassie Stomp (MCA 2-4050)

Count Basie and His Orchestra

December 23, 1938; New York City; "Spirituals to Swing" concert, Carnegie Hall

One O'Clock Jump (Theme) (Vanguard VSD 47/48)
Blues with Lips (Vanguard VSD 47/48)
Rhythm Man (Vanguard VSD 47/48)

Kansas City Six

Probably 1938; Possibly same concert as above

After You're Gone (Unissued)
Way Down Yonder in New Orleans (Unissued)

"Make Believe Ballroom" Jam Session

1938; Broadcast WNEW Studio

I Know That You Know (IAJRC LP-14)

(NOTE: William Gottlieb, in *The Golden Age of Jazz* (New York: Simon & Schuster), tells of a private recording session with Young and members of the Count Basie and Bob Crosby bands, in late 1938, Washington, D.C. One set of the results was definitely destroyed, but another set may survive.)

Count Basie and His Orchestra

Ca. 1938 or 1939 (Source unknown)

Jumpin' at the Woodside (Inc.) (Unissued)

Count Basie and His Orchestra

January 5, 1939; New York City; Decca

My Heart Belongs to Daddy (MCA 2-4108)
Sing for Your Supper (MCA 2-4108)

Count Basie and His Orchestra

February 2, 3, and 4, 1939; New York City; Decca

You Can Depend on Me (MCA 2-4050)
Cherokee Part I (MCA 2-4050)
Cherokee Part II (MCA 2-4050)
Blame It on My Last Affair (Take A) (MCA 2-4050)
Blame It on My Last Affair (Take B) (Decca 78 rpm only)
Jive at Five (MCA 2-4050)
Thursday (MCA 2-4108)
Evil Blues (MCA 2-4108)
[Oh] Lady Be Good (MCA 2-4050)

Basie's Bad Boys

February 13, 1939; Chicago; Columbia

(NOTE: Previously thought to be April 26, 1939; see notes on the LP for explanation.)

I Ain't Got Nobody (Columbia, JG 34840)
Goin' to Chicago [Blues] (Columbia JG 34840)
[Let Me] Live and Love Tonight (Columbia JG 34840)
Love Me Or Leave Me (Columbia JG 34840)

Count Basie and His Orchestra

March 19, 1939; New York City; Vocalion

What Goes Up Must Come Down (Take 1) (Columbia JG 34840)
What Goes Up Must Come Down (Take 2) (Columbia JG 34840)
Rock-A-Bye Basie (French CBS 66101)
Baby, Don't Tell On Me (Take 1) (French CBS 66101)
Baby, Don't Tell On Me (Take 2) (French CBS 66101)
If I Could Be with You (One Hour Tonight) (Take 1) (French CBS 66101)
If I Could Be with You (One Hour Tonight) (Take 2) (French CBS 66101)
Taxi War Dance (Take 1) (Columbia JG 34840)
Taxi War Dance (Take 2) (Columbia JG 34840)

Count Basie and His Orchestra

March 20, 1939; New York City; Vocalion

Don't Worry 'Bout Me (Take 1) (Columbia JG 34840)
Don't Worry 'Bout Me (Take 2) (Columbia JG 34840)
Jump for Me (French CBS 66101)

Count Basie and His Orchestra

April 5, 1939; New York City; Vocalion

And the Angels Sing (Columbia JG 34840)
If I Didn't Care (Columbia JG 34840)
12th [Twelfth] Street Rag (Columbia JG 34840)
Miss Thing, Part I (Columbia JG 34840)
Miss Thing, Part II (Columbia JG 34840)

(NOTE: Discographies used to list Young as the saxophonist on a Jerry Kruger session of April 25, 1939, but this has been shown to be incorrect. See Berger, Berger, and Patrick, *Benny Carter,* published by Scarecrow Press with Institute of Jazz Studies, Volume 2, p. 82. There is a clarinetist audible in the ensembles who remains to be identified.)

Count Basie and His Orchestra

May 19, 1939; Chicago; Vocalion

Lonesome Miss Pretty (Columbia JG 34840)
Bolero at the Savoy (Columbia JG 34840)
Nobody Knows (French CBS 66101)
Pound Cake (Columbia JG 34840)

Count Basie and His Orchestra

June 4, 1939; Chicago; Broadcast, Hotel Sherman

Southland Shuffle (Jump for Me) (Jazz Archives JA-41)
One O'Clock Jump (Theme) (Unissued)

Count Basie and His Orchestra

June 5, 1939; Chicago; Broadcast, Hotel Sherman

Moten Swing (Jazz Archives JA-41)
Darktown Strutters Ball (Jazz Archives JA-41)
One O'Clock Jump (Theme) (Jazz Archives JA-41)

Count Basie and His Orchestra

June 10, 1939; Chicago; Broadcast, Hotel Sherman

I've Found a New Baby (often listed as "I Found . . .") (Jazz Panorama LP-23)
Thinkin' of You (Inc.) (Unissued)

Count Basie and His Orchestra

June 24, 1939; Chicago; Vocalion

You Can Count on Me (Take A) (Columbia JG 34840)
You Can Count on Me (Take B) (Columbia JG 34840)
You and Your Love (French CBS 66101)
How Long Blues (Take A) (French CBS 66101)
How Long Blues (Take B) (French CBS 66101)
Sub-Deb Blues (French CBS 66101)

Glenn Hardmann and His Hammond Five

June 26, 1939; Chicago; Vocalion

China Boy (Columbia JG 34840)
Exactly Like You (Take A) (Columbia JG 34840)
Exactly Like You (Take B) (Columbia JG 34840)
On the Sunny Side of the Street (Columbia JG 34843)
Upright Organ Blues (Columbia JG 34843)
Who? (Columbia JG 34843)
Jazz Me Blues (Columbia JG 34843)

Count Basie and His Orchestra

Summer, 1939; New York City; CBS Broadcast, "America Dances," Famous Door

One O'Clock Jump (Theme) (Unissued)
Swinging the Blues (Jazz Archives JA-42)
Rock-A-Bye Basie (Jazz Archives JA-41)
Don't Worry 'Bout Me (Jazz Archives JA-42)
Time Out (Jazz Archives JA-42)
Boogie Woogie Blues (Unissued)
Roseland Shuffle (Shoe Shine Swing) (Jazz Archives JA-42)
White Sails (Unissued)
Clap Hands, Here Comes Charlie (Jazz Archives JA-42)
One O'Clock Jump (Theme) (Unissued)

Count Basie and His Orchestra

August 4, 1939; New York City; Vocalion

Moonlight Serenade (French CBS 66101)

Song of the Islands (Columbia JG 34843)
I Can't Believe that You're in Love with Me (French CBS 66101)
Clap Hands, Here Comes Charlie (Columbia JG 34843)

Count Basie's Kansas City Seven

September 5, 1939; New York City; Vocalion

Dickie's Dream (1st Take; labeled Take 2 on LP and in text of this book) (Columbia JG 34843)
Dickie's Dream (2nd Take; labeled Take 3 on LP and in text of this book) (Columbia JG 34843)
Dickie's Dream (3d Take; Inc., no solo by Young) (Unissued)
Dickie's Dream (4th Take; mistakenly labeled both as Take 1 and Take 4 on LP; called Take 1 in text of this book) (Columbia JG 34843)
Lester Leaps In (Take 1) (Columbia JG 34843)
Lester Leaps In (Take 2) (Columbia JG 34843)

(NOTE: Ralph Gleason reported hearing Young with Basie on a transcription cut at a dance in Glendale, California, on a portable recorder—probably from October 1939. See *Down Beat,* November 28, 1957.)

Count Basie and His Orchestra

November 6, 1939; New York City; Columbia/Okeh

The Apple Jump (Columbia JG 34843)
I Left My Baby (Columbia JG 34843)
Riff Interlude (Columbia JG 34843)
Volcano (French CBS 66101)

Count Basie and His Orchestra

November 7, 1939; New York City; Columbia

Between the Devil and the Deep Blue Sea (Columbia JG 34843)
Ham 'N Eggs (Columbia JG 34843)
Hollywood Jump (Columbia JG 34843)
Someday Sweetheart (French CBS 66101)

Billie Holiday and Her Orchestra

December 13, 1939; New York City; Vocalion

Night and Day (Take A) (Columbia PG 32127)
Night and Day (Take B, tape exists) (Unissued)
The Man I Love (Columbia JG 34843)
You're Just a No Account (Columbia JG 34843)
You're a Lucky Guy (Columbia JG 34843)

Kansas City Six

December 24, 1939; New York City; "Spirituals to Swing" concert, Carnegie Hall

Pagin' the Devil (Vanguard VSD 47/48)
Good Morning Blues (Vanguard VSD 47/48)
Way Down Yonder in New Orleans (Vanguard VSD 47/48)

Jam Session with Count Basie Orchestra, Benny Goodman Sextet, and others

December 24, 1939; New York City; Same concert as above

Lady Be Good (Vanguard VSD 47/48)

(NOTE: The Vanguard album above wrongly lists Young as present on *'Fore (Four) Day Creep.)*

(NOTE: *Don't Be Late,* listed as a "newly discovered Holiday-Young 1939 recording" on AJ504, features neither Holiday nor Young, nor is it from 1939!)

Count Basie and His Orchestra

February 20, 1940; Boston; Broadcast, Southland Café

One O'Clock Jump (Theme) (Collector's Classics 11)
Ebony Rhapsody (Collector's Classics 11)
Riff Interlude (Collector's Classics 11)
Darn That Dream (Collector's Classics 11)
Take It Prez (Collector's Classics 11)
Baby Don't Tell on Me (Collector's Classics 11)
If I Could Be with You (One Hour Tonight) (Jazz Panorama LP-23)
I Got Rhythm (Jazz Panorama LP-23)

Count Basie and His Orchestra

March 1, 1940; Boston; NBC Broadcast, Southland Café

Indiana (Missing first few piano measures) (Unissued)
Time Out (brief gap in middle) (Unissued)
12th [Twelfth] Street Rag (Inc.) (Unissued)

Count Basie and His Orchestra

March 9, 1940; Boston; NBC Broadcast, Southland Café

Basin Street Blues (Unissued)
St. Louis Blues (Inc.) (Unissued)
Topsy (Unissued)
One O'Clock Jump (Inc.) (Unissued)

Count Basie and His Orchestra

March 12, 1940; Boston; NBC Broadcast, Southland Café

Doggin' Around (Unissued)
Tickle Toe (Missing first few meaures) (Unissued)
I Left My Baby (Unissued)

Count Basie and His Orchestra

March 13, 1940; Boston; NBC Broadcast, Southland Café

Rockin' in Rhythm (Unissued)

(NOTE: Everybody's EV-3006, in preparation at this writing, contains six of the above items from March.)

Count Basie and His Orchestra

March 19, 1940; New York City; Columbia

I Never Knew (Columbia JG 34843)
Tickle Toe (Columbia JG 34843)
Let's Make Hey! While the Moon Shines (Take A) (Columbia JG 34843)
Let's Make Hey! While the Moon Shines (Take B) (Columbia JG 34843)
Louisiana (Take A) (Columbia C2 34849)
Louisiana (Take B) (Columbia C2 34849)

Count Basie and His Orchestra

March 20, 1940; New York City; Columbia/Okeh

Easy Does It (Columbia C2 34849)
Let Me See (Take A) (Columbia C2 34849)
Let Me See (Take B) (Columbia C2 34849)

(NOTE: Young is not on two other titles)

Count Basie and His Orchestra

May 31, 1940; New York City; Okeh

Blow Top (Take A) (Columbia C2 34849)
Blow Top (Take B) (Columbia C2 34849)
Gone With "What" Wind (Take A) (French CBS 66101)
Gone With "What" Wind (Take B) (French CBS 66101)
Super Chief (French CBS 66101)
You Can't Run Around (French CBS 66101)

Billie Holiday and Her Orchestra

June 7, 1940; New York City; Okeh

I'm Pulling Through (Columbia C2 34849)
Tell Me More (Columbia PG 32124)
Laughin' at Life (Take A) (Columbia C2 34849)
Laughin' at Life (Take B) (Columbia C2 34849)
Time On My Hands (Columbia C2 34849)

Count Basie and His Orchestra

August 8, 1940; Chicago; Okeh

Evenin' (Columbia C2 34849)
The World Is Mad, Part I (Columbia C2 34849)
The World Is Mad, Part II (Columbia C2 34849)
Moten Swing (French CBS 66101)
It's Torture (French CBS 66101)
I Want a Little Girl (French CBS 66101)

Benny Goodman Septet Rehearsal

October 28, 1940; New York City; Studio Rehearsal

(Warmup fragment) (Jazz Archives JA-42)
Ad-Lib Blues (Jazz Archives JA-42)
I Never Knew (Jazz Archives JA-42)
Charlie's Dream (Jazz Archives JA-42)
Wholly Cats (Jazz Archives JA-42)
Lester's Dream (actually another take of *Charlie's Dream*—this piece, in F minor, is similar, but not identical, to *Dickie's Dream,* which is in C minor) (Jazz Archives JA-42)

Count Basie and His Orchestra

October 30, 1940; New York City; Okeh

All Or Nothing At All (Take 1) (French CBS 66101)
All Or Nothing At All (Take 2) (Tax m-8027)
The Moon Fell in the River (Take 1) (French CBS 66101)
The Moon Fell in the River (Take 2) (French CBS 66101)
What's Your Number? (Take 1) (Columbia C2 34849)
What's Your Number? (Take 2) (Columbia C2 34849)
What's Your Number? (Take 3) (Columbia C2 34849)
Draftin' Blues (Take 1) (French CBS 66101)
Draftin' Blues (Take 2) (French CBS 66101)
Draftin' Blues (Take 3, Inc.) (French CBS 66101)
Draftin' Blues (Take 4, Inc.) (French CBS 66101)

Count Basie and His Orchestra

November 19, 1940; New York City; Okeh

Five O'Clock Whistle (Take 1) (Columbia C2 34849)
Five O'Clock Whistle (Take 2) (Columbia C2 34849)
Five O'Clock Whistle (Take 3) (Columbia C2 34849)
Love Jumped Out (Take 1) (French CBS 66101)
Love Jumped Out (Take 2) (French CBS 66101)
Love Jumped Out (Take 3) (French CBS 66101)
My Wanderin' Man (Take 1) (French CBS 66101)
My Wanderin' Man (Take 2) (French CBS 66101)
My Wanderin' Man (Take 3) (French CBS 66101)
Broadway (Take 1) (Columbia C2 34849)
Broadway (Take 2) (Columbia C2 34849)

Billie Holiday/"Make Believe Ballroom" program

December 19, 1940; New York City; Broadcast, WNEW Studio

The Man I Love (Saga 6918)
Untitled Jam Session (Unissued)

Matinee Jam Session

December 29, 1940; New York City; Concert, Village Vanguard

(Unknown titles) (Unissued, perhaps lost)

Hot Lips Page

December 29, 1940; New York City; Broadcast, WNEW Studios

Theme (Unissued)
[Oh] Lady Be Good (Unissued)
Theme (different version) (Unissued)
Wham (Unissued)

Count Basie and His Orchestra

Ca. 1940; Green Bay, Wisconsin; Broadcast
(NOTE: The date usually given, March 7, cannot be correct, based on itinerary.)

Louisiana (Jazz Archives JA-42)
Green Bay (Inc.) (Jazz Archives JA-42)

Matinee Jam Session

January 12, 1941; New York City; Concert, Village Vanguard

(Unknown titles) (Unissued, perhaps lost)

Lester Young Band

Probably between February 27 and March 17, 1941; New York City; Broadcast, Manhattan Center

Tickle Toe (Everybody's EV-3002)
Willow Weep for Me (Taxi War Dance) (Everybody's EV-3002)

Una Mae Carlisle with Orchestra

March 10, 1941; New York City; Bluebird

Blitzkrieg Baby (RCA LPV 578)
Beautiful Eyes (RCA LPV 578)
There'll Be Some Changes Made (RCA LPV 578)
It's Sad But True (RCA LPV 578)

Billie Holiday and Her Orchestra

March 21, 1941; New York City; Okeh

Let's Do It (Take 1) (Columbia C2 34849)
Let's Do It (Take 2) (Columbia C2 34849)
Let's Do It (Take 3, tape exists; Inc.) (Unissued)
Georgia on My Mind (Take 1) (Columbia PG 32124)
Georgia on My Mind (Take 2) (Columbia PG 32124)
Georgia on My Mind (Take 3, tape exists) (Unissued)
Romance in the Dark (Take 1) (Columbia PG 32124)
Romance in the Dark (Take 2, rejected but tape exists) (Unissued)
Romance in the Dark (Take 3, rejected but tape exists) (Unissued)
Romance in the Dark (Take 4) (Columbia CG 30782)
All Of Me (Take 1) (Columbia C2 34849)
All Of Me (Take 2) (Columbia C2 34849)
All Of Me (Take 3) (Columbia C2 34849)

Sam Price and His Texas Blusicians

April 3, 1941; New York City; Decca

The Goon Drag (Gone Wid De Goon) (Japanese MCA 3080)
Things 'Bout Coming My Way (Japanese MCA 3080)
Lead Me Daddy Straight to the Bar (Japanese MCA 3080)
Just Jivin' Around (Japanese MCA 3080)

Lee and Lester Young's Band

December 2, 1941; Hollywood; Broadcast, Capri Club

Untitled Piece using riff of *Benny's Bugle* (Everybody's EV-3002)
Untitled Blues (Theme) (Everybody's EV-3002)

Lee and Lester Young's Band

Probably 1941; Probably Hollywood; Private recording, probably in club

Just A Little Bit South of North Carolina (with vocal by Lester Young) (Unissued)

(NOTE: The above item, long a mystery, has been identified with the help of Lee Young. The audible instrumentation, the arrangement, and Lester's solo style all suggest Lee and Lester Young's Band. The vocal solo alternating with the group vocal was also a trademark of that band. Lester wanted to try singing one number and chose this song, written by Sunny Skylar, Cannon, and Shaftel. It was current in 1941 and was recorded between March and September 1941 by Gene Krupa, Dick Robertson, and Raymond Scott. This recording, probably made by a fan in a club, was found dubbed onto an acetate marked "February 19, 1944, Nola Studios, New York City," but that information does not pertain to the original recording.)

Lee and Lester Young's Band

May 6, 1942; Los Angeles; Broadcast, Trouville Club

Frolic Sam (Unissued)

(NOTE: Only this piece, the last of this broadcast, has been found.)

Lee and Lester Young's Band

Ca. June 1, 1942; Los Angeles; Broadcast, Trouville Club

Broadway (Inc.; missing beginning) (Unissued)
I Hear Music (with Billie Holiday) (Unissued)
Pogo Joe (Inc.) (Unissued)

Lee and Lester Young's Band

Ca. June 1, 1942; Los Angeles; Broadcast, Trouville Club

Untitled piece using riff of *Benny's Bugle* (Unissued)
Solitude (with Billie Holiday; Inc.) (Unissued)
Broadway (Unissued)
[Oh] Lady Be Good (Inc.; missing beginning) (Unissued)

(NOTE: Young is reported to have been the "unknown" saxophonist on *Travelin' Light* by the Paul Whiteman Orchestra with Billie Holiday, June 12, 1942, Los Angeles, but probably not on the other three titles recorded at that session without Holiday. He takes no solos.)

Lester Young–King Cole Trio

July 15, 1942; Los Angeles; Philo/Aladdin

(NOTE: This date, questioned by several researchers, is supported by *Down Beat* of August 1, 1942, as well as by style analysis.)

Indiana (Spotlite SPJ 136)
I Can't Get Started (Spotlite SPJ 136)
Tea for Two (Spotlite SPJ 136)
Body and Soul (Spotlite SPJ 136)

Lee and Lester Young's Band

Probably between September 1 and October 31, 1942; New York City; Private recording, Café Society Downtown
(NOTE: *Down Beat* gave September 1 and 8 as opening dates, but 1 appears to be correct.)

The Great Lie (Unissued)
Untitled (Rhythm Changes) (Inc.) (Unissued)

(Also a few unknown titles, possibly including a blues)

Dickie Wells and His Orchestra

December 21, 1943; New York City; Signature

I Got Rhythm (French RCA FXM3-7324)
I'm Fer It Too (French RCA FXM3-7324)
I'm Fer It Too (Alternate Take) (French RCA FXM3-7324)
Hello Babe (Alternate Take) (French RCA FXM3-7324)
Hello Babe (French RCA FXM3-7324)
Linger Awhile (French RCA FXM3-7324)

Lester Young Quartet

December 28, 1943; New York City; Keynote

Just You, Just Me (Take 1) (Trip 5509)
Just You, Just Me (Take 2) (Trip 5509)
I Never Knew (Take 1) (Trip 5509)
I Never Knew (Take 2) (Trip 5509)
Afternoon of a Basie-ite (Take 1) (Trip 5509)
Afternoon of a Basie-ite (Take 2) (Trip 5509)
Sometimes I'm Happy (Trip 5509)

(NOTE: The most problematic part of the Young catalog is his tenure with the Basie band from December 1943 to September 1944. The band made numerous radio broadcasts during this period and many Armed Forces Radio Services (AFRS) transcriptions. The AFRS transcriptions were on discs made for military radio use only, and appeared in various series, for example, "Jubilee," "One Night Stand"

(O.N.S.), "Down Beat," and "Basic Music Library" (B.M.L.) programs. There is an occasional overlap between shows within series as well as between shows in different series. In addition, the same titles appear many times, making it very difficult to specify which versions of each tune appear on the various LP issues. AFRS shows used mostly "live" material, and studio recordings at times. We know the dates that some of these transcription discs were edited, and that some were broadcast, but no one knows the dates of the "live" performances themselves, nor do we know all titles from each performance. The following listing represents the best research as of this writing.)

Count Basie and His Orchestra

December 28, 1943; New York City; Broadcast, probably Hotel Lincoln

It's Sand, Man! (Unissued)

Count Basie and His Orchestra

Probably December 1943 (possibly December 6); New York City; Broadcast, AFRS "Jubilee" 55

One O'Clock Jump (Theme) (Unissued)
Jumpin' at the Woodside (Swing House SWH-23)
Baby, Won't You Please Come Home? (Unissued)
Do Nothin' till You Hear from Me (Swing House SWH-41)
Don't Believe Everything You Dream (Swing House SWH-23)
I've Found a New Baby (Swing House SWH-23)
One O'Clock Jump (Theme) (Unissued)

Count Basie and His Orchestra

January 10, 1944; New York City; Lang-Worth transcriptions
(NOTE: These were studio recordings for radio use only.)

One O'Clock Jump (Theme with Count Basie opening announcement) (Blue Heaven BH-3-308)
Don't Believe Everything You Dream (5 takes; 4 are Inc., of which two last only a few bars) (Unissued)
Don't Believe Everything You Dream (different take) (Blue Heaven BH-6-605)
Don't Cry Baby (Unissued)
Don't Cry Baby (different take) (Palm 30-12)
I've Had This Feeling Before (two takes, one only a few bars long) (Unissued)
I've Had This Feeling Before (different take) (Blue Heaven BH-1-109)
Sent for You Yesterday (And Here You Come Today) (Unissued)
Sent for You Yesterday (And Here You Come Today) (different take) (Palm 30-12)

Shoo Shoo Baby (Unissued on LP)
Wiggle Woogie (Blue Heaven BH-6-605)
9:20 Special (Blue Heaven BH-1-109)
Down for Double (Blue Heaven BH-1-109)
Swing Shift [Swing] (Blue Heaven BH-1-109)
Rockin' the Blues (Unissued)
Rockin' the Blues (different take) (Blue Heaven BH-3-308)
I Couldn't Sleep a Wink Last Night (Blue Heaven BH-6-605)
I've Found a New Baby (Blue Heaven BH-6-605)
Basie Boogie (Blue Heaven BH-3-308)
Do Nothin' till You Hear from Me (Blue Heaven BH-3-308)
Rock-A-Bye Basie (Blue Heaven BH-6-605)
Red Bank Boogie (Blue Heaven BH-6-605)
One O'Clock Jump (Theme as above, but with Count Basie signoff announcement)
    (Blue Heaven BH-1-109)

Kansas City Seven

March 22, 1944; New York City; Keynote

After Theatre Jump (Trip 5509)
Six Cats and a Prince (Trip 5509)
Six Cats and a Prince (Alternate Take) (Queen-Disc Q-051)
Lester Leaps Again (Trip 5509)
Destination K.C. (Take 1) (Trip 5509)
Destination K.C. (Take 2) (Trip 5509)

Kansas City Six

March 28, 1944; New York City; Commodore

Three Little Words (Take 1) (Commodore XFL 15352)
Three Little Words (Take 2) (Commodore XFL 15352)
Three Little Words (Take 3) (Commodore XFL 15352)
Three Little Words (Take 4) (Commodore XFL 15352)
Jo-Jo (Take 1) (Commodore XFL-15352)
Jo-Jo (Take 2) (Commodore XFL-15352)
Jo-Jo (Take 3) (Commodore XFL-15352)
Jo-Jo (Take 4) (Commodore XFL-15352)
I Got Rhythm (Take 1) (Commodore XFL-15352)
I Got Rhythm (Take 2) (Commodore XFL-15352)
I Got Rhythm (Take 3) (Commodore XFL-15352)
Four O'Clock Drag (Take 1) (Commodore XFL-15352)
Four O'Clock Drag (Take 2) (Commodore XFL-15352)

Count Basie and His Orchestra

April 3, 1944; New York City; Fats Waller Memorial Concert, Carnegie Hall

I'm Gonna Sit Right Down And Write Myself a Letter (Unissued)
Ain't Misbehavin' (Everybody's EV-3002)

Count Basie and His Orchestra

April 6, 1944; New York City; Columbia Broadcast, Hotel Lincoln

Swing Shift [Swing] (Unissued)
I've Had This Feeling Before (Unissued)
Blue Room Jump (Andy's Blues) (Unissued)
One O'Clock Jump (Unissued)

Count Basie and His Orchestra

April 10, 1944; New York City; Mutual Broadcast, Hotel Lincoln

One O'Clock Jump (Theme) (Unissued)
My, What A Fry! (Everybody's EV-3002)
Absent Minded (Inc.) (Unissued)
One O'Clock Jump (long version, ending Inc.) (Everybody's EV-3002)

Count Basie and His Orchestra

Ca. April 10, 1944; New York City; Broadcast, Hotel Lincoln, AFRS "O.N.S." 198

One O'Clock Jump (Theme) (Unissued)
Diggin' for Dex (Caracol 431)
My Ideal (Unissued)
Blue Lou (Unissued)
Ain't It the Truth (Caracol 431)
Take Me Back, Baby (Musidisc 5105)
And So Little Time (Unissued)
Journey to a Star (Unissued)
Jumpin' at the Woodside (Caracol 431)
One O'Clock Jump (Theme) (Unissued)

Count Basie and His Orchestra

Ca. April 14, 1944; New York City; Mutual Broadcast, Hotel Lincoln

Bangs (Everybody's EV-3004)

(NOTE: *Irresistible You,* broadcast here, was not recorded.)

Ain't But the One (Son of a Gun) (Everybody's EV-3004)
Don't Cry Baby (Inc.) (Unissued)

I've Found a New Baby (Everybody's EV-3002)
One O'Clock Jump (opening piano measures only) (Unissued)

Count Basie and His Orchestra

Ca. April 14, 1944; New York City; Columbia Broadcast, Hotel Lincoln

King Porter Stomp (Everybody's EV-3004)

Count Basie and His Orchestra

April 17, 1944; New York City; Broadcast, Hotel Lincoln, AFRS "O.N.S." 213

One O'Clock Jump (Theme) (Queen-Disc Q-025)
Avenue C (Queen-Disc Q-025)
Tess's Torch Song (Queen-Disc Q-025)
I'm Gonna Sit Right Down And Write Myself a Letter (Queen-Disc Q-025)
Rock-a-Bye Basie (Queen-Disc Q-025)
And So Little Time (Unissued)
Dance of the Gremlins (Queen-Disc Q-025)
When They Ask About You (Queen-Disc Q-025)
One O'Clock Jump (Theme) (Unissued)

(NOTE: Two other titles were repeated from ca. April 10.)

Johnny Guarnieri Swing Men

April 18, 1944; New York City; Savoy (10 A.M.–1 P.M.)

These Foolish Things (Savoy SJL 2202)
Exercise in Swing (Take 1) (Savoy SJL 2202)
Exercise in Swing (Take 2) (Savoy SJL 2202)
Exercise in Swing (Take 3) (Savoy SJL 2202)
Exercise in Swing (Take 4) (Savoy SJL 2202)
Salute to Fats (Take 1) (Savoy SJL 2202)
Salute to Fats (Take 2; Inc.) (Savoy SJL 2202)
Salute to Fats (Take 3) (Savoy SJL 2202)
Salute to Fats (Take 4; Inc.) (Savoy SJL 2202)
Salute to Fats (Take 5) (Savoy SJL 2202)
Basie English (Take 1) (Savoy SJL 2202)
Basie English (Take 2) (Savoy SJL 2202)

Earl Warren and His Orchestra

(NOTE: Actually, the Basie band minus Basie).

April 18, 1944; New York City; Savoy (2 P.M.–5 P.M.)

Empty Hearted (Savoy 78 rpm only)

Circus in Rhythm (Take 1) (Savoy SJL 2202)
Circus in Rhythm (Take 2) (Savoy SJL 2202)
Circus in Rhythm (Take 3) (Savoy SJL 2202)
Poor Little Plaything (Take 1) (Savoy SJL 2202)
Poor Little Plaything (Take 2) (Savoy SJL 2202)
Tush (Take 1) (Savoy SJL 2202)
Tush (Take 2) (Savoy SJL 2202)

Count Basie and His Orchestra

April 21, 1944; New York City; Columbia Broadcast, Hotel Lincoln

Kansas City Stride (Everybody's EV-3002)
One O'Clock Jump (long version, ending, Inc.) (Unissued)

Count Basie and His Orchestra

Ca. April 21, 1944; New York City; Broadcast, AFRS, "Kate Smith Show"

One O'Clock Jump (Unissued)
Nagasaki (Unissued)
Kansas City Keys (Basie Boogie) (Unissued)

Count Basie and His Orchestra

April 24, 1944; New York City; Mutual Broadcast, Hotel Lincoln

One O'Clock Jump (Theme) (Unissued)
I've Found a New Baby (Unissued)
Tess's Torch Song (Inc.) (Unissued)
Jazz Me Blues (Everybody's EV-3002)
I Couldn't Sleep a Wink Last Night (Inc.) (Unissued)
Blue Lou (the LP says April 21) (Everybody's EV-3004)
My Melancholy Baby (Inc.) (Unissued)
Avenue C (Unissued)
One O'Clock Jump (long version, ending Inc.) (Unissued)

Count Basie and His Orchestra

Ca. April 24, 1944; New York City; Broadcast, Hotel Lincoln, AFRS "O.N.S." 228

Hey Rube! (Unissued)
I Dream of You (Unissued)
I'm Gonna Sit Right Down And Write Myself a Letter (Unissued)
The Basie Blues (Unissued)
Irresistible You (Unissued)
Ain't Misbehavin' (Musidisc 5105)
I'm in Love with Someone (Unissued)

Jumpin' at the Woodside (Musidisc 5105; abridged version, spliced to the one from ca. September 11)
9:20 Special (long version, ending Inc.) (Unissued)

Count Basie and His Orchestra

April or May 1944; New York City; Broadcast(s), Hotel Lincoln, AFRS "Down Beat," 103, 145
(NOTE: Some AFRS programs contained all these titles and others, some included only a few of these. May 6, 1944, may be the date for some titles.)

One O'Clock Jump (Theme) (Queen Disc, Q-025)
I've Found a New Baby (Queen Disc, Q-025)
Avenue C (once falsely called "Catsup") (Queen-Disc, Q-025)
Do Nothin' till You Hear from Me (Queen-Disc, Q-025)
Basie Boogie (Falsely named "Avenue C") (Queen-Disc, Q-025)
Harvard Blues (Queen-Disc, Q-025)
My Ideal (Unissued)
Jumpin' at the Woodside (Queen-Disc Q-025)
One O'Clock Jump (Theme) (Queen-Disc Q-025)

(NOTE: Last two titles may derive from another source.)

Count Basie and His Orchestra

Probably April or May 1944; New York City; Mutual Broadcast, Hotel Lincoln

One O'Clock Jump (Theme) (Unissued)
Swing Shift [*Swing*] (Unissued)
Beaver Junction (Unissued)

(NOTE: *Gee Baby, Ain't I Good to You,* broadcast here, was not recorded.)

Count Basie and His Orchestra

Probably April or May 1944; New York City; Mutual Broadcast, Hotel Lincoln

One O'Clock Jump (Theme) (Everybody's EV-3002)
Dinah (Everybody's EV-3002)
So Little Time (Inc.) (Unissued)
Blue Room Jump (Everybody's EV-3002)
One O'Clock Jump (Inc.) (Unissued)

Count Basie and His Orchestra

Probably April or May 1944; New York City; Broadcast, Hotel Lincoln

Tush (Everybody's EV-3002)
This I Love above All (Unissued)

Lester Young Quintet

May 1, 1944; New York City; Savoy

Blue Lester (Lester's Blues) (Savoy SJL 2202)
(I Don't Stand) A Ghost of a Chance (Take 1) (Savoy SJL 2202)
(I Don't Stand) A Ghost of a Chance (Take 2) (Savoy SJL 2202)
Indiana (Take 1) (Savoy SJL 2202)
Indiana (Take 2) (Savoy SJL 2202)
Jump Lester Jump (Lester's Savoy Jump) (Savoy SJL 2202)

Count Basie and His Orchestra

Ca. May 5, 1944; New York City; Broadcast, AFRS "Down Beat" 5

Dinah (Unissued)
I Never Knew (I Could Love Anybody) (NOTE: This is a different song from *I Never Knew.)* (Unissued)
Baby, Won't You Please Come Home (Unissued)
My, What a Fry! (Unissued)
One O'Clock Jump (Theme) (Unissued)

(NOTE: This prerecorded program begins with an excerpt from the closing theme.)

Count Basie and His Orchestra

May 13, 1944; New York City; Mutual Broadcast, Hotel Lincoln

One O'Clock Jump (Theme) (Unissued)
Hey Rube! (Unissued)
Tush (Caracol 431)
This Is a Lovely Way To Spend an Evening (Unissued)
Rock-A-Bye Basie (Unissued)
Harvard Blues (Unissued)
Jazz Me Blues (Caracol 431)
I Couldn't Sleep a Wink Last Night (Unissued)
I Never Knew (I Could Love Anybody) (Unissued)
One O'Clock Jump (long version, ending Inc.) (Caracol 431; abridged version)

Count Basie and His Orchestra

Probably May 14, 1944; New York City; Mutual Broadcast, Hotel Lincoln

Every Tub (IAJRC 17)

Count Basie and His Orchestra

May 17, 1944; New York City; Mutual Broadcast, Hotel Lincoln

I Never Knew (Unissued)

This I Love above All (Unissued)
Let's Mop It (Unissued)
I Want a Little Girl (Unissued)
Dance of the Gremlins (Caracol 431)
How Blue the Night (Unissued)
Too Much in Love (Unissued)
Blue Room Jump (Andy's Blues) (Caracol 431)
One O'Clock Jump (Theme) (Unissued)

Count Basie and His Orchestra

May 20, 1944; New York City; Broadcast, Hotel Lincoln

Call Me Darling (Everybody's EV-3002)
Ain't It the Truth (Everybody's EV-3002)

Count Basie and His Orchestra

May 24, 1944; New York City; Mutual Broadcast, Hotel Lincoln

Let's Jump (Inc; ending only) (Unissued)
Too Much in Love (Unissued)
One O'Clock Jump (Inc.) (Unissued)

Count Basie and His Orchestra

May 25, 1944; New York City; Lang-Worth transcriptions

Let's Jump (Blue Heaven BH-3-308)
Time Alone Will Tell (Blue Heaven BH-6-605)
This I Love above All (Blue Heaven BH-1-109)
I'm Gonna Sit Right Down and Write Myself a Letter (Musidisc 5160)
Circus in Rhythm (Blue Heaven BH-6-605)
Tush (Blue Heaven BH-3-308)
Ain't It the Truth (Blue Heaven BH-6-605)
I Dream of You (Blue Heaven BH-3-308)

Count Basie and His Orchestra

May 27, 1944; New York City; V-disc studio session (made for Armed Forces servicemen and not for sale to the public)

Kansas City Stride (Jazz Society AA 505)
Beaver Junction (Jazz Society AA 505)
Circus in Rhythm (Jazz Society AA 505)
Aunt Hagar's Country Home (Jazz Society AA 506)
Gee, Baby, Ain't I Good to You (Jazz Society AA 505)
Basie Strides Again ([Along] Avenue C) (Jazz Society AA 505)

(NOTE: There is an undated V-disc title, *Call Me Darling*, which must be from this session, since Young solos briefly. Also, Richard Sears lists an unissued *Basie Strides Again* in his book *V-discs*, but it appears to be the same take, not a new item.)

Count Basie and His Orchestra

May 27, 1944; New York City; Mutual Broadcast, Hotel Lincoln

Broadway (Unissued)
My Ideal (Unissued)
Circus in Rhythm (Unissued)
A Journey to a Star (Inc.) (Unissued)
Tuesday at Ten (Unissued)
Harvard Blues (Unissued)
Rock-A-Bye Basie (Unissued)
Down for Double (Unissued)

Count Basie and His Orchestra

Ca. May 28, 1944; New York City; Broadcast, Hotel Lincoln, AFRS "Down Beat" 151, 185

Beaver Junction (Unissued)
Exactly Like You (Unissued)

(NOTE: More titles were added, from other broadcasts.)

Count Basie and His Orchestra

May 29, 1944; New York City; Mutual Broadcast, Hotel Lincoln

One O'Clock Jump (Theme) (Unissued)
Blue Lou (Unissued)
Call Me Darling (Caracol 431)
Jazz Me Blues (Unissued)
Harvard Blues (Unissued)
My, What a Fry! (Caracol 431)
Time on My Hands (Unissued)
Avalon (Caracol 431)
One O'Clock Jump (Inc.) (Unissued)

Count Basie and His Orchestra

May 30, 1944; New York City; Columbia Broadcast, Hotel Lincoln

Beaver Junction (Unissued)
I'm in Love with Someone (Unissued)
Kansas City Stride (Unissued)

Tess's Torch Song (Unissued)
There'll Be Some Changes Made (Caracol 431)
Let's Jump (Unissued)
Time Alone Will Tell (Unissued)
Jumpin' at the Woodside (Unissued)
One O'Clock Jump (Theme) (Unissued)

Count Basie and His Orchestra

May 1944; New York City; Broadcast, Hotel Lincoln, AFRS "O.N.S." 242

One O'Clock Jump (Theme) (Unissued)
Hey Rube! (Unissued)
Those Same Little Words (Unissued)
Let's Jump (Unissued)
Too Much in Love (Unissued)
There'll Be Some Changes Made (Unissued)
Time Alone Will Tell (Unissued)
Avenue C (Unissued)

(NOTE: *The Basie Blues* was inserted here from ca. April 24.)

One O'Clock Jump (Theme) (Unissued)

Count Basie and His Orchestra

Probably May 1944; New York City; Broadcast, possibly Hotel Lincoln

Blue Room Jump (Unissued)
Fellow on a Furlough (Unissued)
I'm Gonna Sit Right Down and Write Myself a Letter (Unissued)
Beaver Junction (Unissued)
And Now I'm in Love (Unissued)
Tess's Torch Song (Unissued)
Avenue C (Unissued)
Together (Unissued)

Count Basie and His Orchestra

Probably late May 1944; New York City; Broadcast, Hotel Lincoln, AFRS "O.N.S." 269 (NOTE: A reliable source gives May 22.)

One O'Clock Jump (Theme) (Unissued)
It's Sand, Man! (Musidisc 5105)
I Dream of You (Unissued)
Circus in Rhythm (Musidisc 5105)
Time Alone Will Tell (Unissued)
I'm in Love with Someone (Unissued)

Swing Shift [*Swing*] (Musidisc 5105)
Gee, Baby, Ain't I Good to You (Musidisc 5105)
Jumpin' at the Woodside (Everybody's EV-3002)
One O'Clock Jump (Theme) (Unissued)

Jammin' the Blues (Film)

August 1944; Hollywood; Two soundtrack sessions

Midnight Symphony (Jazz Archives JA-18)
On the Sunny Side of the Street (Jazz Archives JA-18)
Jammin' the Blues (Soundtrack take) (Europa Jazz EJ-1011)
Jammin' the Blues (Alternate take) (Jazz Archives JA-18)
Blues for Marvin (Jazz Archives JA-18)
If I Could Be with You (One Hour Tonight) (Jazz Archives JA-18)
Sweet Georgia Brown (Jazz Archives JA-18)

(NOTE: Only the first three titles were used in the film)

Count Basie and His Orchestra

Ca. September 11, 1944; Los Angeles; Broadcast, AFRS "Jubilee" 96, 112

One O'Clock Jump (Theme) (Unissued)
Avenue C (Unissued)
More Than You Know (Unissued)
Basie Boogie (Unissued)
Harvard Blues (Unissued)
I'll Be Seeing You (Unissued)
Jumpin' at the Woodside (Jazz Panorama LP-2)
One O'Clock Jump (Theme) (Unissued)

Count Basie and His Orchestra

Ca. September 18, 1944; Hollywood; Broadcast, AFRS "Jubilee" 97

Let's Jump (Unissued)
Gee Baby, Ain't I Good to You (Unissued)
Snoqualomie Jojo (with the King Sisters) (Unissued)
Do Nothin' till You Hear from Me (Unissued)
My, What a Fry! (Unissued)
One O'Clock Jump (Theme) (Unissued)

Count Basie and His Orchestra

1944; Unknown location; Broadcast, AFRS "B.M.L." 481

Let's Jump (Musidisc 5160)

One O'Clock Jump (Musidisc 5160)
Jumpin' at the Woodside (Musidisc 5160)
Andy's Blues (Caracol 421)

Count Basie and His Orchestra

1944; Unknown location; Broadcast

Jumpin' for Maria (Green) (Unissued)
Blue Lou (Unissued)

Count Basie and His Orchestra

1944 (LP says May 30); Unknown location; Broadcast

Hey, Rube! (Caracol 431)

(NOTE: During 1944 a Young solo titled *Hi Heckler* was published in the folio *Tenor Saxophone Styles,* New York, Capitol Songs, 1944; reprinted in Dave Dexter, *The Jazz Story: From the '90s to the '60s* [Englewood Cliffs, N.J.: Prentice-Hall, Inc., 1964], xii. The solo, three blues choruses in C, was presumably transcribed from an informal recording such as a dictaphone. Perhaps the source still exists.)

(NOTE: Two titles released on the Riff 78 rpm label of Chicago, from sometime between 1944 and 1946, feature a saxophonist known only as "The Man." Some collectors believe this to be Young, but many qualified listeners disagree.)

Lester Young and His Band

December 1945; Los Angeles; Aladdin (NOTE: Usually assigned to October, but Young was in the army until December.)

D.B. Blues (Blue Note LA 456-H2)
Lester Blows Again (Blue Note LA 456-H2)
These Foolish Things (Blue Note LA 456-H2)
Jumpin' at Mesner's (Blue Note LA 456-H2)

Helen Humes and Her All Stars

December 1945 or January 1946; Los Angeles; Philo/Aladdin

Please Let Me Forget (Philo/Aladdin 78 rpm only)
Pleasing Man Blues (Whiskey, Women, and—KM-701)
He Don't Love Me Anymore (Whiskey, Women, and—KM-701)
See See Rider (Philo/Aladdin 78 rpm only)
It's Better to Give Than to Receive (Whiskey, Women, and—KM-701)

Jazz at the Philharmonic

January 28, 1946; Los Angeles; Concert, Philharmonic Auditorium

Blues for Norman (Verve VE 2-2518)
[Oh] Lady Be Good (Verve VE 2-2518)
I Can't Get Started (Verve VE 2-2518)
After You've Gone (Verve VE 2-2518)
Crazy Rhythm (Verve VE 2-2518)
Lover Come Back to Me (Unissued)
The Man I Love (Verve VE 2-2518)
Sweet Georgia Brown (Verve VE 2-2518)

Lester Young and His Band

Probably January 1946; Los Angeles; Aladdin

It's Only a Paper Moon (Bluenote LA 456-H2)
After You've Gone (Bluenote LA 456-H2)
Lover Come Back to Me (Bluenote LA 456-H2)
Jammin' with Lester (Bluenote LA 456-H2)

(NOTE: There is a report of AFRS "O.N.S." 898 with Young, Nat Cole, and Les Paul, from early 1946, but it is not known whether this is unique material.)

Lester Young–Buddy Rich Trio

Late March or April 1946; Los Angeles; Clef
(NOTE: Most sources say December 1945, but the above dating conforms best with the musicians' itineraries.)

Back to the Land (Verve VE 2-2516)
I Cover the Waterfront (probably Take 1) (Queen-Disc Q-051)
I Cover the Waterfront (Take 2) (Verve VE-2-2516)
Somebody Loves Me (Verve VE 2-2516)
I've Found a New Baby (Verve VE 2-2516)
The Man I Love (Verve VE 2-2516)
Peg o' My Heart (Verve VE 2-2516)
I Want to Be Happy (Verve VE 2-2516)
Mean to Me (Verve VE 2-2516)

Lester Young with Nat Cole

Probably early April 1946; Hollywood; Transcription, AFRS "Jubilee" 184

These Foolish Things (with brief spoken introduction by Young) (Spotlite SPJ 119)
Lester Leaps In (Spotlite SPJ 119)

Lester Young Quartet

Probably early April 1946; Transcription, AFRS "Jubilee" 190

D. B. Blues (with brief spoken introduction by Young) (Spotlite SPJ-119)

Jubilee All-Stars

Probably early April 1946; Hollywood; Transcription AFRS "Jubilee" 190/192

One O'Clock Jump (Theme) (Unissued)
I Got Rhythm (Spotlite SPJ-119)
Sweet Georgia Brown (Spotlite SPJ-119)
Lady Be Good (Spotlite SPJ-119)
One O'Clock Jump (Theme) (Unissued)
Unlucky Woman (with Helen Humes) (Unissued)

Jazz at the Philharmonic

April 22, 1946; Los Angeles; Concert, Embassy Theatre
(NOTE: AFRS "Down Beat" 239 contained the first and part of the third title. Also, one reliable source gives April 23 as the date.)

JATP Blues (Verve VE 2-2518)
I Got Rhythm (Verve VE 2-2518)
I Surrender Dear (Verve JATP series, Vol. 4)
I've Found a New Baby (LP says April 23) (Verve 815.1491)
Bugle Call Rag (Unissued)

(NOTE: Six Billie Holiday titles have been issued with the above, but they appear to have been spliced from various concerts and Young's presence is dubious.)

Jazz at the Philharmonic

May 27, 1946; New York City; Concert, Broadcast, Carnegie Hall

[Carnegie] Blues (Verve 825.101-1)
[Oh] Lady Be Good (Jazz Archives JA-18)
I Can't Get Started (Verve 815.1491).
Sweet Georgia Brown (Phoenix LP 8)
Slow Drag (previously thought to be April 22) (Verve JATP Series, Vol. 4)

Jazz at the Philharmonic

June 3, 1946; New York City; Concert, Broadcast, Carnegie Hall

Tea for Two (Jazz Archives JA-18 and Verve 825.101-1; JA omits introduction)
I Cried for You (Billie Holiday on this and the next two) (Phoenix LP 8)
Billie's Blues (Phoenix LP 8)
He's Funny That Way (Phoenix LP 8)

Jazz at The Philharmonic
(NOTE: All titles are reported to be Inc., featuring Young solos.)

June 17, 1946; New York City; Concert, Carnegie Hall

Blues (Verve 825.101-1)
Just You, Just Me (Unissued)
It's the Talk of the Town (Unissued)
I Got Rhythm (Verve 825.101-1)
D.B. Blues (Unissued)

(NOTE: Also reported to derive from the above three concerts are "Sunday" and "Lester Leaps In," but this is unconfirmed.)

Lester Young and His Band

August 1946; Los Angeles; Aladdin

You're Driving Me Crazy (Bluenote LA 456-H2)
[New] Lester Leaps In (Bluenote LA 456-H2)
Lester's Be Bop [Boogie] (Bluenote LA 456-H2)
She's Funny That Way (Bluenote LA 456-H2)

Lester Young and His Band

February 18, 1947; Chicago; Aladdin
(NOTE: Young had been in California at least through February 15, so this session may have been in Los Angeles.)

Sunday (Bluenote LA 456-H2)
S.M. Blues (Bluenote LA 456-H2)
Jumpin' with Symphony Sid (Bluenote LA 456-H2)
No Eyes Blues (Bluenote LA 456-H2)
Sax-O-Re-Bop (Sax-O-Be-Bop) (Bluenote LA 456-H2)

(NOTE: Above two titles are accidentally interchanged on the LP.)

On the Sunny Side of the Street (Bluenote LA 456-H2)

Lester Young and His Band

December 28 and 30, 1947; New York City; Aladdin

Movin' with Lester (Bluenote LA 456-H2)
One O'Clock Jump (Queen Disc Q-051)
Jumpin' at the Woodside (Bluenote LA 456-H2)
Easy Does It (Bluenote LA 456-H2)
Easy Does It (Alternate Take) (Queen-Disc Q-051)
Just Coolin' (Bluenote LA 456-H2)
I'm Confessin' (Bluenote LA 456-H2)
Lester Smooths It Out (Bluenote LA 456-H2)

Lester Young and His Band

November 27, 1948; New York City; Broadcast, Royal Roost

Jumpin' with Symphony Sid (Theme) (ESP 3017; slightly edited version)
Lester Leaps In (ESP 3017)
Ghost of a Chance (ESP 3017)
Just You, Just Me (ESP 3017)
Sweet Georgia Brown (ESP 3017) (Beginning is missing on the LP)
How High the Moon (with Ella Fitzgerald and other guests) (ESP 3017)
Jumpin' with Symphony Sid (Theme) (Unissued)

Lester Young and His Band

December 4, 1948; New York City; Broadcast, Royal Roost

Bebop Boogie (Session Disc 103)
I'm Confessin' (Session Disc 103)
I Cover the Waterfront (Session Disc 103)
How High the Moon (Session Disc 103)
Sunday (Session Disc 103)
Jumpin' with Symphony Sid (Theme) (Ambrosia 10)

Lester Young and His Band

December 29, 1948; New York City; Aladdin

Tea for Two (LP says February, 1949) (Queen-Disc Q-051)
East of the Sun (Bluenote LA 456-H2)
The Sheik of Araby (Bluenote LA 456-H2)
Something to Remember You By (Bluenote LA 456-H2)

Lester Young and His Band

March 19, 1949; New York City; Broadcast, Royal Roost

Bebop Boogie (Charlie Parker PLP-409)
These Foolish Things (Charlie Parker PLP-409)
D.B. Blues (Charlie Parker PLP-409)
Just You, Just Me (Charlie Parker PLP-409)

Lester Young and His Band

March 26, 1949; New York City; Broadcast, Royal Roost

Lester Leaps In (Again) (Alto 707)
She's Funny That Way (Alto 707)
Lavender Blue (Alto 707)
Tea for Two (Alto 707)

Lester Young and His Band

April 9, 1949; New York City; Broadcast, Royal Roost

Lavender Blue (Session Disc 103)
Ghost of a Chance (Session Disc 103)
Mean to Me (Session Disc 103)
Sunday (Ambrosia 10)

Lester Young and His Band

June 28, 1949; New York City; Savoy

Crazy Over J–Z (Take 1) (Savoy SJL 2202)
Crazy Over J–Z (Take 2) (Savoy SJL 2202)
Crazy Over J–Z (Take 3) (Savoy SJL 2202)
Ding Dong (Take 1) (Savoy SJL 2202)
Ding Dong (Take 2) (Savoy SJL 2202)
Ding Dong (Take 3) (Savoy SJL 2202)
Blues 'N Bells (Take 1) (Savoy SJL 2202)
Blues 'N Bells (Take 2) (Savoy SJL 2202)
Blues 'N Bells (Take 3) (Savoy SJL 2202)
June Bug (Lester Digs) (Savoy SJL 2202)

Billie Holiday with Buster Harding's Orchestra

August 17, 1949; New York City; Decca

Ain't Nobody's Business (MCA 2-4006)
Baby Get Lost (MCA 2-4006)

Jazz at the Philharmonic

September 17, 1949; New York City; Concert, Carnegie Hall
(NOTE: Date usually given as Sunday the 18th—could be technically correct if
concert started at midnight.)

The Opener (Verve 815.1501)
Lester Leaps In (Verve 815.1501)
Embraceable You (Verve 815.1501)
The Closer (Verve 815.1501)
Flying Home (with Ella Fitzgerald) (Verve 815.1471)

Lester Young Band

February 22, 1950; New York City; Private recording, Savoy Ballroom
(NOTE: The above date is spoken on one of the source recordings, but it appears
that these titles derive from more than one night.)

Neenah (Blues Tres) (Jumpin' and Stompin') (Inc.; missing beginning) (Charlie Parker PLP-402, CP 504, and Audiofidelity AFE 3-8)

I Cover the Waterfront (Charlie Parker PLP-402 and Audiofidelity 3-8)

These Foolish Things (Inc.; missing first few bars) (Charlie Parker PLP-402)

Lester Leaps In (Inc.) (Charlie Parker PLP-402)

Sunday (Inc.; missing beginning) (Charlie Parker PLP-402 and Audiofidelity AFE 3-8)

Destination Moon (Charlie Parker PLP-402)

Pennies from Heaven (Charlie Parker PLP-405)

Stardust (Inc.; missing first few bars) (Charlie Parker PLP-405)

Mean to Me (Charlie Parker PLP-405)

Stardust (different version, Young on last note only) (Charlie Parker PLP-405)

On the Sunny Side of the Street (Charlie Parker PLP-405)

Three Little Words (Charlie Parker PLP-405)

Jumpin' with Symphony Sid (Theme) (Charlie Parker CP 504; Young's solo abridged on LP)

Up 'N Adam (often listed as "Up and At 'Em" or "Up and Atom") (Charlie Parker CP 504 and Audiofidelity AFE 3-8)

Perdido (Charlie Parker CP 504 and Audiofidelity AFE 3-8)

[Oh] Lady Be Good (Charlie Parker CP 504)

'Deed I Do (Charlie Parker CP 504)

Seventh Ave. Romp (Charlie Parker CP 504 and Audiofidelity AFE 3-8)

Lester Leaps In ending with *Jumpin' with Symphony Sid* (Charlie Parker CP 504 and Audiofidelity AFE 3-8)

Almost Like Being in Love ending with *Jumpin' with Symphony Sid* (Inc.; missing first few bars) (Audiofidelity AFE 3-8)

I Cover the Waterfront (#1) (different version; Inc.; begins midway) (Audiofidelity AFE 3-8)

I Got Rhythm (Audiofidelity AFE 3-8)

Blues Original (untitled; Inc.; begins midway) (Audiofidelity AFE 3-8)

One O'Clock Jump ending with *Jumpin' with Symphony Sid* (Audiofidelity AFE 3-8)

D.B. Blues (Audiofidelity AFE 3-8)

'Deed I Do (different version) (Audiofidelity AFE 3-8)

[Oh] Lady Be Good (different version) (Audiofidelity AFE 3-8)

In a Little Spanish Town (Audiofidelity AFE 3-8)

Blues with a Bridge ending with *Jumpin' with Symphony Sid* (Inc.; missing beginning, splice near end) (Audiofidelity AFE 3-8)

These Foolish Things (different version, with vocalist; Inc.; missing first few bars) (Unissued)

These Foolish Things (different version) (Unissued)

Jumpin' with Symphony Sid (two versions, both different than above, both Inc., begin in progress) (Unissued)

Jumpin' with Symphony Sid (Theme Only) (Unissued)

Blues (untitled; Inc.; two excerpts only) (Unissued)
Indiana (Inc.; missing first few bars) (Unissued)
Indiana (different version, ending Inc.) (Unissued)
Sunday (different version, ending Inc.) (Unissued)
How High the Moon (Unissued)
Up 'N Adam (different version; Inc.; missing first few bars) (Unissued)
Tea for Two (Unissued)
Sometimes I'm Happy (Unissued)
Too Marvelous for Words (Unissued)
I Cover the Waterfront'(different version, with vocalist) (Unissued)

(NOTE: There are also several unissued titles by the band without Young.)

Lester Young Quartet

March 1950; New York City; Clef

Too Marvelous for Words (Verve VE 2-2516) (An alternate take is on Clef 8924.)
'Deed I Do (Verve VE 2-2516)
Encore (Verve VE 2-2516)
Polka Dots and Moonbeams (Verve VE 2-2516)
Up 'N Adam (Verve VE 2-2516)

Lester Young Band

April 2, 1950; Chicago; Private recording, probably in club

Neenah (Lester's Blues No. 2) (Savoy SJL 1109)
Body and Soul (Savoy SJL 1109)
Up 'N Adam (Lester Warms Up) (Savoy SJL 1109)
Big Eyes Blues (Lester's Blues No. 1) (Savoy SJL 1109)
One O'Clock Jump (Savoy SJL 1109)
Lester's Mop Mop Blues (Up and Atom) (Savoy SJL 1109)
Pennies from Heaven (Savoy SJL 1109)
I Can't Get Started (Savoy SJL 1109)
How High the Moon (Savoy SJL 1109)
Jumpin' with Symphony Sid (Savoy SJL 1109)

Lester Young Quintet

April 1950 (possibly same as above); Chicago (LP says New York City); Private recording, probably in club

Tea for Two (Jazz Archives JA-34)
D.B. Blues (Jazz Archives JA-34)
Blue and Sentimental (Jazz Archives JA-34)
Lester Leaps In (Jazz Archives JA-34)

Lester Young Quartet

July 1950; New York City; Clef

Three Little Words (Verve VE 2-2516)
Count Every Star (Verve VE 2-2516)
It All Depends on You (Verve VE 2-2516)
Neenah (Verve VE 2-2516)
Jeepers Creepers (Verve VE 2-2516)

Norman Granz Jazz Concert

September 16, 1950; New York City; Concert, Carnegie Hall

Norgran Blues (Verve 815.1511)
Lady Be Good (Verve 815.1511)
(I Don't Stand) A Ghost of a Chance (Verve 815.1511)
Indiana (Verve 815.1511)

Lester Young Quartet

January 6, 1951; New York City; Broadcast, Birdland

Up 'N Adam (Ambrosia 10)
Three Little Words (Ambrosia 10)
Neenah (Ambrosia 10)
I Cover the Waterfront (Ambrosia 10)
Lester Leaps In (Ambrosia 10)

Lester Young Quartet

January 13, 1951; New York City; Broadcast, Birdland

Up 'N Adam (Session Disc 104)
Too Marvelous for Words (Session Disc 104)
Indiana (Session Disc 104)

Lester Young Quartet

January 16, 1951; New York City; Clef

Thou Swell (Verve VE 2-2516)
September in the Rain (Verve VE 2-2516)
Undercover Girl Blues (Verve VE 2-2516)
Frenesi (Verve VE 2-2516)
Pete's Café (Verve VE 2-2516)
Little Pee Blues (Verve VE 2-2516)

Lester Young Quartet

January 20, 1951; New York City; Broadcast, Birdland

Neenah (Session Disc 104)
Ghost of a Chance (Session Disc 104)
Lester Leaps In (Ambrosia 20)
Up 'N Adam (Ambrosia 20)

Lester Young Quartet

February 24, 1951; New York City; Broadcast, Birdland

Up 'N Adam (Ambrosia 10)
These Foolish Things (Session Disc 104)
Neenah (Ambrosia 10)
Lester Leaps In (Session Disc 104)
Jumpin' with Symphony Sid (Theme) (Ambrosia 10)

Lester Young Quartet

March 8, 1951; New York City; Clef

A Foggy Day (Verve VE 2-2516)
In a Little Spanish Town (Verve VE 2-2516)
Let's Fall in Love (Verve VE 2-2516)
Down 'N Adam (Verve VE 2-2516)
Lester Swings (Verve VE 2-2516)
Slow Motion Blues (Verve VE 2-2516)

Lester Young Quintet

March 17, 1951; New York City; Broadcast, Birdland

Jumpin' with Symphony Sid (Theme) (Ambrosia 10)
Up 'N Adam (Ambrosia 10)
Too Marvelous for Words (Ambrosia 10)
Neenah (Ambrosia 10)
Ghost of a Chance (Ambrosia 10)
Lester Leaps In [*Again*] (Session Disc 104)

Lester Young Quintet

May 19, 1951; New York City; Broadcast, Birdland

Indiana (Ambrosia 20)
Ghost of a Chance (Ambrosia 20)
How High the Moon (Ambrosia 20)
D.B. Blues (Ambrosia 20)

Lester Young Quintet

August 4, 1951; New York City; Broadcast, Birdland

Up 'N Adam (Ambrosia 20)
Blue and Sentimental (Ambrosia 20)
Neenah (Ambrosia 20)
Lester Leaps In (Ambrosia 20)

Jazz at the Philharmonic

April 6, 1952; Paris; Concert, Broadcast, Salle Pleyel

Undecided (Inc.; begins midway) (Unissued)
I Cover the Waterfront (Inc.; begins midway) (Unissued)
Blues (Inc.; begins with a quote of *MopMop*) (Unissued)

Lester Young Quintet

April 25, 1952; New York City; Broadcast, Birdland

Neenah (Ambrosia 30)
Ghost of a Chance (Ambrosia 30)
In a Little Spanish Town (Ambrosia 30)
Destination Moon (Ambrosia 30)
Lester Leaps In (Ambrosia 30)

Lester Young Quartet

April 26, 1952; New York City; Broadcast, Birdland

Tea for Two (Unissued)
I Cover the Waterfront (Unissued)
Up 'N Adam (Unissued)
Three Little Words (Unissued)

Lester Young Quintet

May 2, 1952; New York City; Broadcast, Birdland

Up 'N Adam (Ambrosia 30)
'Deed I Do (Ambrosia 30)
How High the Moon (Ambrosia 30)
Pennies from Heaven (Ambrosia 30)

Lester Young Quintet

May 3, 1952; New York City; Broadcast, Birdland

Up 'N Adam (Ambrosia 30)
'Deed I Do (Ambrosia 30)

Count Basie and His Orchestra

July 29, 1952; New York City; Broadcast, Birdland

Jumpin' at the Woodside (Sabie 5302)
One O'Clock Jump (Sabie 5302)

(NOTE: Young was not in the band, but guested on a few numbers each night. Only those numbers appear in the remaining Basie listings.)

Lester Young Quintet

August 2, 1952; New York City; Broadcast, Birdland

Jumpin' with Symphony Sid (Theme) (Unissued)
Up 'N Adam (Ambrosia 40)
Ghost of a Chance (Ambrosia 40)
In a Little Spanish Town (Ambrosia 40)
Too Marvelous for Words (Ambrosia 40)
Neenah (Ambrosia 40)

Lester Young with Oscar Peterson Trio

August 4, 1952; New York City; Clef/Norgran

Ad Lib Blues (Verve VE 2-2502)
Just You, Just Me (Verve VE 2-2502)
Tea for Two (Verve VE 2-2502)
Indiana (Verve VE 2-2502)
These Foolish Things (Verve VE 2-2502)
I Can't Get Started (Verve VE 2-2502)
Stardust (Verve VE 2-2502)
(It Takes) Two to Tango (Unissued)
On the Sunny Side of the Street (Verve VE 2-2502)
Almost Like Being in Love (Verve VE 2-2502)
I Can't Give You Anything But Love (Verve VE 2-2502)
There Will Never Be Another You (Verve VE 2-2502)
I'm Confessin' (Verve VE 2-2502)

Count Basie and His Orchestra

August 11, 1952; New York City; Broadcast, Birdland (LP says August 31)

Jumpin' at the Woodside (Duke D-1018)
One O'Clock Jump (Duke D-1018)

(NOTE: A different performance of these two titles is reported for August 5, unconfirmed.)

Jazz at the Philharmonic

September 13, 1952; New York City; Concert, Carnegie Hall
(NOTE: Above date confirmed in *Benny Carter,* by Berger, Berger, and Patrick.)

Jam Session Blues (Verve 815.1521)
I Can't Get Started (Young's part in a medley) (Verve 815.1521)
Cotton Tail (Verve 815.1521)
Perdido (Verve 815.1521)

Ella Fitzgerald and All Stars (probably Jazz at the Philharmonic)

1952 or 1953; Location unknown

Lester Leaps In (LP does not list Young, but he is featured) (Europa Jazz EJ-1050)

Count Basie and His Orchestra

January 1, 1953; New York City; Broadcast, Birdland

Jumpin' at the Woodside (Unique Jazz 004)

Lester Young and His Quintet

January 3, 1953; New York City; Broadcast, Birdland

Up 'N Adam (Ambrosia 40)
Blue and Sentimental (Ambrosia 40)
After You've Gone (Ambrosia 50)
In a Little Spanish Town (Ambrosia 50)
Jumpin' with Symphony Sid (Theme) (Ambrosia 50)

Count Basie and His Orchestra

January 3, 1953; New York City; Broadcast, Birdland

Every Tub (Sabie 5302)

Count Basie and His Orchestra

January 6, 1953; New York City; Broadcast, Birdland

Jumpin' at the Woodside (Unique Jazz 004)

Count Basie and His Orchestra

January 7, 1953; New York City; Broadcast, Birdland

Every Tub (Unique Jazz 005)

Count Basie and His Orchestra

January 8, 1953; New York City; Broadcast, Birdland

Pres (Unissued)

Lester Young and His Quintet

January 10, 1953; New York City; Broadcast, Birdland

Lullaby of Birdland (Theme) (Ambrosia 50)
Indiana (Ambrosia 50)
Almost Like Being in Love (Ambrosia 50)
Neenah (Ambrosia 50)
D.B. Blues (Ambrosia 50)

Count Basie and His Orchestra

January 10, 1953; New York City; Broadcast, Birdland

Jumpin' at the Woodside (Sabie 5302)

Count Basie and His Orchestra

January 13, 1953; New York City; Broadcast, Birdland

Jumpin' at the Woodside (Unique Jazz 004)

Count Basie and His Orchestra

January 14, 1953; New York City; NBC Broadcast, "Stars in Jazz," Birdland

Every Tub (Unique Jazz 005)

Lester Young and His Quintet

January 15, 1953; New York City; NBC Broadcast, "Stars in Jazz," Birdland

Lullaby of Birdland (Theme) (Unissued)
Up 'N Adam (Danish Storyville SLP-4107)
Too Marvelous for Words (Unissued)

(NOTE: The Storyville LP contains two more titles from an unidentified Birdland broadcast, *Blues in G* and *Tea for Two* (Inc.). It gives January 15 for them, but the personnel is audibly not that of the above.)

Lester Young and His Quintet

January 17, 1953; New York City; Broadcast, Birdland

Lady Be Good (Ambrosia 50)
A Foggy Day (Ambrosia 50)

In a Little Spanish Town (Ambrosia 60)
Lester Leaps In (Ambrosia 60)

(NOTE: One title by Young with the Basie band, reported for January 17, appears
not to have happened.)

Lester Young Quartet/Quintet at JATP

March 3, 1953; Paris; Concert, Salle Pleyel

Flashes of Prez (NOTE: Bruyninckx reports that this was a long segment including
   These Foolish Things, I Cover the Waterfront, Lester Leaps In, and *How High The
   Moon.* This is unverified.) (Unissued)

Lester Young Band

July 4, 1953; New York City; Broadcast, Birdland

Up 'N Adam (Ambrosia 60)
I Can't Get Started (Ambrosia 60)
Lester Leaps In (Ambrosia 60)

Metronome All Stars with Billy Eckstine

July 9, 1953; New York City; MGM

How High the Moon, Parts I and II (English MGM 2353 071)
St. Louis Blues, Parts I and II (English MGM 2353 071)

Lester Young Band

July 11, 1953; New York City; Broadcast, Birdland

Lullaby of Birdland (Theme) (Ambrosia 60)
Indiana (interrupted by Korea bulletin, spliced out on LP) (Ambrosia 60)
In a Little Spanish Town (Ambrosia 60)
[New] D.B. Blues (Ambrosia 60)

Jazz at the Philharmonic

September, 1953; Hartford; Concert, Bushnell Auditorium
(NOTE: Usually given as Carnegie Hall, September 19 (not 23). This new
information is suggested by Pablo LP.2308-240.)

One O'Clock Jump (NOTE: Young is not audibly present on the other title, *Flying
   Home.)* (Verve 815.1531)

Lester Young Quintet at JATP

September, 1953; Hartford; Same concert as above

Lester's Blues (Up 'N Adam) (Verve 825.101-1)
I Cover the Waterfront (Verve 825.101-1)
Lester Gambols (Lester Leaps In) (Verve 825.101-1)

Lester Young and His Band

December 11, 1953; New York City; Norgran

Willow Weep for Me (Norgran MGN 1071)
This Can't Be Love (Verve MGV-8308)
Can't We Be Friends (Norgran MGN 1071)
Tenderly (Norgran MGN 1071)
New D.B. Blues (Verve MGV-8308)
Jumpin' at the Woodside (Verve MGV-8308)
I Can't Believe That You're in Love with Me (Verve MGV -8125)
Lady Be Good (Verve MGV-8308)

Lester Young with Count Basie and His Orchestra

September 25, 1954; New York City; Concert, Carnegie Hall

Pennies from Heaven (Roulette RE-127)
Jumpin' at the Woodside (Roulette RE-127)

Lester Young and His Band

December 10, 1954; New York City; Norgran

Another Mambo (Verve VE 2-2538)
Come Rain Or Come Shine (Verve VE 2-2538)
Rose Room (Verve VE-2-2538)
Somebody Loves Me (Verve VE-2-2538)
Kiss (Touch) Me Again (Verve VE-2-2538)
It Don't Mean a Thing (Verve VE-2538)
I'm in the Mood for Love (Verve VE-2538)
Big Top Blues (Verve VE 2-2538)

Count Basie and His Orchestra

December 16, 1954; New York City; Broadcast (Radio and TV), Birdland

Jumpin' at the Woodside (Sabie 5301)

Count Basie and His Orchestra

December 17, 1954; New York City; Broadcast, Birdland

Jumpin' at the Woodside (Sabie 5301)

(NOTE: There is a report of a tape ca. 1954 with Young, Charlie Parker, and Sonny

Rollins. Also, Columbia Records once announced a six-minute track by Parker with Young singing, of unknown date, but this was never issued. Parker died in March 1955. Just Found: three titles by Young with Basie, February, 1955.)

Billie Holiday

May 6, 1955; New York City; Concert, Carnegie Hall

Stormy Weather (Everest Archive of Folk and Jazz Music FS-310)

Count Basie and His Orchestra

Probably 1955; New York City; possibly same concert as above

Lady Be Good (Hall of Fame JG 629)

Lester Young with Norman Simmons Trio

Probably between July 22 and August 11, 1955; Chicago; Private recording, Bee Hive Club

(Unknown titles) (Unissued)

Jazz at the Philharmonic

October 2, 1955; Chicago; Concert, Chicago Opera House

The Blues (Mail Order Blues) (Verve 815.1551)
The Modern Set (Chris 'N Diz) (Verve 815.1551)
I Didn't Know What Time It Was (Young's part in a medley) (Verve 815.1551)

Jazz at the Philharmonic

Probably 1955; New York City; Concert, probably Carnegie Hall

The Modern Set (Chris 'N Diz) (Hall of Fame JG 632)
I Didn't Know What Time It Was (Hall of Fame JG 631)

Lester Young—Harry Edison All Stars

November 1, 1955; Los Angeles; Norgran
(NOTE: Usually listed as December 1, New York City.)

Mean to Me (Verve VE 2-2538)
That's All (Verve VE 2-2538)
Red Boy Blues (Verve VE 2-2538)
Pennies from Heaven (Verve VE 2-2538)
She's Funny That Way (Verve VE 2-2538)
One O'Clock Jump (Verve VE 2-2538)

It's the Talk of the Town (Verve PR(S) 2–3)
I've Found a New Baby (Unissued)

The Jazz Giants '56

January 12, 1956; New York City; Norgran

I Guess I'll Have to Change My Plans (Verve VE 1-2527)
I Didn't Know What Time It Was (Verve VE 1-2527)
Gigantic Blues (Verve VE 1-2527)
This Year's Kisses (Verve VE 1-2527)
You Can Depend on Me (Verve VE 1-2527)

Lester Young—Teddy Wilson

January 13, 1956; New York City; Verve

Pres Returns (Verve VE 2-2502)
Prisoner of Love (Verve VE 2-2502)
Taking a Chance On Love (Verve VE 2-2502)
All of Me (Verve VE 2-2502)
Louise (Verve VE 2-2502)
(Our) Love Is Here To Stay (Verve VE 2-2502)
Love Me Or Leave Me (Verve VE 2-2502)

Lester Young and His Quintet

August 7, 1956; New York City; ABC Broadcast, Birdland

Lullaby of Birdland (Theme) (Unissued)
Lester Leaps In (Unissued)
Polka Dots and Moonbeams (Unissued)
Up 'N Adam (Unissued)

(NOTE: Three titles are reported to be from an August 15 broadcast—*In a Little Spanish Town, Three Little Words,* and *These Foolish Things.* Other sources report another Birdland broadcast on September 5, titles unknown. These are unconfirmed.)

Lester Young Band

Probably October, 1956, Frankfurt; Private recording, club date

Lestter Leaps In (Onyx 218)
These Foolish Things (Onyx 218)
There Will Never Be Another You (Onyx 218)
Lullaby of Birdland (Onyx 218)
Lester's [European] Blues (Onyx 218)

Lester Young Band

Probably October, 1956; Paris; Possibly broadcast

Three Little Words (Unissued)
I Cover the Waterfront (Unissued)
D.B. Blues (Unissued)

(NOTE: The above session is under consideration for possible release by Xanadu Records.)

Birdland All-Stars with Lester Young and Miles Davis

November 2 1956; Paris; Concert, Salle Pleyel

[Oh] Lady Be Good (Unissued)

Birdland All-Stars: Lester Young with the Rene Urtreger Trio

November 12, 1956; Freiburg; Broadcast

Indiana (Unique Jazz 14)

Birdland All-Stars with Lester Young, Miles Davis, and Modern Jazz Quartet

November 12, 1956; Freiburg; same as above

How High the Moon (Unique Jazz 14)

Lester Young with the Kurt Edelhagen Orchestra

November 12, 1956; Freiburg; same as above

Lester Leaps In (Unique Jazz 14)

Lester Young Band

November 19, 1956; Zurich; Concert

Jumpin' with Symphony Sid (Unissued)

Lester Young Band

Probably November 1956; Europe (city unknown); TV broadcast

Polka Dots and Moonbeams (Onyx 218)
Lester Leaps In (Onyx 218)

(NOTE: Broadcast on January 2, 1957.)

Lester Young with the Bill Potts Trio

December 7 and 8, 1956; Washington, D.C.; Private recording, Olivia's Patio
Lounge
(NOTE: Recorded on Friday night, Saturday afternoon, and Saturday night the 8th;
not known which titles are from which session.)

A Foggy Day (Pablo 2308 219)
When You're Smiling (Pablo 2308 219)
I Can't Get Started (Pablo 2308 219)
Fast Bb Blues (Pablo 2308 219)
D.B. Blues (Pablo 2308 219)
Tea for Two (Pablo 2308 219)
Jeepers Creepers (Pablo 2308 219)
Lester Leaps In (Pablo 2308 225)
These Foolish Things (Pablo 2308 225)
I'm Confessin' (Pablo 2308 225)
Three Little Words (Pablo 2308 225)
Jumpin' with Symphony Sid (Pablo 2308 225)
Almost Like Being in Love (Pablo 2308 225)
Lullaby of Birdland (Pablo 2308 225)
Just You, Just Me (Pablo 2308 228)
Sometimes I'm Happy (Pablo 2308 228)
Up 'N Adam (Pablo 2308 228)
Indiana (Pablo 2308 228)
G's, If You Please (Pablo 2308 228)
There Will Never Be Another You (Pablo 2308 228)
It's the Talk of the Town (Pablo 2308 230)
I Cover the Waterfront (Pablo 2308 230)
Pennies from Heaven (Pablo 2308 230)
G's, If You Please (different version) (Pablo 2308 230)
Almost Like Being in Love (different version) (Pablo 2308 230)
D.B. Blues (different version) (Pablo 2308 230)
I'm Confessin' (different version) (Pablo 2308 230)

(NOTE: There are also unissued versions of some of the above titles from these
sessions, including *G's, If You Please, Up 'N Adam,* and *Lullaby of Birdland,* the
latter in several versions, some comprised of the theme only.)

Lester Young with Earl Swope and the Bill Potts Trio

December 8, 1956 (afternoon); Washington, D.C.; Private recording, Olivia's Patio
Lounge

Lady Be Good (Jazz Archives JA-34)
Up 'N Adam (Jazz Archives JA-34)

Jumpin' with Symphony Sid (Jazz Archives JA-34)
Lullaby of Birdland (Jazz Archives JA-34)

(NOTE: LP does not specify date.)

Lester Young Band

December 8, 1956 (night); Washington, D.C.; Broadcast, "Bandstand U.S.A.,"
Olivia's Patio Lounge

Jumpin' With Symphony Sid (Musidisc 5174)
These Foolish Things (Musidisc 5174)
Three Little Words (ending Inc.) (Musidisc 5174)

(NOTE: LP gives wrong location.)

Lester Young Band

December 15, 1956; New York City; Broadcast, "Bandstand U.S.A.," Café
Bohemia
(NOTE: The LP mistakenly gives December 29.)

Lester Leaps In (Danish storyville SLP-4107)
These Foolish Things (Danish storyville SLP-4107)
Three Little Words (Danish storyville SLP-4107)

Lester Young Band

December 22, 1956; New York City; Broadcast, "Bandstand U.S.A.," Café
Bohemia

Pennies from Heaven (Musidisc 5174)

(NOTE: Here Leonard Feather presents Young with Musicians' Musician Poll
award)

Polka Dots and Moonbeams (Musidisc 5174)
Indiana (Ambrosia 60)

Lester Young Band

December 29, 1956; New York City; Broadcast, "Bandstand U.S.A.," Café
Bohemia

Jumpin' with Symphony Sid (theme not played) (Unissued)
(I Don't Stand) A Ghost of a Chance (Unissued)
Tea for Two (ending Inc.) (Unissued)

Count Basie and His Orchestra

July 7, 1957; Newport, R.I.; Concert, Newport Jazz Festival

Polka Dots and Moonbeams (Verve MGV-8243)
Lester Leaps In (Verve MGV-8243)
Sent for You Yesterday (And Here You Come Today) (Verve MGV-8243)
Boogie Woogie (Verve MGV-8243)
Evenin' (Verve MGV-8243)
One O'Clock Jump (Verve MGV-8243)

Lester Young All Stars

July 31, 1957; Los Angeles; Verve

St. Tropez (Verve MGV-8298)
Flic (Verve MGV-8298)
I Cover the Waterfront (Young's part in a medley—preceded by *A Ghost of a Chance,* a trumpet solo.) (Unissued)
Our Love Is Here to Stay (Verve MGV-8298)
Sunday (Unissued)
Perdido (no take number assigned—may be Inc.) (Unissued)

(NOTE: A Hollywood Bowl concert of August 22, 1957 was reportedly recorded by Norman Granz. If so, Young would be present on certain titles, including a *Blues, Polka Dots and Moonbeams* as part of a medley with other artists, *Goin' To Chicago,* and *How High the Moon.* Verve 825.101-1, just issued, contains a *Polka Dots and Moonbeams* from a JATP medley in Chicago, October 19, 1957.)

Jazz at the Philharmonic

October 25, 1957; Los Angeles; Concert, Shrine Auditorium

The Slow Blues (Verve MGV-8267)
Merry-Go-Round (Verve MGV-8267)
Polka Dots and Moonbeams (Young's part in a medley) (Unissued)

(NOTE: The winds also play a brief theme at the end of an unissued drum feature. Both of these numbers actually were issued, by mistake, on at least one copy of MGV-8267.)

Ella Fitzgerald and the JATP All Stars

October 25, 1957; Los Angeles; same concert as above
(NOTE: LP suggests wrong location.)

Stompin' at the Savoy (Verve MGV 8264)
Lady Be Good (Verve MGV 8264)

Count Basie All Stars

December 5, 1957; New York City; Studio rehearsal for "The Sound of Jazz"

Dickie's Dream (Columbia CSP JCL-1098)

I Left My Baby (Columbia CSP JCL-1098)

(NOTE: Some sources say December 4.)

Billie Holiday with Mal Waldron's All Stars

December 5, 1957; New York City; Studio rehearsal for "The Sound of Jazz"

Fine and Mellow (Columbia CSP JCL-1098)

Billie Holiday with "The Sound of Jazz" All Stars

December 8, 1957; New York City; TV broadcast, "The Sound of Jazz"

Fine and Mellow (Everest Archive of Folk and Jazz Music FS-310)

(NOTE: Young appears on the above title only. He had rehearsed with Basie but was unable to appear with him on the broadcast.)

Jazz at the Philharmonic

Probably 1957; New York City; Concert, probably Carnegie Hall, September 14

The Slow Blues (Jam Session Part 2) (Hall of Fame JG 628)

Lester Young All Stars

February 7, 1958; New York City; Verve

Waldorf Blues (Verve MGV-8298)
Sunday (Verve MGV-8298)
You're Getting to Be a Habit with Me (Verve MGV-8298)

Lester Young All Stars

February 8, 1958; New York City; Verve

Romping (Verve MGV-8316)
Gypsy in My Soul (Verve MGV-8316)
Please Don't Talk About Me When I'm Gone (Verve MGV-8316)
They Can't Take That Away from Me (Verve MGV-8316)
Salute to Benny (Verve MGV-8316)
Medley (The Very Thought of You, I Want a Little Girl, Blue and Sentimental; Young
    plays on the last one only) (Unissued)
Mean to Me (Unissued)

(NOTE: It is tempting to suggest that the Verve label holds enough unissued Young, from this and earlier sessions, to compile a new LP. No such LP is now planned.)

Lester Young All Stars

March 23, 1958; New York City; Verve

Clarinet Blues (Unissued)
Jeepers Creepers (Unissued)
Mean to Me (Unissued)
Sunday (Unissued)

(NOTE: This session is unconfirmed.)

Newport All Stars

July 5, 1958; Newport, R.I.; Broadcast, Newport Jazz Festival

I Cover the Watefront (Unique Jazz 14)
Muskrat Ramble (Unissued)
Royal Garden Blues (Jump the Blues) (Unique Jazz 14)

Lester Young Interview with Chris Albertson

Probably August 26, 1958; probably New York City; Private recording (Unissued)

Art Ford's Jazz Party

September 25, 1958; New York City; TV Broadcast

Mean to Me (Enigma 301)
Jumpin' with Symphony Sid (Enigma 301)

Lester Young with Jodie Christian Trio

December 26, 1958; Chicago; Private recording, Pershing Hotel

Mean to Me (Unissued)
D.B. Blues (Unissued)
Polka Dots and Moonbeams (Unissued)
Three Little Words (Inc.) (Unissued)
Jumpin' with Symphony Sid (Inc.) (Unissued)
I Cover the Waterfront (Inc.) (Unissued)

Lester Young and His Quintet

Probably late 1958; New York City; Broadcast, "Bandstand U.S.A.," Birdland

Lullaby of Birdland (Theme) (Unissued)
Three Little Words (Unissued)
I Can't Get Started (Unissued)
Blues in F (Inc.) (Unissued)

Lester Young Interview with François Postif

Ca. February 18, 1959; Paris; Private recording (Unissued)

Lester Young Band

Probably February, 1959; Paris; Private recording, possibly broadcast, Blue Note

Lester Leaps In (Unissued)
Blues (not *Lester Gambols,* as listed by some collectors) (Unissued)

(NOTE: A third title, *Mean to Me,* is reported. All three titles are under consideration for release by Xanadu Records.)

Lester Young Quintet

March 4, 1959; Paris; Verve

[Oh] Lady Be Good (Verve MGV 8378)
I Didn't Know What Time It Was (Verve MGV 8378)
Almost Like Being in Love (Verve MGV 8378)
Three Little Words (Verve MGV 8378)
I Cover the Waterfront (Verve MGV 8378)
I Can't Get Started (Verve MGV 8378)
Indiana (Verve MGV 8378)
Pennies from Heaven (Verve MGV 8378)
New D.B. Blues (Verve MGV 8378)
Lullaby of Birdland (Verve MGV 8378)
There Will Never Be Another You (Verve MGV 8378)
Tea for Two (Verve MGV 8378)

Lester Young Band

March 11, 1959; Paris; Private recording, probably at a radio station

D.B. Blues (Unissued)

(NOTE: A Blue Note broadcast with unknown titles is also reported for March 11.)

Lester Young Band

Probably March, 1959; probably Paris; Broadcast

There Will Never Be Another You (Unissued)

Selected Discography of LPs

This section includes the LPs listed in the Catalog of Recorded Works, alphabetically by record label, with some annotations. I give the main artist or title and, except for American issues, the country of origin, along with the dates of the sessions represented on the LP, so that one may use this list as an index to the Catalog. (Of course, the Catalog lists only relevant titles from each LP, not necessarily all titles.) An excellent source for the foreign recordings is Oak Lawn Jazz, Box 2663, Providence, Rhode Island 02907. Unfortunately, some of the LPs have gone or will soon go out of print, and must be sought in second-hand shops and on auction lists. Recordings known to be out of print as of this writing are marked with asterisks (*). Note that many deleted Verve LPs are becoming available on Japanese pressings.

The three-record set, *Lester Young*, issued as Time-Life STL-J13, is not listed below but is worth mention; it provides a good cross section of his work, with an excellent 50-page booklet (available directly from Time-Life Records, 541 North Fairbanks Court, Chicago, Illinois 60611).

Alto 707. Lester Young. March 26, 1949. (Also contains parts of November 27, 1948, and March 19, 1949.)

Ambrosia 10, 20, 30, 40, 50, 60. *Lester Young: The President*, Volumes 1 through 6. Contain titles from broadcasts of December 4, 1948, through December 22, 1956, that are not available on other LPs.

Blue Heaven BH-1-109, BH-3-308, BH-6-605. Count Basie and His Orchestra. January 10, 1944, and May 25, 1944.

*Blue Note LA 456-H2. *Lester Young: The Aladdin Sessions*. Aladdin sessions from December 1945 through December 29, 1948. (Aladdin sessions are still available on a French label.)

*Caracol 421 (France). *Count Basie and Lester*. 1944 (Unknown location); contains other 1944 titles also.

*Caracol 431 (France). *Count Basie*. Ca. April 10, 1944; May 13, 17, 29, and 30, 1944; and 1944 (Unknown location).

CBS 66101 (France). *The Complete Count Basie, 1936–1941*. Ten-record set. See Catalog for various Basie sessions in 1939 and 1940; also includes all other Basie titles for Vocalion and Columbia from 1936 through 1941.

CBS 66274 (France). Teddy Wilson. May 11, 1937

*CBS-SONY YBPC1/SOPH 61-70 (Japan). Billie Holiday. November 9, 1938. Boxed set plus bonus disc.

*Charlie Parker PLP-402, PLP-405, PLP-409. Lester Young. March 19, 1949, and February 22, 1950.

Charlie Parker CP-504. *The Pres—Lester Young*. February 22, 1950.

Collector's Classics 11 (Denmark). *Swing Music from the Southland Café, Boston.* February 20, 1940.

Columbia CSP JCL-1098. *The Sound of Jazz.* December 5, 1957.

*Columbia CG 30782. *Billie Holiday: God Bless the Child.* March 21, 1941.

Columbia PG 32132, PG 32124, PG 32127 (also found as KG . . .). *The Billie Holiday Story,* Volumes 1, 2, 3 (formerly *The Golden Years,* in two volumes). See Catalog for various Teddy Wilson and Billie Holiday sessions between May 11, 1937, and March 21, 1941

*Columbia CG 33502, JG 34837, JG 34840, JG 34843, C2 34849. *The Lester Young Story,* Volumes 1, 2, 3, 4, 5. All Vocalion, Brunswick, and Columbia titles on which Young solos from 1936 through 1941, mostly with Count Basie and Billie Holiday.

Commodore XFL 14937, XFL 15352. Lester Young. The former documents September 27, 1938, the latter March 28, 1944.

Duke D-1018 (Italy). *Count Basie: The Birdland Era, Volume 2.* August 11, 1952; also contains January 14, 1953.

Enigma 301. *Coleman Hawkins and His Friends at a Famous Jazz Party.* September 25, 1958.

*ESP 3017. *Lester Young—Newly Discovered Performances, Vol. 1.* November 27, 1948; also contains part of December 4, 1948.

Everest Archive of Folk and Jazz Music FS-310. *Billie Holiday, Volume 2.* May 6, 1955, and December 8, 1957.

Everybody's Ev-3002. *Historical Prez: Lester Young 1940–1944.* Probably between February 27 and March 17, 1941; December 2, 1941; and various 1944 dates. (Marlor Productions, P.O. Box 156, Hicksville, N.Y. 11803.)

Everybody's EV-3004. *The Basie Special—Count Basie and His Orchestra 1944–1946.* April 14 and 24, 1944. Address as above.

*Extreme Rarities 1002. *Hot Jazz on Film.* December 8, 1957.

Fanfare 18-118. *Count Basie and His Orchestra, 1938 Live.* July 9, 1938.

*Hall of Fame JG 628, JG 631, JG 632. Various artists. Probably 1955 and Probably 1957.

*Hall of Fame JG 629. *Count Basie.* Probably 1955.

IAJRC LP-14, LP-17. Various artists. July 23, 1938; 1938; and probably May 14, 1944. (International Association of Jazz Record Collectors, c/o Paul Stites, 1917 Schwier Drive, Indianapolis, Indiana 46229.)

Jazz Archives JA-16. *The Count at the Chatterbox 1937: Count Basie and His Orchestra.* February 8, 10, and 12, 1937.

Jazz Archives JA-18, JA-34. *Jammin' with Lester,* and *Jammin' with Lester—Volume Two.* August 1944; May 27 and June 3, 1946; April 1950; and December 8, 1956.

Jazz Archives JA-41. *Count Basie at the Famous Door 1938–1939.* Various dates from August 9, 1938, through Summer 1939.

Jazz Archives JA-42. *Lester Young and Charlie Christian 1939–1940.* Summer 1939; March 7, 1940; and October 28, 1940.

*Jazz Panorama LP-2 (Sweden). *The Swing Era.* July 23, 1938, and September 11, 1944.

*Jazz Panorama LP-23 (Sweden). *Count Basie: Early Basie, 1938–1940.* August 23 and 24, 1938; June 10, 1939; and February 20, 1940.

Jazz Society AA 505, AA 506 (Sweden). *Count Basie.* May 27, 1944.

MCA 3080 (Japan). Various artists. April 3, 1941.

MCA 2-4006. *The Billie Holiday Story.* August 17, 1949.

MCA 2-4050, 2-4108. *Count Basie.* Most of the Decca recordings from January 21, 1937, through February 4, 1939.

MCA 510.167-510.170 (France). *Count Basie and His Orchestra: Early Count.* August 9 and October 13, 1937. Contains all the other Decca recordings of this period also.

MGM 2353 071 (England). Metronome All Stars. July 9, 1953.

Musidisc 5105, 5160 (France). Count Basie. Ca. April 24, 1944; May 25, 1944; probably late May, 1944 and 1944 (Unknown location).

Musidisc 5174 (France). *Lester Young, Vol. 2.* December 8 and 22, 1956.

*Norgran MGN 1071. Lester Young. December 11, 1953.

*Onyx 218. *Lester Young: Prez in Europe.* Probably October 1956 and probably November 1956.

Pablo 2308 219, 2308 225, 2308 228, 2308 230. *Lester Young: "Pres,"* Volumes 1, 2, 3, 4. December 7 and 8, 1956.

*Palm 30-12 (England). *Count Basie.* January 10, 1944.

*Phoenix LP 8. *In Concert—Coleman Hawkins.* May 27 and June 3, 1946.

Phontastic NOST 7639 (Sweden). *Lester—Amadeus!: Lester Young.* June 30, 1937, and June 3, 1938.

Phontastic NOST 7640 (Sweden). *Count Basie: Basic Basie.* November 3, 1937. Also contains some of July 9, 1938.

Queen-Disc Q-025 (Italy). *Count Basie: Big Basie.* April 17, 1944, and April or May 1944.

Queen-Disc Q-051 (Italy). *Tenor Triumvirate.* March 22, 1944; March or April 1946; December 28 and 30, 1947; and December 29, 1948.

Raretone 24011 (Italy). *Billie Holiday: "Me, Myself, and I."* November 9, 1938.

*RCA LPM-6702. Benny Goodman. March 9, 1938.

RCA AXM2-5557. *Benny Goodman, Vol. 5.* March 9, 1938.

RCA 731.092 (France). *Benny Goodman.* March 9, 1938.

RCA FXM3-7324 (France). *Saxophone Giants: The Signature Label.* December 21, 1943.

Roulette RE-127. *Birdland All-Stars at Carnegie Hall.* September 25, 1954.

Sabie 5301, 5302. *Count Basie.* July 29, 1952; January 3 and 10, 1953; and December 16 and 17, 1954.

*Saga 6918 (England). *Billie Holiday.* December 19, 1940.

Savoy SJL 1109, 2202. *Lester Young.* April 18, 1944; May 1, 1944; June 28, 1949; and April 2, 1950.

Session Disc 103, 104. *Hooray for Lester Young,* Volumes 1 and 2. December 4, 1948; April 9, 1949; and various 1951 broadcasts.

Spotlite SPJ 119 (England). *Jubilee All Stars/Prez and the Hawk.* Probably early April 1946.

Spotlite SPJ 136 (England). *Nat Cole Meets the Master Saxes.* July 15, 1942.

Swing House SWH-23, SWH-41 (England). *Count Basie and His Orchestra.* Probably December 1943.

Tax m-8027 (Sweden). Count Basie. October 30, 1940.

Trip 5509. *Lester Young—Pres at His Very Best.* December 28, 1943, and March 22, 1944.

Two Flats Disc T-5006 (Italy). *Billie Holiday: "Guess Who?"* January 12, 1938.

Unique Jazz 004, 005 (Italy). Count Basie. Several dates in January 1953.

Unique Jazz 14 (Italy). *Lester Meets Miles, M.J.Q. & Jack Teagarden All Stars.* November 12, 1956, and July 5, 1958.

Vanguard VSD 47/48. *From Spirituals to Swing.* December 23, 1938, and December 24, 1939.

*Verve JATP Series, Vol. 4, Vol. 9. April 22, 1946; June 3, 1946; and September 19, 1953.

*Verve PR (S)2-3. Various artists. November 1, 1955.

*Verve MGV 8125, MGV 8298, MGV 8308, MGV 8316, MGV 8378. Lester Young. December 11, 1953; July 31, 1957; February 7 and 8, 1958; and March 4, 1959.

*Verve MGV 8243. *Count Basie.* July 7, 1957.

*Verve MGV 8264. *Ella Fitzgerald at the Opera House.* October 25, 1957.

*Verve MGV 8267. *The JATP All Stars at the Opera House.* October 25, 1957.

Verve VE 2-2502. *Pres and Teddy and Oscar.* August 4, 1952 and January 13, 1956.

Verve VE 2-2516. *Lester Swings.* March or April 1946; March 1950; July 1950; January 16, 1951; and March 8, 1951.

Verve VE 2-2518. *Jazz at the Philharmonic/Bird and Pres: The '46 Concerts.* January 28, 1946, and April 22, 1946.

Verve VE 1-2527. *The Jazz Giants '56.* January 12, 1956.

Verve VE 2-2538. *Lester Young/Mean to Me.* December 10, 1954, and November 1, 1955.

Verve 815.1471, 815.1491, 815.1501, 815.1511, 815.1521, 815.1531, 815.1551. *Jazz at the Philharmonic,* various artists. April 22, 1946; May 27, 1946; September 17, 1949; September 16, 1950; September 13, 1952; September 19, 1953; and October 2, 1955. (Also 825.101-1, just released.)

Whiskey, Women, And—KM-701 (Sweden). *Helen Humes: "Be-Baba-Leba," 1944– 1952.* December 1945 or January 1946.

Index